FOREVER GRATEFUL

by Silas Turman

Dedicated to my wife Marie,
my five children,
all my grandchildren,
my relatives,
and my friends.

Chapter One

Life is full of ups and downs. That is what my Dad always said, and I have found that to be true. However, I prefer to write about the enjoyable and amusing side of life, dwelling less on the down times.

My life began differently than most in that my mother died when I was born. Since my father already had several small daughters and young sons, he decided to let his brother, who had no children of his own, raise me.

My aunt and uncle, who later adopted me, were the only father and mother I really ever knew. I did not meet my brothers and sisters until I was a teenager and then seldom saw them.

I was born December 13, 1920 in what is now known as the "notch years" by the social security system. People born in the years 1917 to 1926 receive half the benefits of those in other years.

My eleven-year old brother carried me through the woods to meet my uncle and aunt, who were traveling in a horse and buggy, when I was a few hours old. My brother and I cried as he carried me through the cold, snowy woods in Mayberry, Virginia, located in the Blue Ridge Mountains.

We crossed a creek that was frozen over. He laid me on the ground, broke a hole in the ice, pulled a leaf from a mountain laurel and dipped up some water in the cupped leaf and gave me a drink of the cold mountain water. I stopped crying. When my brother got me though the woods to where my parents-to-be were waiting in their buggy, he handed me over to them and they drove me to their home. I was soon given unpasteurized cow's milk in a bottle. This was to be my formula until I was old enough to eat from the table.

My Mother was very sanitary and careful in every way that they knew in those days. I had great parents. They did their very best with what they had and I did all I could for them in the years to follow.

Perhaps the most vivid memory I had as a three year old was a trip by a horse drawn wagon, from our home in the Bell Spur community, down to Mount Airy, North Carolina. We traveled a distance of about 20 miles each way; we spent one day going, then spent the night, and returned the next day. I remember the stores in town and the candy I saw.

The most vivid memory I have was crossing the river in the wagon. Because there was no bridge, the horses pulled the wagon through it. On the other side, we fed the horses corn and oats while we ate our packed lunch. On our way back we had to go up the very narrow and unpaved mountain road where, if we met someone coming down, we had to pull way up on the bank to give them room to get by so they wouldn't run off the mountain on the other side. I remember my fear of falling of the edge of the mountain.

I plan to write about my love of these mountains, the people I've known and heard about in my lifetime, and the grandparents I heard about more than I knew. I had a step-grandmother who was a very wonderful person. I had aunts and uncles who made great impressions on my own children when they were growing up whenever our families found time to get together.

My Great Grandfather was a well-known Primitive Baptist minister who preached in churches in the Patrick, Carroll, and Floyd counties in Virginia. He was a good-sized man in his day. At six feet, two inches tall, he was a strong and capable man, who used to tell about such activities as wood choppings and log rollings. To clear the land for farming, they could cut and burn logs or otherwise make use of them. They said they would take the butt cut, the biggest part of the tree, and finish it. Then he would go around them and start on the third cut before they would have finished the second. He used a seven-pound axe, while most men used a three and one half pound ax.

He served in the Confederate army during the Civil War and was in Atlanta when the war ended. By the war's end, all of his company were either dead or badly wounded. Because his horse was shot out from under him, he walked all the way home from Atlanta to Carroll County. It took him a month to get home because he traveled by night to avoid union troops and robbers.

His name was Matt Blancett, and he was named on my parents' wedding certificate as the man who married them. He married many people in this area around the turn of the century and on into the early nineteen hundreds, and many people in the area named their children after him.

I have heard stories about him that might be embarrassing to some preachers. One weekend when he was preaching away from home, the Matt Bowman family asked him to pass the night with them. They had a very young son who bore the full name Matt Blancett Bowman. Since they were having an extra person in the house that night, the older children asked where they were going to sleep.

"Sleep in your usual places. Matt Blancett is going to sleep with your mother," their father said, referring to the little boy.

Of course, Reverend Matt Blancett was embarrassed as he didn't know the child's full name and that he was supposed to sleep in the young Matt's bed—and not with Mrs. Bowman.

When he was a young lad, my Dad tramped haystacks for Great-Grandfather Matt. If a storm was approaching, Matt could throw up such big bunches of hay so fast that Dad had to climb up the pole to keep from getting covered up.

Matt Blancett baptized many people during his ministry. One story that has been passed down concerns a ministers' meeting (made up of ministers from different denominations) he attended. During a discussion over the rights and wrongs of different Christian doctrines, Matt related that he had a vision of going to heaven and entering into a great hallway. Down this hall were many doors. The different doors had inscribed on them the different denominations-Baptist, Methodist, Presbyterian, Catholic, and so on. He told them that he went through his door-the Baptist door-to find that all the doors opened to the same big room.

In his older days, he wore a beard white beard that covered his chest. In his later years, he was unable to walk and sat in a chair for periods of time.

My mother by adoption was the only mother I ever knew. I am sure I could not have chosen a better Mother in this world had I been able to choose a mother myself. She was neat and clean, and very careful in every way regarding my health and safety. She made sure I got the right food that I ate regularly, that I got rest and was dressed properly. She also saw to it that I spoke proper English. I owe it to her that I never smoked or drank alcohol.

Sometimes we wore patched clothing, but they were always clean. I certainly did not wear clothes with holes in them as my grandchildren might now do in the name of fashion. I had the things I needed as a child-good food, clothing, and loving care-but I was not spoiled as an only child might have been. I had a few toys, but only a few. I always had chores to do as soon as I was old enough to do anything. Mother was sick a lot with high blood pressure and heart trouble.

I learned to wash clothes, iron, sweep floors and cook some. I could never cook like Mother. We cleaned our clothes on the washboard at first, heating water outside in a big black cast iron pot at the spring. We had no running water when I was a little boy. I ran to the spring and got a bucket full several times a day. Later, when I was eleven years old, we installed a hydraulic ram and pumped water from the spring long before electric power was available in our area of the country.

I learned there were lots of wrong ways to do things but only one right way to do things as far as my mother was concerned. I churned milk to make butter for her often. She would put an apron on me so I wouldn't splatter milk on my pants. She knew just when the milk was turned, or clabbered and ready to churn. It was interesting for me to watch her take the butter to the spring to leave in the cold water to keep cool. We also kept the buttermilk in the spring. It sure was good with the golden flecks of butter floating in it.

Mother always chose my friends and whom I visited. Mother and Dad always agreed. I never heard them arguing. I did not have other children to play with except occasionally on Sundays.

I learned to work in the garden when I was five or six years old. I could pull weeds and use a small hoe. I enjoyed helping in the garden. I even had a little garden of my own.

I guess the seasons have changed some and the varieties of vegetables planted are different but, back then, Mother always had her first mess of beans by the first Sunday in June and corn on the cob by the fourth of July. I haven't been able to have them come in that early for several years now.

We had peach trees that produced bushels of peaches, apple trees of many varieties that bore good apples without spraying. We kept the apples all winter in the root cellar or leaf-lined pens. We grew several varieties-Delicious, Staymen, Champions, York, Black Ben, Ben Davis, Vine, Limber Twig, Rome Beauty, Grimes Golden, Yellow Transparent, Early Harvest, Red June, and Henry Clay.. We also grew a large apple called "Wolf River" that was good for drying in the late fall. We canned and dried apples and peaches. We built a rock furnace and covered it with metal and build a wooden house over it. It contained shelves of screen wire dryers on which thinly sliced apples were placed to dry. Sitting by the fire at night I would use the apple peeler to remove their skins. I would then slice them with a knife and have them ready to put on the dryer in the morning.

My parents were pretty much self-sufficient. I feel that one of the greatest problems in this country today is that we are no longer self-sufficient, depending too much on the government. Years ago we did things for ourselves and for one another. There was a shoemaker or cobbler in every neighborhood. There was a tanning yard where everyone did his or her own butchering and meat curing. Everyone had chickens for eggs and for eating and a cow for milk and butter. We hatched our own chickens from eggs put under a mother hen. The hen would set on the eggs for three weeks and hatch out the sweetest baby chicks.

Kids these days miss a lot if they never see a mother hen hatch out a nest full of eggs, and especially if they have never been flogged by a mother hen for getting too close to her nest of young hatchlings. Before I was old enough to milk the cows my job was to shell the corn, feed the hens, and gather the eggs. I always dreaded getting the eggs out from under a setting hen, as she could peck the blood out of your hand. Sometimes a hen wanted to set when we didn't want another batch of chicks, and the eggs needed to be gathered from the nest. Sometimes there would be a fighting rooster defending the chicken yard from all visitors, including me. There were times when a hen would build her nest in the woods or outside somewhere, and it was my job to find it. I would listen for the hen to cackle to locate her. I once found a nest far back under an old building with 30 eggs in it. Later, when a visiting cousin told me about all of the interesting places he had been in order to point out that I had not been anywhere, I replied, "I've been further back up under a house hunting for a hen's nest than you ever have!"

We also kept turkeys-hens, and one big gobbler. Early in the spring, these hens would lay out in the woods and I would be sent out to watch where they went so we could get the eggs and put them under a chicken hen. Sometimes their nests would be several hundred yards from the house, hidden in tall weeds.

We had a turkey gobbler that would fight. Once I hit him over the head with a stick and his head turned black.

"Wonder what happened to that turkey gobbler?" Mother kept asking.

I never told her because I was afraid I might get a spanking. Children did get spanked, or "switched," in those days. (Sometimes today children still need that).

We had geese when I was small. I hate them because they would follow me and pinch a plug out of my butt. It sure did hurt. We saved the geese feathers and made feather ticks and pillows for company to sleep n.

I'd never heard of mattresses. We slept on straw ticks. Once a year, when the machines would come around to thresh wheat, we would save the straw and restuff all our bed ticks. I would fall out of the newly stuffed bed several times until the straw would finally settle down.

We kept guineas, a black and white feathered bird. They were like good dogs in that they would always, with their clucking, let you know when a stranger came around. In the summer, they laid lots of eggs which we ate because they were smaller than hen eggs, and harder to sell I had lots of fun finding their nests in the tall grass of the meadows. Guineas were good at catching insects out of the garden. They were also good to eat, even if they did have darker meat than chickens, although they were so fast you could not catch one. My Dad would have to shoot them in the head with a twenty-two rifle because their heads were always moving, I never was as good as shooting them as they were.

Sometimes mother would can chickens. There were no freezers in those days or, for that matter, any other way of preserving the meat I think one of my favorite dishes was chicken and dumplings. I can no longer eat it for health reasons, but I can sure remember the taste.

Thanksgiving meant pork, which, for our family, meant hog butchering. It usually took place during Thanksgiving week. The first real cold day of the season. An important and very exciting day on the farm. The first butchering day I can remember will always stay with me.

The wooden scalding box was filled with water from the spring and left to set for a day or two so it would swell and be watertight. Then we cut dry wood- usually pine or dead chestnut- and split it into pieces about four feet long. We put down a layer of flint stones on top of that. These layers were stacked up six to eight times.

Dad fired this stack early in the morning, about 4 a.m. on that particular butchering day. As the wood burned down, the rocks became very hot. Then he took a pitchfork and picked up a rock and held it in the water. He kept doing this, rock after rock, until the water got hot. Dad passed his fingers through the water three times very quickly to be sure the water was hot enough. He always seemed to know when the water was just right.

Dad had previously shot the hogs and stuck their necks with a sharp knife to bleed them. As soon as the water was ready, the hogs, which were hauled in on a horse drawn sleigh, were rolled into the water one at a time using chains. A man on either side used the chains to roll and turn the hog to make sure it was evenly scalded. During this time, they used knives or an old hoe to remove all of the hair. When the hogs were clean, they were hung up to dress in much the same way they are today.

I always looked forward to fresh pork. Tenderloin was my favorite. We cured the ham's middlings (bacon) and hog jaws, made sausage from the shoulders, and souse meat from the liver, head, and small scraps. We used the cured side meat, or fat back, for seasoning vegetables. The bacon was often sold. Hams were sometimes sold in early spring. Dad used the money to buy grass and clover seed or fertilizer to go on the fields.

We raised our own pigs. One or more sows usually had two litters a year, one in the spring and one in the fall. Neighbors came to buy pigs at weaning time. Once I remember going with my Dad below the mountain in a horse drawn wagon with pigs in a coop to sell.

One man bought one and opened his burlap sack for dad to put him in. When Dad dropped it in, the bottom of the sack burst and the squealing pig fell out and ran away. The man gave me fifty cents to catch it. He thought he would have fun watching chase after it. What he didn't know was that it was a pet and it wasn't afraid of me, so I had no trouble catching it.

Pigs made great pets. I prefer lambs, but cats and dogs are better than either. When an old sow gets upset over someone catching her pigs, she can be pretty mean. Once, a neighbor who was carrying a pig and running from a sow, said the old hog's nose was actually bumping his legs. "If the hog's mouth had been split the other way, she would have gotten my legs," he said.

My uncle said he had a pig that he fed twice a day. He said that he picked it up and set it in the pan every time he fed it, saying that he could still do it when the pig weighed 500 pounds. I didn't believe him then and still don't.

Back during the Depression, a certain neighbor who bought and sold pigs, bought several and could not sell them. He had to keep and feed them and was quite upset over it. One day, when he went to feed them in the pen beside the road, something didn't look right. He started counting them and found someone had left him six more pigs

At one time we raised sheep, and I became quite attached to them. They usually had lambs in late winter. We kept them in a building at night, and often they would send me out late at night with a kerosene lantern —of course, we didn't have flashlights yet— to check on them. Sometimes the ewes would not own the lambs at first, so we had to work with them. Sometimes they had twins and would not suckle both. It was my job to bottle-feed them and they made great pets. Like Mary's little lamb, they "followed me everywhere I went."

I'll never forget the one I called "Billy." He would wake me in the middle of the morning walking across the porch bleating for his breakfast. If I didn't get up he would get on our porch and pounce up and down stiff-legged to make a big noise and awaken me. I had a little red wagon that he liked to ride in while I pulled it around. He would also get in with me and coast down hill. Later, this would create a problem. When Billy grew larger, he became jealous and even fought with the neighbor boys who came to ride the wagon with me. He would back up, then charge them and knock them down. I didn't have many other children for playmates so I became very attached to him. Then it came time to sell him.

I didn't want to, but Mother and Dad insisted and I had to give in. I remember not being to sleep the night before we sold Billy. When we sold the lambs we walked them, along with all their mothers, about two miles to Jimmy Bowman's floor scales, where the lambs were weighed and sold to buyers. As we drove the ewes back home the day we sold Billy, it was a sad time for me. Dad would walk in front with a bucket of chop and the flock would follow. Mother and I would walk behind and keep the strays in line. About a mile from home we would enter the public road coming out of our road. The ewes always had a worried, sad look on the return home without their lambs. I sure knew how they felt when I came home that day without Billy. I mourned for him for a long time and tried to avoid such attachments to animals in the future.

Walking the lambs to the Bowman Market was a rather complex event. The farmers would talk to each other on the crank telephone to make sure that only one man at a time would be on the road so the flocks wouldn't get mixed up. Sometimes the sheep would fight each other. The males, or buck sheep, never went on these drives unless they were being sold. They created too much havoc by fighting.

One year we had an unusually large buck weighing about 250 pounds. My friends and I would ride him. Riding a sheep requires a firm grasp on its wool since their skin is loose and one has a tendency to roll from one side to the other. I ended up putting a collar and chain on the big buck. I would hook the chain to my little wagon, letting him pull me. Once the buck ran off with the wagon and a young cousin who happened to be inside it at the time. After throwing my cousin out, the buck tore through the yard and jumped the fence. Only then was he stopped because the wagon remained on the other side of the fence.

My cousin jumped up and yelled, "Catch him, Silas! Catch him!" My Dad, who was watching, roared in laughter.

During one of our winter storm nights the wind caused so much drifting that the next morning Dad could not find the white sheep in the white snow. He walked and walked, crossing over the top of a rail fence covered by the drift. That's when he fell through, right on top of the sheep that had taken shelter against the fence, where they'd been buried by the snow. They would survive to be sheared in the spring.

Sheep-shearing, in those days, was quite a job. It was done by hand, using shears that were no more than large scissors. I would hold the sheep while Mother and Dad did the sheering. We then stuffed the wool into burlap bags to be sold by the pound. We took some of the wool to a Floyd County carding plant to be woven into yarn.

Sheep-shearing occurred in the spring. If it was done too early and it turned cold, the sheep would become sick. We tried to keep the sheep clean so the wool would be clean.

In the winter, mother would spin the yarn on the old spinning wheel. I always enjoyed watching her do that. Then she would knit socks, gloves and sweaters. Today, that old spinning wagon rests in my attic. That, and an old blue bedspread she spun, are cherished reminders of the many joys and travails of sheep raising.

Everyone around us had sheepskins tanned by Simon Scott of Mayberry, Virginia. On a cold, blustery winter night, I would curl up on a sheepskin by the fire and drift off to sleep. We would sit by the fire and talk, and when we got ready to read, or Mother to knit, we would light the old kerosene lamps.

We read the Bible a lot more in those days. The Southern Planter magazine came once a month and the newspaper Enterprise came once a week. No colored pictures or funny papers were in our home at first. All that came later.

Chapter Two

There used to be a country store every few miles in Carroll County when I was a boy. People didn't go to town more than two or three times a year, so they did most of their buying and selling at the local country store. There were four or five stores within a mile or two of my home when I was a youngster. The nearest one was at Bell Spur. It's owner, Hub Stanley, was the first store-keeper I knew.

Sometimes we carried an old hen to the store when she quit laying. The first time I saw my wife to be she was carrying a chicken to the store. She was a small girl and I was a boy of twelve. I loved to carry eggs to Stanley's store. Mother would count out seven dozen eggs, making sure they were clean and fresh. The basket held seven dozen and that was all I could carry. I often carried an empty metal kerosene can with me. A potato would be stuck on the pouring spout to keep it from leaking on the walk back home.

Eggs usually brought between 15 and 30 cents a dozen then. Mother would give me a list of things to get at the store: coffee was 16 cents a pound; sugar was 25 cents per five pound; kerosene was 15 to 20 cents a gallon; and a big box of stick matches were 5 cents per box. We seldom bought soap since my Mother could make that at home. Often there were sewing and embroidery threads on the list.

Mother did lots of embroidery work, drawing designs freehand on pillow-cases, bedspreads, table covers, and dresser scarves. The store kept fabric for skirts, dresses, and most any kind of clothing. Most of it sold for 20 or 30 cents a yard.

Mother always gave me instructions not to stay at the store any longer than was necessary or waste time by playing on the way back. But Mr. Stanley's store was a colorful place for a youngster. There were glass jars with pepper-mint, chocolate, horehound, coconut, and other kinds of candy. There was a big metal barrel with peanuts in the shell. Occasionally, I was allowed to have 5 cents worth of candy, which was a lot back then. This treat would last me several days. Chocolate was my favorite. Before there were cracker jacks, peanuts came in a small box containing a surprise. It sure was exciting buying a box for 5 cents and finding jack snapper or a marble in the box. Once I got a nickel as a surprise.

In the winter, Mr. Stanley always had a barrel of salt fish. It was exciting to buy a few pounds of them from the sell of a basket of eggs. I sure did love those salt fish. I would also have to bring Dad back a couple of plugs of chew-ing tobacco. He never smoked but he did chew tobacco back then.

Sometimes I carried butter to the store to sell. Mother had printed a flower on it in the butter printer. If we didn't need as many groceries as the butter and eggs brought, the store clerk would give us credit in the form of a hand written slip of paper.

I brought so much I would have to rest on the way home. It would be a heavy load for me, with a gallon of kerosene for the lamps at home, five pounds of sugar, a pound of coffee, and other goods such as nails or horseshoes. There could also be baking soda, salt, flavoring like vanilla. There might also be some medicines like caster oil or black draught.

One reason I loved to go to the store was the beautiful scenic walk. Going through the open meadows, on a clear day I could see as far away as Pilot Mountain and Sorry Town, both in North Carolina. The Blue Ridge Mountains were always beautiful with their seasonal colors. Progressing through the pasture, I had to go down a steep hill to Squall Creek. As I neared the creek I could hear it gurgle as it poured over a small waterfall. I crossed a very beautiful little stream of cold water by stepping on stones so as not to get my shoes wet, while being careful not to fall and break the eggs.

A road, densely lined with laurel bushes, wound up a grade along a wagon trail through the woods. Sometimes I would be afraid there might be a bear or mad dog in the woods, although I ever saw were rabbits, groundhogs, and lots of squirrels. I did see a fox once or twice and once thought I saw a bobcat. There were no deer in this area at that time.

Often I would see a stranger at the store who would pick on me. In the winter, several men sitting around the pot-bellied stove would tease me. There was a very large man named Charlie Branch who would sometimes pass the store in a wagon drawn by a team of horses. He liked to pick at small boys and we were afraid of him. The store had a double door and most of the time just one door was open. He was so large he had to turn sideways to get his shoulders through the door and then his stomach would drag on the way in. When I heard the door rattle I would look up to see if it was he. My cousin, Mr. Stanley's grandson, and I would all hide under the counter until he left.

Charlie told lots of stories, some of which many have been true and some of which were obviously tall tales. He said that one early spring he had an old sow covered with lice. Someone told him to pour kerosene on her to kill them. He did, but, since the lice were still crawling, he set a match to her in another attempt to kill them. As soon as he set her on fire, she ran circles in a dry broomsage field setting it on fire. The fire quickly crossed to the woods and burned a large area. This may or may not have been true.

Another story of his that I didn't believe concerned his coon dogs. He had a female that liked to run with a pick of other dogs. However, because it was time for her to have pups, he tied her up one day. That night, as the rest of the pack started to run and bark, he claimed he could heard her familiar bark and she knew she had broken loose. After a while, he also heard some youthful yipping with the pack and knew she'd had the puppies and they had joined the race, too.

I met many characters at the store. One lady who came to the store had we today know as "osteoporosis." She was very drawn and stooped over in the shoulders. Someone told her he was sorry for her, adding that she once was very pretty and had a good figure. Her husband replied, "She still has a good figure. Her head is just on backwards."

An old fellow who lived down on the side of the mountain and liked to read was questioned by some of the young people just to see what kind of answer he would give them. They asked if he liked novels. "I'm not sure," he said. "I never eaten any, but I did like ground hogs."

When they asked him if he had eaten any poultry, he replied, "I planted some one time but the chickens scratched it all up."

Being raised in the mountains is different from growing up in the flatlands, but not as different as my relatives in Richmond, Virginia thought. They actually asked if we had room for a garden on the mountain. Many of my cousins lived on the flatter lands at the foot of the mountain.

Some people lived on the side of the mountain. In those days when people were mostly dependent on what you could grow and raise yourself, the people who lived on the sides of the mountain did not fare as well as the ones living on the upland plateaus like us, or on the flatlands below the mountain. One man, who lived on the side of the mountain, met and married a woman from Mount Airy. When he brought her home to his two-room cabin one hot summer there were two hogs in the fireplace. His wife returned to her mother and would not come back to him.

Where I live there is farmland on the north and west side of my home. On the southwest side and east side it is only a few hundred yards to where the mountain begins to drop off. Kibler Valley, and what is now the city of Danville's power plant, is only a mile and one half east of me. I used to walk to Kibler Valley as a teenager - it took me thirty minutes down and ninety minutes back up. The altitude is 1200 feet less at the bottom.

There are beautiful places in the surrounding mountains I explored as a teenager: the Pinnacles of Dan, Squall Creek Falls, Cedar Bluff, Santa Clause Rock and, very near by, Arrat Creek Falls and Jumping Off Rock.

Some of these places are hard to get to and people don't visit them much anymore. When I was small my Mother said "Don't go toward the mountains, stay out of tall weeds and watch out for snakes." Dad was always killing copperhead moccasins and occasionally a rattlesnake during the summer months. We always found them every year in the meadows. Where you found one copperhead you usually found a second one. None of my family ever got snake bitten but some of the neighbors did. Mr. Jake Radford got bit on the hand, after dark one night, as he picked up an armload of cook stove wood, and picked up the snake with it. He was very sick and almost lost a finger. The rest of his life he would have a small stiff middle finger.

Late in my teenage years as they were building the City of Danville Powerhouse they shot off so much dynamite that it scared many snakes out of the mountain. In a three-hour period one July afternoon we killed seven copperheads and one rattlesnake.

Once I was tying some oats into bundles by hand when my Dad saw a rattlesnake. The rattlers were sticking out from under a bunch of oats I was starting to pick up. We killed it and it had thirteen rattles. Each rattle indicates a year of age for the snake.

Later in life I had a collie dog. He killed every snake he could find. He saved me from getting bit as I was getting corn from the corncrib.

I did not see the snake until my collie jumped in front of me and grabbed it. My wife was going into an old cellar with a concrete floor to get some fruit jars. I asked her to let me check the building. Sure enough I found a copperhead lying beside the jars and killed it. My uncle, Earnest Stanley, was driving a truck near Dan River when a bag of fertilizer fell off. He stopped the truck and went back to get the fertilizer. A rattlesnake was lying beside the bag. He killed the snake. He used to kill snakes by grabbing the tail and cracking it like a whip and snapping its head off. Once he was showing some of his friends how he did it with a dead copperhead. He gave it a big jerk and the head flew off and the fangs hung in Mr. Jesse Smith's shirt. Mr. Smith was almost bitten by a dead snake. If the fangs had broken the skin he would have been. Uncle Earnest had a great sense of humor and could tell great stories.

I, nor anyone else in our community, ever went to the doctor much when we were growing up. Sometimes a doctor would come to someone's house if they were very sick. I did split my wrist open with a knife, stuck a sharp snag into my thigh and stuck a nail deep into my foot when I was small. All of these were treated at home. After the wounds were washed, spirits of turpentine was poured over them and they were bound up. I was lucky, blessed by God or the treatment was good because I healed up without infection. Mother did soak them in hot Epsom salts water.

Just before I started to school my parents decided that because I had lots of sore throats I should have my tonsils and adenoid out. We didn't yet have a car as was true of most people so Uncle Earnest Stanley took us to Mount

Airy to see Dr. Cundiff in his model-T Ford truck. The Doctor promised me a big bag of oranges, more than I had ever seen. I don't know if it was because he was putting me to sleep or what it was for. When I woke up I was very sick and had an awful sore throat for a long time and I could eat only oatmeal. Either made me very sick on my stomach. I eventually got over it and was better. I never saw a doctor again until I was thirteen and had a bout with pneumonia.

A Dr. Glenn Cox from Hillsville came to see me twice. Antibiotics were not around then and it took two weeks to break the fever. I came through that all right also.

I remember my real blood daddy came to see me a few times and brought my sisters with him. He gave me a silver dollar when I was five years old. I didn't see my sisters often. I remember Lelia and Maude walking out here to see me and spending the night when I was about five years old. We had a good time playing, then they had to walk the five miles back to their home.

When it came time to go to school I did not want to go, I had not been with other children much and did not know how well I would get along. My parents had begun to teach me. I knew my letters and could count a little.

They read stories from the bible to me and I was anxious to learn to read for myself. The school was a little over a mile from home. It was up and down steep hills and through woods. If I had gone around the road it would have been three miles. I took the nearest way possible. Dad went with me the week before school was to start. We cut bushes and briars out and made me a good path through the woods. He put me a footlog across Squall Creek. I came into the road just above Bell Spur Church. Sometimes I would meet the Scott children when I reached the road or get with the Light children at the church, or the Stanley and Turman children coming up the road from south of Bell Spur. There were Bowmans, Hortons, Cullers, Kimbles and others in the school.

I had to walk one mile going and coming through the woods by myself. It seemed like a long way for a small boy of six to travel alone. I enjoyed the woods, the evergreens in the winter and the creeks I crossed. We crossed near the baptizing pond of Bell Spur Church.

The school was a one-room school with one window and a few desks. The heat was a big iron pot-bellied stove in the center of the room. There were a few nail kegs near the stove we could sit on when we got too cold at our desk. The winters were cold then and there was lots of snow. Seldom were the schools closed because of bad weather. I guess because no one came on buses. We would wade through the snow and go through driving rain.

I can remember going when the ice-coated limbs were crashing all around me. My Mother packed good lunches, many times more than I could eat. There were ham or sausage biscuits, jelly biscuits and a piece of homemade pie or cake. I liked to play so well I did not take time to eat it all. Mother would get on me if I brought some home so I learned to throw some away on the way home and my Dad found it. I was in real trouble then and I did not do that anymore.

At school the water was carried from the nearest spring, which was a long way from the school. Two of the older children were responsible for bringing the water. The water bucket had a dipper that all the students drank from. Mother told me never to drink after anyone and would put me a little can of water in my lunch box. I don't recall ever drinking from the dipper. She was careful about keeping everything clean and not spreading germs.

My lunch was better than some. Some children brought a lard bucket filled with cornbread crumbled into milk. Three members of the same family ate out of the same pail with a spoon each. Some carried a cold sweet potato or a buckwheat cake with molasses on it. Dad said he saw a little fellow bring a few walnuts with a hammer to crack them for his lunch.

The wood for the school stove was usually cut by the older boys and carried in by the smaller boys and girls.

It took a lot of wood and much time was spent cutting wood with a cross cut saw and axes. We learned to use the cross cut saw at an early age. The word survival applied.

We didn't have an outside bathroom. We just didn't have any bathroom at all. If you needed to go you asked to be excused and went to the woods that were nearby.

My first teacher was Eva Croft. Later she was married to Buford Croft and moved to North Carolina.

I think we only went to school six month of the year then. I missed days when I was sick with a cold or the flue. I never had a perfect attendance year until I was in the sixth grade. I don't recall ever having a fight in school but I remember breaking up a few fights between younger boys. I enjoyed reading and arithmetic and was better in spelling than I am now. I was slower at learning to write and have never been really good at it. I should have been a doctor since no one could read my handwriting.

Walking to school wasn't the only place I walked. I walked a mile to get the mail. We didn't go every day as we didn't get much mail then. That was in the days before junk mail, and we did not get a daily paper. We got more letters from relatives than we do now. The Sears Roebuck and Montgomery Ward Catalogues were an important part of our mail. Most of my clothes and shoes that weren't made at home were ordered from them.

It was exciting to get a package and see if everything fit. My parents made sure it was large enough. They didn't want me to outgrow it before I wore it out. This meant that my clothes were too large at first. I usually wore bib overalls at school and at home. Mother saw that they were clean and that I changed when they got dirty.

The first mail carrier I remember, when I went to mail a letter with an order to Montgomery Ward was Mr. Yeatts. He was driving a horse and buggy. I still remember the quiet clucking sound he made to his horse when he wanted it to get going. Sometimes he would ride one horse and lead another one with the packages and mail on it. In the winter he had a blanket across his lap as he rode in the buggy, or surrey as it was called. later a Mr. Alvin Barnard would drive a car and carry the mail. His brother was married to my mother's sister, Bertha. In the winter He, Uncle Guy Barnard, would carry the mail out on this end of the route.

Early one morning Aunt Bertha rode with him out here to visit my mother. She would lay down in the back seat of the car when she saw anyone since no one was supposed to ride with the mail carrier. That morning there was sleet and ice on the ground when a young man came out to meet the mail. He fell down and slipped and fell on the ice.

Uncle Guy said to him, "You need a board to slide on this morning." The young man said, "I don't need a board; I can just slide on my ass." He didn't know Aunt Bertha was in the back seat. In those days people didn't use the today's popular three and four letter words in mixed company.

After the first year in school I enjoyed the summers at home more than ever. I enjoyed the garden and animals. My Dad had bought a new grain drill and I waited on it as he drilled spring oats. I would keep the buckets filled with fertilizer and oats to be poured into the drill each time he came around the field. The drill had a box for clover seed and small grass seed also. It did a good job, better than the old broadcast method. After our oats were drilled we took our horses and went to the neighbors and drilled oats for them.

Mother and I planted potatoes. Dad laid off the land in straight rows before he left to do other things. I remember that mother and I planted ten bushels of potatoes in one day. We dropped the fertilizer and potatoes, which had been cut into small pieces the day before and then covered them with a hoe. We sure were tired at the end of the day.

Of course the chores had to be done no matter how tired we were. Two cows had to be milked, hogs fed, eggs gathered, chickens fed, water carried, wood for the cook stove brought in. Sometimes wood had to be cut unless we already had enough on hand. Early the next morning the chores had to be done again. Someone from the city once asked if we had to milk twice a day. We thought that was funny.

Mother grew her own sweet potato plants or slips as they were called. When the potatoes were ready for harvest she would wrap each one in newspaper after they had dried awhile in the open air. Then she put them in a pasteboard box and put them in a closet near the fireplace where they wouldn't freeze during the winter.

In April, I would clean out the sweet potato plant bed. It was about 5 feet long by 3 feet wide, and 30 inches deep with a wood frame around the top. After cleaning it out I would cut white pine twigs in small pieces and pack them in the bottom about a foot deep. On top of that I packed a thick layer of horse manure from the horse stalls. This was covered with about 6 inches of dirt. The sweet potatoes were buried in this about 2 inches below the surface and the wooden frame was covered with old glass windows. After awhile the potatoes would sprout from the hot bed and produce hundreds of plants. Enough for us and many of the neighbors.

I helped plant all kinds of plants in the garden each year and mother would save the seed. We hardly ever had to buy garden seed.

I tried to lay off the rows with a horse when I was 7 years old. The rows were so crooked Dad laughed at me. I did eventually learned to lay off a straight row. Everything took time and practice. I started planting corn when I was 7 years old. Dad would lay off the rows with one horse, and I followed with the second horse and planter. Dad had bought a new one horse drawn planter. You would put fertilizer in one box and corn in another box. This

way we could plant a lot of corn in one day. The horse was so well trained he would stay right in the row. All I had to do was hold up the planter and keep up. One day while planting there was a large straw rack on top of a solid rock in the middle of the field. Dad lay off a row up to the stack and went around it and started up on the other side. When my horse came to the straw rack he climbed on top and walked across to the other side. I just hung on to the planter and followed along. Dad got a good laugh about that.

There were many things to do on the farm and I enjoyed most of them. We had horses and colts back then. They were workhorses and not just riding horses. We did ride them. My mother had a sidesaddle and I still have it. She took me riding on trips when I was a baby, holding me in her lap. On one occasion she and Dad rode to Claudeville, VA to see her sister Nora Burge. She said that when she crossed Dan River the horse got in deep water up to its belly and she got really nervous.

She was afraid she would fall off or the horse would fall with me in her arms and she was not a swimmer.

I became very attached to different horses as a boy, and especially later as a teenager. I did all kinds of work with horses on the farm as well as logging for the sawmill. Dad was very good with horses as he grew up working with them.

He tells of hauling lumber down Squirrel Spur Mountain and of runaway teams. He also tells of hauling to and from the trains that ran on the narrow gauge railway in Kibler Valley. That was before my time.

I use to hold the tools, nails and such, while he shoed horses. We had several horse-drawn tools that we loaned to other neighbors. The horses worked for others, also, usually for man-hours in exchange for work. Two horses worked for an hour in exchange for one man hour. People would come and work for Dad in exchange for the horse hours. We had two horse turning plows as well as a hillside plow that turned both ways back and forth across the hillside. You swung the plow over and locked it in place as you changed directions. We had harrows, disc, and several types of cultivators. We had a mower and rake for hay, wagons, ground sleds that we made and the grain drill and corn planter.

At the age of seven I could only hoe the garden and cornfield as Dad cultivated them.

I would get very tired of digging the weeds out of the rows all day long. He cultivated a cornfield in a checked pattern one year. He laid it off in three-foot rows, north, south, east and west. He planted the corn, four seed to the hill, where the rows crossed. This eliminated hoeing as he could cultivate it in both directions but it did require planting by hand. He made real good corn that year.

At seven I began to mow with a scythe while Dad cut with horses and a mower. I would mow the corners and especially the rail fences. Mowing with a scythe was hard work that I got better at as I got larger and older. I could put the hay in shocks as Dad raked it. Carrying it up on poles and stacking it came a little later. I did start tramping the haystacks at about seven. Dad would pitch it up with a fork while I went round and round the pole until I topped it off and slid down to the ground.

The rail fences were made from the once plentiful trees that grew on the mountain. Around the time I was born the chestnut trees were dying because of blight. That was a great catastrophe to this area. Many people were dependent on the sale of chestnuts as part of their cash crop. A few trees were still producing. I remember one tree in particular where I picked up chestnuts by the bushel. I put them in sacks and Dad had to carry them while I carried two bucketfuls.

Those old trees were huge. I remember one tree that divided at the ground, each side was three and one half feet in diameter. Dad and Matt Light would cut those old trees for lumber. It would take them all day to cut them down and into saw logs. They would cut in one direction for a while and then in another direction on another side for a while. They used cross cut saws and axes. It would take them until noon to get them on the ground, and they did real well to do that.

Dad told of how they gathered the chestnuts in the fall, and took them to the market for sale. Two-horse wagon loaded with bags full of them. Imagine a wagonload, or two tons of chestnuts. It was a money crop, and a big loss to families in the area when they were gone. They told of how they hurried out to get them early in the morning, whole families working together trying to beat the animals, especially hogs, from eating them all. When most of the chestnuts were gathered the hogs would be turned out and they would feed well on them and save feeding them corn.

I can remember the forest standing full of big dead and dying trees. The big sound trees were cut for lumber and the wind shaken ones were split for rail fences. The small ones were used for wood in the cook stoves. I never knew of another wood that split or burned as well for firewood as chestnut. I split many a block of it.

Many big hollow unsound trees remained in the woods to decay and fall down. Some stood for many years. I'm sure many people still living will remember the big old tree that stood at the bend of the road south of Bell Spur Church.

Chestnut lumber and framing made very good building material. Later the wormy boards that had been discarded back then, became a premium on the market and sold for very high prices. Chestnut fence posts were almost as good as locust. Chestnut logs were easily split into rails. I remember Dad splitting them as fast as I could carry them and lay them into a zigzag fashion for a fence. You could build a fence pretty fast that way. We had many rail fences. They would have reached for two miles if they had been laid end to end. Every field was fenced with rails and many fence lines and outside boundaries were in the woods.

These fences lasted for many years. They were built 6 and 8 rails high, and were superb for holding sheep. Most cattle stayed in their boundaries as well. Horses sometimes pushed them down and they had to be rebuilt. It seemed that we had more rail fences than most of our neighbors - we had more chestnut trees I think.

The loss of the chestnut trees was a sad thing to a farm boy or a forest lover. Chestnut lumber also made nice furniture. The only bad thing I can say about a chestnut tree was that it was a pretty rough thing to step on a dried chestnut burr when barefoot. The taste and flavor of the old chestnut was far better than the Chinese chestnut of today. There was a difference in the flavor and size of the fruit from different trees.

Chapter Three

Summer came and cabbage along with buckwheat were the last crops to be planted. We burned a brush or log pile and later sowed the cabbage seed in the burned over bed. No weeds came up in this soil and the plants grew well. We lay off the rows, made the hills and set the plants with a peg. We carried water and watered each plant. This was a hard chore in dry weather. After cultivating and hoeing the cabbage in late fall, we cut them and hoped we had a buyer.

Sometimes we stored them in a straw rack. Often we would plough a furrow and lay it full of cabbage pulled up by the roots with the roots turned up. They would keep all winter this way and when the ground was thawed we got them out, trimmed off the outside leaves and sold them. Usually the price was a dollar to a dollar and a half a hundred pound. We grew from one to two acres of cabbage.

About the time we were getting ready to go back to school it was potato-digging time. We usually plowed through the row once with the horse drawn plow. Then we went through the rows with the potato digger. We would let the potatoes sun for a few hours and then pick them up, separating them according to size. At first we did not have a root cellar or basement to put them in so we would dig a hole three feet into the ground.

We could put in about 25 to 30 bushels of potatoes, cover it over with boards and a mound of dirt. I got money for my first saving account from potatoes grown this way. With that much hard work you felt like you had really earned it.

Here it was time for my second year of school. I had enjoyed the summer so much I really didn't want to go back to school. I wanted to learn to read better so I went, not that I had a choice in the matter.

This year I was going to set some rabbit gums along my pathway through the woods. I had already been building some. I took boards 6 to 8 inches wide and cut them 30 inches long. Three were cut the same length and one was an inch and one half shorter. Then I nailed them together making a box. I nailed a board over one end. The shorter board was the topside. A trap door was made to fit inside this end with a narrow strip nailed to top and bottom. The trap door must slide easily up and down. Then a half-inch hole was bored in the top, eight inches from the back, and another half way between the first hole and the trap door. A small stick with a notch in it was put through the back hole. That was the trigger. It had to be half the size of the hole. A second stick was fit tight into the second hole. A stick was balanced across the tight stand stick, and tied to the trap door with a nail in the top.

I then tied to the trigger stick with twine. With correct adjusting this made a trap. The lid was held up in place when the trigger notch was engaged. A piece of apple, cabbage or some salt placed in the back of the trap attracted the rabbit. When the rabbit went in after the bait he bumped the trigger and the trap door fell, fastening the rabbit inside. Each morning as I went to school I stopped and checked my rabbit traps. I was always excited to see my trap door down. Sometimes I would have a rabbit and sometimes something had tripped it from the outside. If I had one I would leave it until I was on the way home from school in the afternoon.

We ate rabbits sometimes. They were very good fried with gravy. The country stores also bought them. They bought them in December through February when the weather was cold. I would take the entrails out and put a little salt in them and hang it in a cool out building. The first chance I got I would take them to the store and get 15 to 20 cents apiece for them. I sold enough to get me a good pair of lace up shoes one winter and a pair of leggings to wear when it snowed.

Later I set steel traps along Squall Creek near my pathway. I would have to leave early to check all my traps each morning before school. On weekends I would check each morning. I caught lots of opossums, a few raccoons, a few gray foxes and one red fox.

I skinned them out and put their skins on a board to dry for a while and then shipped them to a fur company. I made 30 or 40 dollars each winter this way. The money was added to my savings account. Opossum furs brought 2 to 4 dollars each, raccoons 10 to 12 dollars, and a red fox 20 dollars. It was really a thrill to catch a red fox. Once I caught a mink and got 30 dollars for it. I never caught a bobcat but Dad did, when I was small. Something caught one of our big turkeys out of an apple tree one night. Only half of it was eaten and the rest left. Dad set steel traps around it that evening. The next morning before daylight he gave me the kerosene lantern and said go check on the traps. I was eight years old at the time and felt nervous going out in the dark. When I checked the traps, one was gone. I began walking around the board fence that surrounded the field very much aware that the lantern was giving a very poor light.

All of a sudden a big bobcat stuck his head up over the fence and hissed at me. I ran all the way to the house with my hair standing straight up, somehow managing to hold onto the lantern. The cat had climbed over the fence caught in the trap and got hung up. Dad went back and killed him. I was shaking all day.

Our neighbor, Gracie Quesinberry, caught one and sold him to a zoo.

Sometimes I would catch a skunk. I sure hated this; it messed up the traps and they were worth nothing.

A neighbor boy Arles Quesinberry, Garcie's son, followed my example and caught a skunk one morning and got too close to it. He went on to school and the teacher sent him home. She said either he went home or the rest of the school would have to go home.

I found many ways to make a few dollars as we went along. I saved some and spent some trying out new things. I liked to read and I spent some on books. I would read anything I could find including the Bible, with Mothers encouragement.

I was not really afraid of going to school until I was in the fourth grade. One of my classmates saw a strange animal near the edge of the woods I had to go through. He thought it looked like a gorilla or maybe it was a bear. Then the teacher saw a strange animal as she came home from school after the students left. She was boarding with my Uncle Deck and Aunt Menerva Turman, who lived near Bell Spur Church. Most of the teachers did board with them. We never did find out what the animal was.

On the first week of school following summer vacation we would work to help clean up the schoolyard. We would take mowing scythes and axes and cut down the tall grass, briars and small bushes that had grown up during the summer. The girls washed the window, swept, dusted and cleaned out the inside of the school.

The schoolyard was very small so a neighbor, Mr. John Collins allowed us to make a place to play baseball on his property. Usually he would allow wood to be cut to heat the school.

We would bring a ball from home to play with. It was often a ball of tightly rolled yarn. Occasionally we had a rubber ball to play with. The cleared area was so small the balls were often lost in the high weeds. We also played Etna Over. We would have a team on either side of the schoolhouse and the ball would be thrown over the school. Whoever caught the ball would be followed by the rest of the team and run to the other side of the school seeing how many people could be hit with the ball on the opposing team before they got back to the other side. People that got hit became team players on the side that hit them. We started out with equal number of players and the team with the most players when the game was decided to be over, won.

We played Bull in the Pen, which was a game of throwing the ball at someone. Finally we built a volleyball court and bought ourselves a net and volleyball.

When I was four and one half years old my Mother needed cataract surgery. John Collins was Mothers cousin and the only person around that I knew that had a car. He took Mother to Roanoke to have the surgery. Roanoke seemed so far away. We went by Radford and crossed the New River on a ferry.

I had never seen a river so big. We spent the night with Uncle Fred Harrell and Aunt Annie. They had an indoor bathroom! A flush toilet and a tub to take a bath in! I remember being so worried about Mother and the trip seemed so far away.

On the way back, near Radford, Mr. Collins steering rod came loose and he ran down a bank and through the fence. No one was hurt and the car hardly had a scratch. People didn't worry about little scratches on cars those days anyway. I think the car was called a Star, anyway it wasn't a Chevrolet or Ford. Mothers operation was a success.

Mother had high blood pressure, sick headaches, and some heart problems so I helped her out with the housework a lot. She taught me many things including reading the Bible. She tried to teach me to sing but was not very successful at that.

I would help her with the canning and we canned almost everything imaginable. We didn't have a pressure cooker canner so for years the canning was done outside in a big tub over a fire. One of my jobs was keeping the fire going. We canned pork. mutton, beef and chicken. I would grind the sausage by hand in a grinder and she would make patties and fry them, then they would be put in a can. It all sure was good.

She dried beans, apples and even sweet corn over the wood stove. She pickled beans, beets, cucumbers and peaches.

She would also, in the cold wintertime, pack stone crocks with sausage and cover them over with grease and set them in the springhouse. Every morning when we wanted sausage she would cut some out of the crock and fry it. It kept very well that way. I ground up the meat scraps from hogs and it was heated to draw the grease out. This was our lard. We never had to buy any. Cooking oil was unheard of. The beef and sheep (mutton) fat was saved in the same manner and was used to make candles and rubbed on shoes and boots to soften and waterproof them.

Most kids went barefoot in the summer months, this saved buying so many shoes. Sometimes it was hard on our feet. Once I got a stone bruise on my heel and had to walk on my tiptoe for days. We had to be careful about stepping on bees as well.

We kept lots of bees when I was small. My Dad was good at working with them. We always had plenty of honey. We once had 40 stands of bees. Some of our bees were kept in old time stands and some were in the newer type with frames and separate sections called supers. The honey could be removed easier from the newer type. With a bellows blowing smoke you could drive the bees from the top, back into the main hive, and lift the top section off. We checked them to see when they were filled with honey. There were lots of different kinds of honey depending on what type of bloom the bees got the nectar from. The best was sourwood, which we didn't have much of at this elevation.

Locust and poplar made from the blooms of the locust and poplar trees was good honey. Sweet clover was also good honey. Honey made from the bloom of mountain laurel was supposed to be poison. Old timers said uncapped honey, honey that the bees had not completely sealed in the comb, was also poison. Maybe the bees knew it wasn't good and wouldn't finish storing it. Much honey was made from the bloom of buckwheat. Bees really flocked to the buckwheat when it was white in bloom. Buckwheat was used for feed grain for farm animals and for flour.

Some people sowed sweet clover for bees. Bees gathered pollen from fruit tree blooms to feed their young and at the same time pollinated the fruit trees. They also got pollen from some vegetables as well as corn, and many weeds and flowers. Sometimes we fed the bees sugar water in the early spring after a hard winter. A worker bee lives only about 30 to 60 days. Sometimes we would find bee trees in the woods. This would be where the hive had swarmed or decided to divide and instead of going into a hive like the owners would hope for, they would settle in a hollow tree in the woods. Some of our neighbors would cut them down for the honey. Swarming would take place in May, June or July. When they would swarm a group would gather and follow a new green from the old hive.

Dad had a saying: "A bee swarm in May is worth a stack of hay; a swarm in June is worth a silver spoon; a swarm in July is worth an apple pie."

After July it was not worth hiving since the blooming season was almost over. Hiving a swarm of bees is an amazing thing. It was my job sometimes when Dad was out in the field to watch the bees to see if they swarmed. When they did, we hoped they would settle on a lower limb so we could get them down easily, we would put down wide boards and set a new bee hive stand on them. We called it a bee gum. Then we cut off the limb or twig so the bees would be crawling up a slight incline. Some people pecked lightly on the hive with a stone or piece of metal. I never knew why, but it did seem to work. The bees usually went right in and were moved to a permanent place that night. Sometimes if something would happen to the queen they would come out and return to their old stand. Sometimes they would just leave and fly away to the woods to a place their scouts had already picked out. Sometimes we would chase after them throwing dirt sticks or anything available into them or beating on a wash tub or something to make a loud noise and they would slow down and settle in a tree where we could hive them. More often they just rose higher and went on their way.

You usually did not get stung while hiving bees if you remained calm and not fight them or mash them.

If they seemed ill we would wear a veil. You could tell be the noise they made if they were mad.

Robbing them was a different matter, they did not like you to take their honey. Bee keeping is a science and anyone going into the business should study and prepare for it.

Harvesting corn in those days was quite a task. We cut it with corn knives in late September and tied it up in big shocks. It stayed there until the first of November. At that time we hauled it together and began shucking (removing the outer covering) the ears. We set a ring of fodder around us for a windbreak and pitched the corn into a pile as we shucked it. Shucking corn was a cold job. Sometimes we shucked at night by the moonlight or lantern light. Shucking was easily done if the fodder was damp.

My parents tell the story how they were shucking corn by moonlight when my birth Dad came to ask them to take me since my mother had just died. It was December 13.

We would stack the fodder in stacks to be used as feed for the cows during the winter months. Sometimes we pulled the fodder below the ears while it was green in the field and tied it in small bunches and hung it on the ears to dry. After the bunches dried we tied them into larger bundles and stored them in the barn to feed the sheep.

We would then cut the corn tops above the ears in bunches in the field to dry. They were used as cow feed. Later the ears were pulled off and hauled to a building and stored.

We usually drilled wheat and rye every fall about the first of October. We did not buy seed but saved our own from year to year. In the spring we drilled oats and in June or early July we drilled buckwheat. We would stack the wheat, rye and oats close together and what we called a thresh yard. The buckwheat was piled into a big stack too. Cutting all this with a grain scythe or grain cradle was a big hard job. I could not do this until I was twelve but I got very good at it. When I was seven years old I learned to bind the bundles and help put them in shocks to dry and into stacks later. Mr. Cook Quesinberry and I cut 5 acres of oats one day with the grain scythe. I was 14 years old then. I sure was tired and sore the next day.

The day that the threshing machine came was a big day. I can remember the treadmill powered by horses that Dad talked about. I also remember hauling some grain to machines powered by a steam boiler. One belonged to Gnat Stanley and another by Lee and Merion Smith. Getting the straw home after the grain was removed was no easy matter. It was piled high on the wagon and a pole was tied across the top to help hold it on.

What I remember most is the threshing machine and working crew coming to our farm.

The first ones were pulled by a tractor with metal wheels. It took six men to work around the machine. My job as a small boy was to hold the burlap bags for the men to empty the grain into. If everything was working good the grain, especially oats, came through fast. It kept a man moving to empty the half bushels pails, putting one half bushels to the bag. We usually had about a short day of threshing to do. It took time to set the machine down and get ready to start, it might be ten o'clock getting everything going. The best part was quitting at noon for lunch. Mother had a big task preparing all that food. Meats, vegetables and desserts. I can taste it now. I remember one year we had 160 bushels of buckwheat, over 100 bushels of rye, over 100 bushels of wheat, and 200 bushels of oats. We had to haul all this and pour it into grain bins. These bins were in the old house where Dad and Mother lived when they were first married in January 18, 1914. They built a new house in 1921 when I was a baby.

The threshing machine owner got paid by taking toll, one bushel out of every sixteen. Farmers from all over the community went with the machine helping one another get their grain threshed. My uncle Guy Barnard did the threshing around here for several years. Someone got to stealing the gas out of his tractor wherever he left it at night. One night he burned all the gas out of the tank and closed a valve below the tank. Then he put some water in the tank.

The next morning a pickup was setting about one hundred yards from the tractor. They had drained water out of his tank and put it in theirs and their motor quit running. He knew who the truck belonged to.

Chapter Four

Going to the mill has been a big part of my life. The mill when I was a lad was almost as important as the country store. There were numerous mills everywhere in the county. Almost as many mills as stores. The first mills were water powered. By the late 1920's some were steam powered and soon became gas powered.

The first mill was George Terry's. Joe Terry was the operator I remember. In those days we had corn meal ground, Wheat for flour and occasionally rye flour. We were always having buckwheat ground for buckwheat pancake flour. There was no such thing as buying flour at the store. You might buy your flour at the mill. It would be very good in those days.

Mills were always interesting to me as a boy, watching the old water wheels and seeing the many pulleys and belts, watching the miller hurrying about his work, and adjust the mill. It was quite a sight seeing the people go and come in buggies and wagons. Some even rode horseback with a bag of grain thrown up behind them on the horse's back. Sometimes Dad would send me on a horse to mill with a sack of corn and I would hope it did not fall off the horse. I would have had a real struggle lifting it back on the horse. We would take wagonloads of grain to be ground for feed for the hogs and sheep. Milk cows also got ground grain but horses and chickens ate whole grain.

There was always the wheat and buckwheat bran, by-products of flour that were used for feed.

Times were changing fast. In 1927 and 1928 we started seeing cars and trucks. Roads were being built. They were still dirt roads that got very muddy during the winter.

One day as we were working in the field we heard a strange noise. It seemed to be coming from overhead. I looked up. It was an airplane! I had never seen one, though I had been hearing and reading about them. Dad had talked about the few he had seen when he fought in Europe in World War I.

On the Fourth of July we were cutting and putting rye in the shock and I was excited as I had been promised that we would take the whole afternoon off and go to Laurel Fork to the Fourth of July Celebration. Laurel Fork was only five miles away but I seldom got that far from home as a small lad. There was going to be an airplane there in the afternoon. Doris Webb was flying his little plane down from Maryland.

He landed on a dirt strip and my parents took me up close and we watched it take off and fly. What a thrill that was. Little did I know that later I would be in the air force.

I was always reading and hearing talk about radios. Soon I would get to hear one. Our neighbor, Tyler Quesinberry, had ordered all the parts and was building one. He was a very smart man, he did lots of reading and studying and educating himself.

For some time had been making and developing pictures in the area. He built his own cabinet for the radio and put the works in and bought the batteries. When he had finished it, we were invited over to hear it. I don't think there was another radio anywhere around. How unbelievable it was hearing people talking, singing and making music hundred of miles away!

People flocked in to hear the "Grand Ole Opry" on Saturday nights. I got to go at other times when there weren't so many people around. The batteries at that time didn't last very long. Later they would be improved.

Tyler put a water wheel on Squall Creek about one half miles from his house and hooked it to a generator and ran two wires all the way to his house. He had electric lights and could recharge the six-volt batteries used in cars and some radios. I was so interested in the radio I had wires running all over the place in my playhouse which was located in a room in the old house. I imagined I had a radio. Tyler later became the best radio and TV repairman I ever knew. I started saving money for a radio and was able to get a R.C.A. battery radio in 1932.

We were buying more milk type cattle, especially Guernseys. We bought a registered bull from Hamm Newman. Other farmers brought their cows to breed with our bull. We charged a $1 breeding fee. We had lots of milk and were looking for a market.

We had a market for cream so we got a cream separator, which we still have.

Many people have never seen a cream separator. It was turned by hand at that time. It had a gearbox and ran a high speed. The milk was poured into a holding reservoir and it went down through a series of discs turning at a high speed. It was hard to turn at first until it picked up speed. When it picked up speed you poured the milk in either warm or cold. We usually poured the milk in fresh from the cow. It turned so fast it made high-pitched sounds. It had two spouts we sat buckets under. A stream of skim milk came out one and a smaller stream of cream came out of the other one.

We put the cream in five-gallon cans and kept it in the springhouse in cold water. Every third day a hauler picked it up. We were still milking by hand and it would be a long time before we got electric power. I loved the cows and we had some very good Guernseys. They produced more cream than the Holsteins. Dad sold some of the older cows that did not produce so well. The skimmed milk we fed to the hogs. We fed quite a few and they really did grow on skim milk and corn. I was liking farming better all the time. I was also enjoying school and reading. I would sit down to read on a rainy day but there was still work to do. Mom would say, "Go get a bucket of water."

I would answer, "As soon as I get to the bottom of the page."

She would reply, "I need it right now."

We didn't have a weatherman then so we had to forecast our own weather. If the sunset behind a cloud it would rain before it set again. Thunder before seven meant rain before eleven. There were dozens of old Indian signs like sundogs at sunset means change in weather within 24 hours. Dad said there was only one sign you could be sure about. Thick clouds all around and pouring down in the middle. This was a sure sign of rain.

The neighbor boys came to visit and play with me more often now. One Sunday afternoon I got a little red wagon and it was called a radio flyer. We rode down the hills and built roads through the woods to ride on. We built the trucker wheel wagon all by ourselves. It was all wood, the wheels were made from a black gum log. They were drilled in the center and the axles were made from locust or hickory wood.

My cousin Wilton Stanley made some real good ones using some metal. He had access to his dad's blacksmith shop. Uncle Earnest was in the sawmill business and he had a log skidder. He pulled logs out of the mountain with a cable. I made a play log skidder. I planted post in the ground and made a drum to hold the wire from a dogwood trunk, used telephone wire for the cable, drilled holes in the post and put a hand crank in one end.

I would turn the crank and wind the wire around the drum. I pulled pieces of wood out of the forest, to the area where Mother did her laundry near the spring. She used them to heat water in the cast iron pot. That way gathering wood was a play job, and I had fun. If I had to have carried it out in my arms it would have been work.

One day when I was winding out the wood she was washing. I had gotten very dirty. She made me take off my clothes and put them in the wash pot to boil so she could wash them. I was so embarrassed and didn't know what to do but she had broken off a switch and knew I must do it. I had no clothes down there. The house was about a hundred yards away and she told me to go to the house and dress after I washed up. What if someone came up while I was naked? Then horribly, we heard someone talking as they came down the spring path from the house. It was two neighbor girls that were a little older than me. Mother called them to come on down to the spring! There wasn't anything to do but to run to a nearby laurel thicket and hide!

It sure was a good thing the weather was warm. They visited with Mather a long while and I could hear them giggling about me. They pretended they were coming in my direction, but didn't. They finally left and I went to the house and got on some clothes. I was more careful about getting my clothes dirty after that.

Washing was a hard job for Mother back then.

I remember sometimes scrubbing the clothes on the washboard and wringing the water out by hand. The soap was usually homemade lye soap, and if it were store bought it was the same type yellow cake soap. The only bleach that was bought was in a small wooden box and was called bluing.

Mother made most of the soap we used for laundry and bathing. It was made from trimmings from butchering pigs, pork skins and such. All of this was put in the big iron pot that we boiled the laundry in. The heat was kept low until all the grease was melted out. The fat scraps were saved for cracklings and the meat skins were dried in the oven and used for snacks as the same pork skins are today.

She needed lye to mix with the grease to make soap. That was homemade too. It was made from wood ashes. A wooden barrel with both ends removed was set on some boards and filled with ashes. The barrel was set so it slanted slightly in one direction then water was poured in at the top and drained through the ashes and was caught underneath in a stone crock. This was a slow process and took several weeks. The crock was covered so rainwater could not get in it. The water in the crock was lye water. It was mixed with the pork grease and boiled to make soap. It was boiled until it became thick and was poured into a pan and allowed to cool and cut into squares. This was our soap.

Chapter Five

Dock and Pricilla Bowman lived on the south side of our property when I was a lad. They were in their declining years and could not see well. Some said his vision was better than he pretended it was. He had a long gray beard and moved slowly. She always wore black and usually had on a black bonnet and a big apron. They didn't seem to have many of this life's material blessings but seemed happy. Mother would send me to take them milk and butter, vegetables or sometimes just a pone of corn bread. They had chickens and a small garden. If they had any income I don't know what it would be from. Of course they had no rent to pay or light and water bills or anything else that I know of. Their old house had three rooms and one room upstairs. There was a root cellar underneath it. The house had two fireplaces that as well as the chimneys were made from local rock. On of the chimneys still stands, although the house is long gone.

There was a small barn, chicken house and corncrib. The place was in a small cove on Squall Creek with the hills rising up all around it. From there you could not see another house or even know there was an outside world.

In those days there was a small apple orchard with about 50 trees of many varieties on the south slope above the house.

Some of the apples were early apples and they would have plenty of good apples from late summer until late fall.

I remember going down to the Bowmans and seeing long strings of whole green beans strung on a sewing threads and hung in front of the fireplace to dry. They had no cook stove and did all their cooking in the fireplace. For this reason they kept a fire in the fireplace winter and summer. Once I was down their and their son Tom was there and he was drunk. I was afraid of him. He lived on a ridge across the valley from us. Sometimes he would work for my Dad. I remember now of hearing them carrying a conversation from one hill to the other.

Like Dad would call in a very loud voice, "Hey, Tom, can you come over and help me today?"

"No, I got too odd barn much to do here today" or "I'll be over tar", he might answer.

He must have been a strong man because I would see him passing here from Willie Shelor's store carrying on his shoulder a 100-pound bag of daisy wheat middlings to feed his hogs. He would carry it for at least a mile and a half up and down steep hills. Some of the men in those days were strong and had lots of endurance from having to do hard work.

There were a dozen peach trees with large juicy peaches and two big plum trees stood in the front yard. They had access to these without cost.

Dad hauled apples out of there by the wagonload. We use to give these away and may have sold a few. Apples with no worms, no disease, and no spray stuff on them.

This seemed such a peaceful place and I felt the peace of God when I was down there all alone as a small child. Years later when our children came home from college all up tight they wanted first thing to go down there and walk by the creek. They would come to the house having left their troubles behind them.

Here in this place the hills of evergreens, white pine, and mountain laurel rose up around you, and there was no sound of the outside world, just the murmur of Squall Creek as it flowed along on the way to Dan River. There were two good springs near the house and not far to carry it. Now it seems too hard to get to this place but not back then when every one walked or went by wagon or horseback, and my legs were young. You had to go up hill to get out from there in any direction unless you went down the creek. If you went down the creek you soon came to where Squall Creek tumbled over the mountains on its way to Kibler Valley. People don't have time to appreciate the beauty and peace of things like this anymore.

Progress has its advantages and disadvantages and it does not always make for peace and happiness and the joy of life.

My uncle Jim Turman was a big strong man who could lift an enormous amount of weight.

He was always playing pranks and got into trouble as a boy. Then all the guns were muzzleloaders. He had been hunting and was passing a neighbors house when the lady of the house was hanging out laundry.

He said to her, "Look out Old Haley, I am going to shoot." He raised the gun, which was not loaded but had a firing cap in it and pulled the trigger. When she heard the explosion she thought she had been shot and fell over in a dead faint. She took him to court and he had to pay a fine for it.

I heard stories of him lifting logs that two ordinary men couldn't lift. He coals really swing a scythe in cutting rye or wheat. In his older days he got a stiff neck and someone talked him into going to a chiropractic doctor.

When the doctor popped his neck he jumped up and drew back his fist and said, "If you do that any more I will bust your head."

The doctor ran out and didn't even come back to give him the bill.

We saved all our seed back then. Mother shelled the different varieties of green beans and other types of beans and carefully labeled them, storing them in brown paper bags. Sugar corn and all other types of garden seed were saved.

Dad even saved grass seed he cut with the scythe.

There was orchard grass and randall grass he tied in bundles and put it in small shocks to dry. Then he put it on a canvass and threshed it out with a stick or frail. Then he winded it, that is, he tossed it up in the air on a windy day, and the chaff would blow away and the heavier seed would fall back onto the canvas.

Mr. Cook Quesinberry and his sons would go into the mountain in late summer and fall ginseng hunting. They called it Sang. Some days they could make more money that way than working for wages. They would wander over the mountains watching for snakes as they gathered the Ginseng roots. It was not an easy job.

Mr. Cook got interested in growing flowers in his older days and would have huge beds of dahlias with all different colored blooms. He would carry the bulbs from door to door and sell them in early spring. His wife Mallie contacted influenza during World War One and never really recovered. She lay bedfast thirty some years that way. She would do beautiful embroidery and artwork. Later after she had died it all burned up in a house fire.

Dad decided to sell some of the old cows that were not producing so well. This was just before the depression and he got $600 dollars for six cows. A little later after the depression hit they were selling for $20 each. He decided to buy a car. He bought a 1929 Model a ford for the price of six cows.

Now in the early 90's it would take 25 or 30 cows to buy a car. Mr. Edgar Barnard sold him the car and brought it up from Mount Airy. Dad had never had a driving lesson so Mr. Barnard gave him one lesson. The first thing Dad did was to run through the wire fence. It didn't hurt Dad or the car. Later Dad drove the car to the store and bought a jug of vinegar. The vinegar turned over and he grabbed for the jug and ran through the fence again. He drove for 40 more years and never had another accident. He drove that Model A for nine years.

We lived on a private road and Dad mostly kept the car in the garage in the winter months. The battery would run down from not being used. Our road was narrow and muddy. I would help fill the ruts with rocks and beat them in with a hammer during the winter months. Often we would shovel snow or we would just give up and just stay in or walk or ride horseback. I recall Dad taking me to school a few times when it was raining. I didn't get to drive any until I was sixteen. By that time we had to get driving permits.

The year 1929 was a very dry year and not a good crop year. I remember it was the year the mountain burned. The mountain burned on the east side of Dan River from Tater Hill Mountain (now known as Ground Hog Mountain) to The Pinnacles of Dan. The trees on the mountainside were all dried up by September.

The fire lasted for two weeks. At times we could hear the roaring of it as it raced up the steep mountains. It sounded just like thunder and it made the windows shake in the house. My mother would pray and pray, we were so afraid to go to sleep at night. The fires seemed to calm down at night and be the worst in the afternoon. The hot sun would be beating down while the fire raged. We were afraid it would cross the river and race up the mountain toward us. If it had it would have burned all our property. It did finally cross the river near the Pinnacles but men fighting the fire and a shower of rain stopped it. I could stand in our mountain field and watch the red blaze stretch up the mountainside at times.

Much of the time the smoke lay around us like a heavy fog, and made breathing difficult I have seen other forest fires since then but nothing to compare to this one.

Mother was not well that year. She prayed a lot and read her Bible a lot. We went to church once or twice a month. Usually just once a month in the wintertime at Bell Spur Church. We walked to church back then before we got the car. My parents were not members at that time.

Being an only child and not being with people much, I was shy and bashful. Once my parents bought me a little blue suit with short pants. They thought it was so cute for me to wear to church in the hot summer months.

We walked to church one Sunday when I was wearing my suit and was so embarrassed with my legs showing. When some of the other boys and girls laughed or grinned at me I thought I would die. Once when Mother sent me to the store in a hurry I was wearing pants and a short shirt. I begged her to let me change but she wouldn't. I felt so embarrassed. When I got near the store a group of men were telling stories as usual, and when someone told something funny they all laughed. I turned and started to run away thinking they were laughing at me. I finally sneaked back a little later.

Two of my aunts lived in Illinois several years after the married. What a joy when they came for a visit. I had been seeing Ford and Chevrolet cars occasionally. They were driving big Packard cars and I had never seen anything like that in my life. Another relative got to come into Stuart on a train and I got to go with Dad to meet them. I had not been close to a train before. All the steam engines I had seen before were sitting still.

School was getting more interesting all the time. One teacher came and looked at the school grounds grown up with weeds, briars and everything else and just stayed two days and left. We finally got Miss Mamie Marshall to teach that year. She was a very good teacher. She was strict and very good for a bunch of rowdy kids.

Chapter Six

Dad said that the automobile would be the ruin of God's earth. I listened and smiled and thought he was foolish. Now I can see the logic to his thinking.

We say that the car and airplane have brought the world closer together. It has brought the world closer together but the family further apart. When travel was slower man had time to visit his neighbors and learn to love him instead of rushing off to Hawaii or Mexico on vacation, to get acquainted with the girl next door and marry her. He married someone of the same background as he had and worshiped the same God and had similar values. Today, many times peoples of different cultures and backgrounds are physically attracted to each other and marry. This doesn't last and many times divorce is the result.

The car and modern transportation has helped bring this about. People are always in a hurry to make more dollars to buy two or more cars. They are busy to make another dollar to make payments on the cars, to buy the gas, to get the insurance, to keep it on the road. This takes a big chunk of man's income. The car has also taken the Mother out of the home because she, too, is helping keep the two cars on the road so she and her husband can go their separate ways. The children get on a school bus to go great distances; that is supposed to be better.

It brings our children together in groups but our educational systems are for the most part getting worse every year.

The automobile helps the criminal get the scene of the crime and to get away quickly from his crime.

Without the car and our great transportation system that we have we would not have all the imports we have. Cars and toys from Japan, plastic items from Korea instead of leather ones from next door. We would not have had the Asian flu or the Japanese beetle or maybe not the blight that killed the chestnut trees. We would not have the polluted air and water. True, the automobile has its good side, but I'm afraid Satan is driving in it these days, and using it to destroy man and God's beautiful earth.

The Bible tells us that God has said you shall have no other God before me. Man tends to put his car and T.V. before God. Children are so glued to the T.V. that they haven't time to learn to read and if the power goes off they are at a loss for anything to do.

Man is making a god out of the computer but it will be a tool of the devil. Man has many plans but only God's plans will prevail. Ages come and go and man's plans come and go. There was a stone age, an iron age and now a plastic age. Ages will come and go until God sees fit to make an end to it all.

The great depression came suddenly. I think Dad was expecting it but didn't know what to do. He was better prepared financially than some people and having a small family helped. Some of our neighbors who had large families had a hard time. I recall some of them borrowing money from Dad. Some of them just on their word without giving a note. I believe most of them paid him back as soon as they could.

Our near neighbors the Quesinberrys cleared off a mountainside near Squall Creek. It was very steep. They dug holes with a maddox or grubbing hoe and planted corn and beans and even potatoes without any plowing or turning the soil. They made a lot of corn and survived. I remember Tyler coming by carrying a bag of beans and a big rattlesnake he had killed while picking the beans. People really helped out with one another in their hardships and shared in one another needs in 1930. This was quite a hard year on the farm.

The big thing for me and the rest of the community in 1930 was that the association meeting that was being held at Bell Spur Primitive Baptist Church. The church had a large membership then and even non-members took part in the preparation. Houses all around the neighborhood were repaired and painted inside and out. Food of all kinds was prepared before time. Preparations were made for lots of people to spend the night.

Straw tick beds were made and placed on the floor in every available room. Chickens were killed and dressed and extra sheep and pork had been canned ahead of time. Plenty of sugar, flour and coffee were stocked in the pantries for the baking. Mother kept me running, there was so much for me to do. I had never seen her bake so many cakes and pies.

There would be three days, Friday, Saturday and Sunday at the church. Some people began to arrive about mid-week. Most every one came by car but a few nearby came by horse and buggy. Cars came from other states. I had never seen so many cars in my life. Uncle Deck Turman provided them with a big field to park in next to the church. The weather was warm and dry. Someone had hauled ice from Mount Airy in 50-pound blocks. I had never seen ice in warm weather before. People from below the mountain were there with truckloads of watermelons. Three refreshment stands had been built at separate locations. They were temporary shelters made of rough lumber.

They sold candy, chewing gum, peanuts, fruit, oranges, and strawberry flavored drinks. I liked them. I had prepared also and had saved some change for those days too. They had strawberry and vanilla ice cream and orange pop. I had never seen ice cream before other than the snow cream we made at home in the winter time. Boy, was it good. They soon sold out.

I roamed through the fields of parked vehicles. I had never seen such large cars and trucks like these and so many of them.

They preached from nine until twelve. I would get close enough to listen to some of it, but the crowd was too big to get near the outdoor stands and rows of seats where they were preaching. The church would not have held all the preachers that were there much less the people.

When lunchtime came I was not hungry after all the ice cream, peanuts and drinks I had enjoyed. It's a good thing I wasn't. I couldn't get near the long tables because of the crowd. I had never seen so much food that was carried and put on the tables. Everyone seemed to have a good appetite. Back then : children were made to wait until the last to eat, but there was some food left, chicken wings, beans and cake crumbs. Children thought they would starve until their turn came to eat.

After church there was more preaching and singing until late afternoon. We hurried home and Mother got busy in the kitchen preparing a big evening meal for some relatives and friends that lived a long way off that would be spending the night.

Some people ate so much they got sick. Dad said eating too much honey was what had made them sick. They talked and visited until late that night before going to bed.

Then early the next morning Mother was up early preparing a big breakfast.

She had ham and eggs, sausage and gravy and lots of biscuits with honey and jelly of all kinds. Then we packed another big lunch to take to church again. The second and third day of the association was pretty much the same.

When it was all over Mother came home and went to bed tired and worn out and had to go get medicine for high blood pressure. I had to do the house cleaning, wash the dishes, do the laundry and ironing for two weeks. Dad did some cooking. We were really behind on the farm work also. Dad hired a little help and we got caught up.

I had not been interested in girls at age ten. I liked both boys and girls to play with. I got rather lonely at times but was much too busy with all the farm work to think much about it. I would read every spare minute I had. I bought the "Grit" paper once a week for a nickel and looked forward to it. I had read a big part of the Bible, but did not understand it, or at least parts of it. I guess I had as much understanding as most ten year olds.

Cutting timber and saw milling was a big thing for me and others back then. It helped a lot toward our income I was not allowed to help cut the trees at that age, but I did log some. The horses were very gentle.

Dad and Taylor Scott were cutting the trees and he would hook up the logs or help me to do so. The horses pulled them into the mill.

One horse could pull one log while big logs took two horses. They were so well trained they did not need lines. I just followed them in and unhooked the logs and took the horse back to the woods for another trip. The Terry's, Sam, Herbert and Hugh, were running the first mill where I logged here at our place. Herbert fired the big steam boiler while Sam operated the saw and other men off-barred and packed the lumber. They were sawing the chestnuts before they all went bad and rotted. They were cutting some oak, pine and poplar too. All were good size trees. I remember them moving the big steam engine with a big yoke of steers and horses in front of it. They moved it down a steep grade with one team and had a big tree lap behind it to hold it back. Dad and others hauled the lumber out with horses and wagon up Squall Creek by the Dock Bowman house, then on up by Jake Radford's house to the top of the mountain where route 614 now is. There it was loaded on trucks and taken to Mount Airy. Later Joe Kimble sawed the chestnut up that was near our house where it was easier to get to. Gude Bowman fired up the steam boiler while Dad and Matt Light cut the trees. Dalton Culler logged a yard with his steers. I logged the second yard with horses. I was in school when the first yard was logged.

Our old barn was falling down. It had been built by Bill Overby from whom Dad bought the farm.

He had also built the first house Dad and Mother had lived in when they had first got married. We finally tore it down in the thirties. Barnie Shelor built us a new barn in the 1930's. It was still in good shape sixty years later when hurricane Hugo wrecked it. I never saw Bill Overby, or Bill Obe as he was called but I heard many tales about him. How he bootlegged moonshine whiskey and never was caught, how he kept a wild cat tied to his front porch and they said he rolled a big rock into the back of his fireplace and told his wife that was the back stick and she could cut the small wood.

At that time there were still some big trees standing here, old dead oaks when I was a lad. The limbs had been cut off of the laps about 40 feet from the ground. Dad said Bill Obe climbed the trees and cut the limbs off when he lived here. He moved to West Virginia and sometime later when he died he was brought back and buried at Bell Spur.

When I was eleven I started plowing with the two-horse plow. I loved to plow and smell the newly plowed ground as it turned over. We plowed a few acres for corn and a few acres for oats where we had planted corn the previous year. In addition to the corn land there was six or more acres for potatoes, maybe two acres for cabbage and three or four for buckwheat. Then in the fall we plowed some more for wheat and rye. It took six to eight hours to plow

41

an acre with our team. They stepped pretty fast.

They had been logged with so much that when someone blew a whistle or steam engine somewhere they would try to head to the barn for lunch. They had gotten use to having a rest and something to eat when the sawmill shut down for lunch. You could hear these steam engine whistles for miles on a quiet day.

I got in practice and could hitch and harness a team up in about five minutes. I plowed our fields and many of the neighbor's fields with our horses.

I use to love to listen to the tales the men told as we ate lunch. Some of them including Dad who had worked in Kibler Valley for the lumber company around 1910. They told of peeling the logs and watching them slide down the mountains. And tales of the lumber shoot where lumber was slid down Bent Mountain into Kibler Valley, about the splash dams and watching the logs float down Dan River. I remember Mr. Hub Stanley telling of the big man that brought more lunch for himself than he did for the horses. He said during sweet corn season he would bring twelve rosin ears for himself and ten ears of corn for the horses.

Some days he would bring a half-gallon of beans, a pone of cornbread.

Chapter Seven

I continued to like school at Bell Spur. We studied History and Geography, which I really liked and did well in. We also had spelling bees, which I enjoyed; grammar I was not so fond of.

We would have programs at Christmas to which a few parents would come. We also had box suppers to raise money. The girls would bring a pie that would be auctioned off. There would be a pretty girl cake and a jar of sour pickles for the ugliest man. Mother baked a guess cake. She would bake a small item in the cake and people would pay a nickel and guess what was in it. The one that guessed what it was won the cake.

Miss Helen Boyd taught and then Mrs. Fannie Agee Cruise. Mrs. Fannie used the money we made and bought a few library books. I was delighted. There were a couple of Zane Grey books in them which I really liked as well as Gulliver's Travels, The Last of The Mohicans and David Copperfield. I really enjoyed having some good books to read that I didn't have to buy.

Lewis Culler was a good pal of mine. Sometimes we would play Fox and Hound. One day at lunch time we were playing and he was the fox. He ran and ran and no one could catch him. He finally quit when the bell rang, but he was completely worn out. When he went home that night he came down with pneumonia and never recovered. This was a heartbreak for me and the whole school.

There were no antibiotics in those days, or anything else of much value to take when you were sick. There was influenza and diphtheria around. The only vaccine was for small pox. I had chicken pox and missed three days of school.

Mrs. Ethel Watson taught me in the seventh grade, my last year at Bell Spur.

There had been very little change in the school. The School Board had made no improvements. The few books we had bought and were in the home-made book case, the bell that hung on a pole outside the door, which the teacher rang for us to gait playing and come inside were all bought with the money we had raised with our box suppers.

We visited Dad's mother a lot on weekends. She was a sweet lady always smiling and good to everybody. I never remember my grandfather. He passed away before my time. Dad told me how he made furniture and the boys would turn the lathe by hand, how he made apple brandy in the days when it was legal. He just had to buy a license. He would haul it all the way to Danville in wooden kegs with the horse and wagon. That was a way to market the apples when there was no other way to market them.

Dad would tell me stories of the time he served in the army during World War I. He had a history book about and I read it through several times.

He was a machine gunner and was in France for about one year. He fought in the battle of Argonne and was gassed with mustard gas. He would forever have a scar on his back where he was burned with the mustard gas. He told stories of near disaster and how he was blessed to come through all right and to get home to Mother. They both told of how she lived alone some of the time while he was gone and the loneliness and how much letters meant to both of them. Mather had gone to Camp Lee to be with Dad before he went overseas. He went over on his birthday, June 1, and would be returning the next year on his birthday and on the same ship. There were a lot of men in this area that served in the war.

Dad was so glad to get back to his farm. He had a good neighbor a Mr. Asia Shelor. He and Dad exchanged work and he would borrow our team in exchange for labor. I never heard him use a curse word. He told us of being raised on Dan River near Kibler Valley. His Dad had died while fighting fire in the mountains when he was a young lad. He said one year about 1888 or 1889 was a very dry year. He said Dan River was so low he could walk across it without getting his feet wet. Mr. Asa never got to attend school and he didn't know how to read or write his name. He managed very well though, he could count money in his head as well as most people with a pen and paper.

He was telling about when he was a small boy he was after a rabbit when it went a hollow tree that had fallen down. The tree was laying down hill and when he tried to back out he was going up hill and he could hardly move. He wondered if he was going to get stuck in there and no one would know where he was. After a long struggle he managed to get out...without the rabbit.

After his father's death he moved to Floyd County to be near some other relatives. They lived on Little River. His mother married a second time.

Mr. Asa married a sister of Cook Quesinberry and they had five boys and three girls. They were all raised on his 30-acre farm. They were all older than me.

When I knew Mr. Asa he was healthy and ate what he wanted. This included lots of pork and bread and plenty of sweets. After his breakfast of ham, two eggs and gravy, he liked lots of real butter on lots of biscuits and brown sugar, sometimes syrup, different kinds of jellies and preserves. The doctor kept telling him it would kill him. I guess it finally did at three months before his 95th birthday. I guess we must be doing something wrong now what with our interest in diets.

Mother continued to have poor health and I helped her out all I could.

From time to time she had to have some neighbor girls in to help out while she stayed in bed. Dad and I bought a nice radio that we all enjoyed.

It was our first radio, an R.C.A. in a cabinet. She enjoyed listening to the news and the gospel music.

I bought Mother a gas iron that I put gas into. It was lighter in weight than the ones that had to be heated in front of a fire in the fireplace or on the stove. I also bought her a gas lamp that gave a brighter light so she could see better since she also had eye problems.

We bought her a washing machine with a gas motor and wringer. We put it down at the spring and still had to heat the water in the black iron pot. I had to pour the water in and crank the motor for her.

Mother's brother Uncle Dewey Stanley was the youngest child of a family of nine children. Their father, Willie Stanley had died of injuries from being kicked by a horse. Mother was always worrying about Dad and me getting hurt while working with the horses.

Dewey went to work in West Virginia when he was 23 years old. In December 1925 he had a severe accident that resulted in head injuries and was hospitalized for a good while. He recovered with a silver plate in his head but was never able to hear again. I can remember Dad and, Dewey's brother, Walter going to West Virginia to be with him. Mother stayed here to do the chores and look after me. We kept uncle Dewey's dog.

He was a good dog, his name was Old Pale, a watchdog and a good rabbit dog. I can remember he also caught weasels and opossums that got after the chickens. We didn't have a dog of our own back then and I enjoyed him a lot.

Uncle Dewey could read lips and carry on a conversation with people he knew well and would bother to talk to him. He loved to play card games especially Set Back. You really had to do well to beat him. He could figure out the cards you had in your hand. We visited him a lot in the summer and played croquet. He loved to play and was impossible to beat at this game. I played with him many Sunday afternoons but don't remember ever winning. He lived in a world without sound. He worked hard and provided well for his wife and five children. His children he never heard speak! Even so he seemed to enjoy life. I heard him laugh a lot.

Once Uncle Dewey was working for someone who had a reputation for chewing out his workers without cause. He approached Uncle Dewey and chewed him out real good. When he told him he hadn't heard a word he said was the first the man knew that Uncle Dewey was deaf. This angered the man a lot when everyone standing around laughed. Although he was handicapped and couldn't communicate very well, he could do most anything he decided to do. He couldn't drive and lived in a quiet world but he dealt with his problems better than anyone I knew. He had a family and many friends that stood by him.

He loved to hunt and was an excellent shot with a gun. When we had target practice he was hard to beat. He loved to be independent and did not want anyone to be sorry for him. He was a good father and raised a great family. He was very gifted as a carpenter and made many lovely things, which now his family treasure.

The only Grandmother I knew was my step-Grandmother or grandmother by adoption. This made no difference with her or myself. We only lived three miles from her when I was small. That seemed like a long way back then. I did not see her a lot. I went with my parents to visit, and not by myself until I was eight years old. I remember the good meals we ate there.

I remember that she had a modern churn she helped me use. It has a crank with gears and a revolving dasher. Our churn had a wooden dasher that we churned up and down to make butter and buttermilk. She was such a loving person and always smiling. She had a little bite of something good to eat between meals.

I remember when we visited her around Christmas time she got pleasure of saying Christmas gift before you could. That was a ritual at that time. You tried to see who could say Christmas Gift first. Families didn't have big gift giving, get together then like families try to do now.

People had, for the most part, very large families and not much money. She had many grandchildren and tried to give each one something for Christmas. She gave me a little penny bank shaped like an elephant once and on another occasion a Bible storybook. Grandmother had nine children, eight boys and one girl. I believe there were 34 grandchildren and a number of step-grandchildren. Grandfather Landin Turman passed on before I was born. He was married twice and my real grandmother died very young. There were six children by his first wife, four boys and two girls.

One teenaged boy was killed by a runaway horse. My real grandmother was the daughter of Matt Blancett. My step grandmother was Isabell Bowman before her marriage. She had several sisters who I remember visiting us from time to time when I was a lad. She also had one brother whom I vaguely remember. Little boys are noted for being mischievous as well as being somewhat accident-prone. I had my share of accidents as a lad. Some when I was too young to remember. Mother told me of the time when I was a toddler she and I were crossing a pasture field when a fighting buck sheep got after us. While trying to cross a board fence I hung my shoe in a crack in the fence, and was hanging head down on the fence. She was trying to push my shoe out of the fence and threw her thumb out of place.

Another time she said I fell off the porch headfirst into a tub of ice water in which she was soaking my diapers.

With my first knife, which I very well remember, I slashed my wrist. This I did by breaking a rule that I later learned, always whittle with the blade turned away from you. I was thrown off of horses while learning to ride, but never really hurt. My pride was hurt but it soon healed and I was ready to ride again.

A young horse struck me in the chest with its front foot and I was sore and hurt in my upper chest for days. Much later in life an x-ray showed that my collarbone had been broken and healed. I still have a knot there to show for that.

My parents would not let me have anything to do with a gun until I was eleven years old. Not even an air rifle. Some of my friends had air rifles and I was jealous. My first experience with a gun was with a cap buster. I bought it and lots of caps with the rabbits I trapped and sold. My mother lectured me about wasting money. I also bought firecrackers around Christmas time and enjoyed shooting them. Wilton Stanley and I shot a lot of them. At that time you could get them in various sizes up to five inches long. One day while out playing and shooting some firecrackers we passed by his Grandpa's hog house. Two big hogs were lying there asleep. We each lighted firecrackers and threw it into their house. The hogs leaped out, one in one direction and the other on the opposite direction.

The house was old and they knocked the boards off in all directions. It was a complete shambles. Mr. Hub said he did not know what was wrong with his hogs, they had knocked their house down and wouldn't come when he called them to eat. The blast had deafened them. Wilton and I didn't dare tell anyone. Boys will be boys in spite of all adults can do.

We heard stories of the pranks his Dad and my Dad had pulled when they were boys. How they leaned a barrel half full of water against a man's front door, when he opened the door the barrel fell inside the door spilling water over the living room floor.

Finally—I bought me a single shot bolt action 22 rifles. It only cost a few dollars back then. Dad carefully taught me how to use the gun, and all the safety rules. We had a lot of target practice back then. A box of 50 cartridges was twenty cents. Since those old guns were very accurate we used a small target. A penny at 100 feet from us or something similar. Uncle Joe Turman was a good one to target practice with and hard to beat. I use to visit him and my cousins and spend an hour or two shooting at a target.

Mother always worried when there were guns. I never had an accident or near accident. I began to hunt small game, squirrels and rabbits. We did not have deer or wild turkey back then. When Dad and I killed squirrels we would dress them and mother would cook them. She made squirrel dumplings and gravy.

The heads were on the platter too. The brains were considered a delicacy. Once when we had city relatives from Richmond, we had a large platter of squirrel on the table for breakfast. The children had been told to eat what was set before them. They did eat some but told their mother said later they were horrified because in the city they saw squirrels as pets. Ouch! All the time we thought we were serving them the best we had! It could have been old country cured ham, sausage, bacon, steak but we served them the best. It's all a matter of taste and what one becomes accustomed to. The food that is served and that you cultivate a taste for as a child will be one that you will likely always want. Cow milk was what my life began on and what I still love.

Chapter Eight

I became a teenager as I completed the seventh grade and was surprised that I didn't feel much different. I was even more shy than ever as well as tall and skinny. It didn't help much when some of the kids kidded me about the fuzz that was coming out on my face.

I got my first suit of clothes and it cost a fortune $15. I became more interested in sports but had little choice to participate in them. We played some basketball and volleyball at school and occasionally volley ball on Sunday afternoon during the summer, but nothing like that during the week. There was too much work to be done.

My parents said things like "That's a waste of time."

Things were changing with the automobile becoming more common as a way of transportation and the truck the means of moving material things.

There was no longer any sale for tan bark. I had helped Dad peel the bark from chestnut oak logs and pile it high on the wagon to be sold to the tanning yard.

We now were cutting dogwoods out of the forest that were used in the cloth weaving factories to make winding spindles or shuttles. They had to be four inches or more in diameter, cut in sections four or six feet in length.

There were many large and tall dogwoods in the woods then. You don't see them like that anymore. We were still splitting some chestnut rails from the dead chestnut, but these would soon be gone, but rail fences still stood for many years. We cut and split locust for fence post, and began to use barbwire fences and wove wire in the place of the rail fence. People began to move out of some of the more remote and rough areas of the mountains and to an area where they could get in and out with a car or truck, we begin to see a few pickup trucks. The depression was beginning to ease a little. You begin to see ladies wearing a new dress or the men a new suit, buying a new plow or a new pickup truck.

I began to take notice of girls. I was too shy to talk with them much though, and was never around girls a lot since I had no sisters that I hardly ever saw. I went to the store one day and saw a mother and two little girls. They were carrying chickens to the store to sell. I came back and told Mother that I saw two of the prettiest little girls I had ever seen. The oldest girl smiled at me and had such beautiful black hair. Mother told me who they were, and what fine people they were. Little did I know that one day this little girl would one day be my wife. She seemed so much younger than me and was six years younger. I did not see them again for a long time. It was four years later that she moved near my home and we became friends.

My parents and friends were talking about high school. None of them had been to high school, and they didn't know whether it was necessary or not. They were afraid if I went I might learn more meanness than anything else. It might just be a big waste of time they said. I decided I would like to go if I had the opportunity. They finally said it was up to me to decide what I wanted to do. Dad and Uncle Earnest went to talk with the school board, and after several trips to Stuart it was decided that Robert Stanley could drive a pickup school bus to Red Bank School in Claudeville. He built a wood frame and cover on the back of his pickup. The back was left open and two wooden seats were built crossways to sit on. I bought pants and a belt with matching shirts to wear. I had worn bib overalls all way through grade school.

Robert Stanley drove the bus. He was a senior that year. His sister Thelma rode in the cab with him. Wilton and I rode in the back. Wilton's sister rode in the front. Violet Rakes and Vestie Kimble rode in the back with us. Later Vestie dropped out and all three girls packed in the cab. The weather was cold and damp, with the back of the bus open we got very cold. Wilton and I didn't mind though. I did get sick once or twice from the exhaust fumes coming back into the open bus.

Squirrel Spur was just a dirt road and they picked that year to do roadwork.

They widened it out a little and it was muddy and rough all winter. Sometimes Wilton and I had to get out and push and at times we had to have the bus pulled out of the deep mud. I still had to walk out a mile to catch the bus. Mother was not well that winter and Dad had asthma or what was later to prove to be emphysema.

I would get up at five o'clock to kindle the fires and go out to feed the cattle, hogs, and whatever else there was to be fed. Sometimes I had to milk also. At night there were more chores to do as well as homework and lots of reading. The kerosene lamp didn't give as good a light as I wanted. I sat up late at night and Mother tried to get me to go to bed.

I really enjoyed school and the new things I was learning. Science was very interesting to me. I had good teachers. Wayne Blackard was the Principal and my math teacher also. Ruth Clark and Margaret Clark were my teachers also. I met and made many friends. I had known my cousins the Burge boys and their sister Gladys for a long time, but I didn't know anyone else below the mountain. Some of the ones in my class in the eighth grade other than Wilton were Sam Heath, Frances Bateman, Arthur Mills, Charles Mills, Glenn Mills, Goldie Cox, Alma Collins and Wilton's sister Hava. I can't recall others right now.

Upper classmen that were good friends were Garnett Bateman, Lewis Flip-pin, Mildred Heath, Winford Burge, Hope and Thelma Anderson and many more.

They had basketball teams, both boys and girls. I had never seen a basketball game before, we'd played around with a basketball at Bell Spur but didn't know anything about the rules of the game. I was interested but knew nothing about playing. George Haden I thought was a star. He could make a lot of his long shots from near mid court. They had an indoor court that wasn't quite full size. I enjoyed watching and hoped to play someday.

I still enjoyed my radio and listened when I had time. Amos and Andy, Lum and Abner along with the "Grand Ole Opry" were programs I tried never to miss. I still did not go out on Saturday nights much to parties or socials. I usually stayed at home and listened to the "Grand Ole Opry" from Nashville, Tennessee. I could get shortwave radio programs on my radio and liked to tune London, England, Berlin, Germany and Rome, Italy. I liked to study and learn about other countries and wished they would continue the study of geography in high school. Bill and Charlie Monroe came to Red Bank School for a show one night and I persuaded my parents to go and take me. This was the first country music or any other kind of show I ever attended. We all enjoyed the blue grass and gospel music.

I got to attend most all of the basket ball games. Robert played on the team, and hauled some of the players to the away games. The games were played in the afternoon. Most of the courts were outside and unlighted. Meadows of Dan had not yet organized a team. The teams Red Bank played were Blue Ridge, Woolwine, Buffalo Ridge, Stuart and Critz. I can't remember the tournament that year. If they had one I did not attend. My parents were upset with me going to all the games anyway. I needed to hurry home and help with the farm work. Work, Work, Work.

Dad had bought two young horses that needed to be broke to work. We started them out one at the time working beside one of the older horses. Plowing the land was a big job and I needed to find time to help.

We went to school that year rain or shine, clod, snow , sleet or mud. I don't remember the weather ever keeping us home from school. I had to stay home a few days in the spring to plow though.

The eighth grade was not hard at all and the time passed quickly. At lunch time some of us would go to Mr. Anderson's nearby store and get cola or other soft drinks. I had only drank a few in my life before and soon developed a habit of drinking them. I had been told by my parents not to get in the habit of drinking them, but I did. Some of the boys started smoking cigarette but I didn't then or ever.

We did make corncob pipes and smoked rabbit tobacco prior to that time.

It was a weed found in old fields in the fall after it dried down. Old people before our time had smoked a weed called life ever lasting.

Near the end of the school year the Red Bank High School set a date for an outing (fun trip). On a Friday in late April the entire school would take a trip to the Pinnacles of Dan. It was a beautiful spring day sunny and warm with just a light breeze. The tiny buds of leaves were just beginning to put forth, apple trees were budding, sarvis was in full bloom, the cherry trees were white with bloom and the honey bees were out in full force looking for nectar. Wilton and I lived only three miles from the Pinnacles so we thought, why ride a bus? We got an early start and started walking and our parents grumbling. It was such a good day to be home plowing they did not want us out wasting time and doing foolish things.

We arrived to where the road ended near the Pinnacles long before the bus was due there. We had too much energy to set and wait for the rest so we climbed on up first to the small pinnacle and then to the top of the big one. Not many people went on to the third one. There are a couple of rather dangerous places to cross on the climb, and care must be practiced along the way.

We hurried back down, and were back at the foot in time to go back up with the rest of the school class when they arrived, going up was a lot slower this time. Some of the girls were rather nervous, but I believe they all made it to the top of the large pinnacle. This was not my first trip on the Pinnacles or my last. Most everyone far and near took that trip back then, and some of them many times. It was the thing to do. For one thing the view was really something.

I had heard many stories about the Pinnacles that had been passed down. An ancestor of Mr. Hub Stanley and others in this community were captured by the Indians and held for a while. The Indians built a fire on or near the Pinnacles and melted silver from the rocks. The story goes that he later escaped and returned to get some of the silver for himself, but never revealed to anyone the exact spot. There are some old muzzle loading mountain rifles still around that have front sights made of silver said to have come from the Pinnacles. Several people have searched extensively through the area and have not found anything that I am aware of. Garcie Quesinberry combed the area thoroughly and said the only silver in the Pinnacles was in the pocket of whoever was climbing it.

Mr. Asa Shelor told me when he was a boy he went with two men that took some silver from rocks near the Dan River below the Pinnacles. He wanted me to go with him to find the place.

After he told me he was too old and not able to make the trip.

From the top of the Pinnacles looking southwest you can see the mountains near and below my home, mountains I was and still am familiar. From there you can see Squall Creek Falls that no one visits any more because they are difficult to get to. From the Pinnacles you can see the white streak of water down the mountainside. The falls are not 90-degree falls but more like 60 degree falls. The main falls plunge down the mountain about 700 feet before there is a break. Then there are other shorter falls. It is a beautiful place to see and hear and very worthwhile for any strong rugged individual to make the trip.

I went down these falls several times when I was a teenager. The first time with my Dad. We went to the foot of the falls. The first break in the big falls there was a big pool of water. We had fishhooks and lines and cut us a pole. We had worms for bait. We carried the bait in a Prince Albert tobacco can Dad had emptied. We caught twelve rainbow trout, which averaged about 14 inches long. We put them in a cloth flour sack and carried them home. It was very difficult to get to the pool. We had to go on the left side of Squall Creek. Much of the ground was covered with a thin coat of decaying leaves, and the rock was wet. We had to just inch our way down step by step.

One wrong move and you could slide a very long way. Coming back up was even harder and tiring.

There were beautiful old trees down there in an area where no one has been able to get them out. Some were tall hemlock. Later years when I decided to go down there, I knew I didn't want to go alone. It was too dangerous. If I should and break a leg no one could hear me calling because of the noise of the falls. It would also be difficult to carry anyone out from down there.

In one of my early trips there I found an area where several good size trees had been twisted off by a windstorm. I thought it might have been done by the storm that turned Jake Radford's house bottom side upwards. The trees had been destroyed several years before I saw them. I can't remember much about their house being turned over, but I heard lots of talk about it. I can remember them living in the old house on the lower end of our farm. They lived there while their house was being repaired.

I can remember Mother would say sometimes when a real bad storm was approaching, "It looks like a Jake cloud." It must have been a tornado to have turned a large house over.

Jake and Jenny Radford were very interesting people. They had raised three sons Lewis, Arthur, and Oatis. They called them Lou, Art and Oat.

I would pass near their home on the way to the store. They would sound like they were arguing but I am sure they enjoyed it. I could never get by without being seen.

Back then when shoe soles wore out they were resoled. Once Mr. Jake resoled a pair of Jenney's shoes. They had been sitting in front of their warm fireplace in the cold winter when he finished resoling them. He handed her shoes to her and asked how she liked them. She said they were the biggest mess she had ever seen and tossed them into the fire. He just sat there and watched them begin to burn.

She said, "Just sit there, you old fool and watch them burn up." She grabbed them out. They just told this story and laughed about and bought her a new pair of shoes.

Families had to entertain each other before radio and T.V. I think I went to see my first movie when I was in the ninth grade at school. Later as a teenager I saw a number of movies. My parents never approved of them and I don't recall that they ever went to see one. Dad did enjoy television but Mother never lived to see it.

Meadows of Dan became a senior high school in 1936, so after one year at Red Bank the school board made arrangements to run a bus from Bell Spur to Meadows of Dan.

I had a good year on the farm that summer and made a few dollars with potatoes and calves. We had sold the sheep.

I decided to try something new for money and decided to raise onions that year. I planted a few bushels of onion sets and cultivated them. They grew well and I must have made a hundred bushel. I learned that you have to have a market. I sold only about forty bushel and had bushels to decay. I had a stinking time and never tried to grow onions again to sell.

I did grow some peanuts that year and harvested about five bushel. After they had dried we enjoyed roasting them in the wood stove oven. My peanuts were very popular with the neighbor children that winter. I carried some to school to give away.

We were still selling cream and milking the cows. We didn't go to the store much any more because a delivery truck came by once a week and bought our eggs. We used the old crank telephone to call in our order for groceries and feed for the chickens that we had started buying. Almost everyone had a telephone. We all had to keep up our own lines, replace the wire and poles and buy the batteries for our telephone. We cut locust for poles and stretched the one wire from each pole to the other, nailed a wooden bracket to the pole and screwed on a glass insulator on which to tie the wire. Laurel Fork was the central and there was an operator who connected the line from one to the other. There were ten or twelve phones on each line and each one had a different ring.

Ours was a long, short and a long. You wound the crank around for a long and gave it a quick jerk for a short ring.

There was always some eavesdropping. No such thing as a private conversation and it was hard to get the line when you wanted it. A small fee had to be paid the company for the operator and supplies. It was hard to hear when you needed to talk long distance for business or needed a doctor. The system worked very well for near by neighbors. Lightning often burned out the lines or phones during the summer. I was old enough to help work on the line when I was fourteen. Sometimes we would be tying a broken line while someone was ringing a phone somewhere and it would give you a shock. At times the switchboard would give trouble. Tyler Quesinberry would be called in to repair it. The switchboard was in someone's house in Laurel Fork. It was moved from time to time. The telephone keeps being improved as the years go by and the cost of having keeps on going up.

There weren't so many steam engines around anymore. Gas powered units were replacing them at sawmills and there were a few tractors around. A very few in our area.

Dad had to have a hernia operation that year and I had a double load of work. I really felt the responsibility taking care of all the animals. I knew how to do all those things but to have full responsibility of deciding which came first and when to do everything.

Dad spent a week in Mount Airy hospital and it cost him $300. It seemed like a lot of money when we were still in the depression. Franklin Roosevelt had been elected president and things began to change for the better. He talked about the new deal and the federal work force but we had just begun to see the effects of it.

Finally a few people began to get jobs that had been out of work for a long time with the W.P.A. They did different projects like improving roads and such. Some people that were really poor got free coffee, flour, and other staples as well as clothing. Locals received 25 to 30 cents an hour. This was much better than the 10 or 15 cents an hour they previously got if they could find a job.

Surveyors were beginning to survey for the Blur Ridge Parkway. One surveyor who surveyed through Floyd County from Bent Mountain to Meadows of Dan said if he could step on Floyd County and flatten it out it would be as large as Texas. Other surveyors were looking at the City of Danville Power Plant Project.

Money had been provided through President Roosevelt's program that was designed to put people to work and get them out of poverty. Social security was born then, too. Most of us never really understood at that time what was going on. Great changes were being made and some thought it was wonderful and others did not agree. Anyone who wished to work could find a job.

They began buying the right of way for the Parkway. Some people were happy to get the money in those hard times, others would have preferred keeping their land. Some small farms were divided and the best land taken. It was another case of paying the price for progress. The farmers paid the price of letting their land go at a low price in exchange for a road that seemed of little benefit to them at that time. Tourist has enjoyed the parkway and it did bring tourist business to the area. Mountain people, because of the Parkway have changed their ways and lives forever.

Mother always told me not to curse or use foul language, have good manners, and be careful of the company I kept. So I didn't hear much cursing as I grew up. Some of the men did curse when they were angry. Some used funny words instead of cursing, like "Dog gone if I know; you're dod burn right; I'll be odd burn if I know."

Other words mountain people used that you don't hear anymore are: fetch, like fetch me a hammer, or, toat that bucket of water. Instead of calling for someone you hollered for them, and a paper bag is still a poke. Many words are pronounced differently but not so much anymore.

Mother always said, "Act like a gentleman and remember who you are, and, whose you are."

She said tend to your own business and don't gossip or repeat gossip, stay out of pool halls and don't go to moving picture shows, never go into a place where are drinking, and above all keep good company.

She always asked who I had been with, and if their grandpa was a chicken thief, or a person of low morals. She said avoid them. It's in their bloodline. Open the door for a lady and give a lady your seat.

I asked her how you could tell if someone was a lady, she said if they were clean, quite and dressed nice, with little or no make up. They should attend church, and that was where I should go to meet a girl.

Chapter Nine

Each generation thinks the young generation is meaner than the last. I leave that to each individual to decide.

This year at school would be my first at Meadows Of Dan. There were several eight graders, considered freshmen at that time, going from the Bell Spur area. Wilton Stanley, Thelma Stanley, Burnice Shelor and I were ninth graders. Some students from Carroll County were allowed to go to the Patrick County schools. Thomas Smith got the bus route. We still were riding a home-made bus, but a larger one. It was very noisy on the rough roads and so were the students. Meadows of Dan was only seven miles from my home in Bell Spur, but it was a different world. I had not been out there enough to know many people. I'd always been home working and never got far from home on my own, then with my parents when they were visiting relatives or going to a church other than Bell Spur.

Some of the students thought they were more uptown than we were at Bell Spur. They liked to pick on us and make fun. That didn't bother me and I soon made lots of friends.

Fred Clifton was the school principal as well as the history teacher. He was strict and a very good history teacher. I remember him as being a teacher that taught practical things in life as well as what was in the book.

He taught us how to live and make friends, how to support your county and community. He taught us how to take care of our bodies and health and many things a young person needs to know to get along in this life. He also taught a very interesting class in Biology.

I met Dorn Spanglar that year and learned to love and respect him as an educator. He taught many subjects and did a superb job in all of them. We were assigned the lesson for the next day and were supposed to always be prepared. Because of his guidance I would study well. When we got to class he would start writing a test or quiz on the board. There would be ten or more questions daily and your answers determined your grade for the six-week period.

We sat around the outer walls, in back of tables in some of the classrooms, in the old frame building. In other rooms we had individual desk. All of the rooms had a wood stove in the center of the room for heat. A partition could be slid back into a hallway so that two rooms became one. This way we had a small auditorium for giving plays or having assembly when we had a speaker. There was a bell outside on a high pole with a long cord that was pulled to ring the bell and announce the end of recess.

Mr. Spangler began to try to teach us to play basketball. The other boys and I knew very little about basketball.

His first teaching was to get us to follow rules and not just fight over the ball. We had an outside clay court, so our practice was mostly limited to fair, early fall days. We had to buy tennis shoes to practice in. Some of the boys would wear brogans and would hurt other players' feet when playing. We had no suits or shorts so I wore bib overalls in my first game. I could not keep pants up and was afraid of loosing them. I was very self conscious and bashful.

Learning to dribble the basketball on an uneven dirt court was not easy. As I was taller than the other boys I was chosen to play center. We just had enough players for a team and one or two substitutes. There were no substitutes for center. All practice was at noon hour or during school. All games were played after school in the daylight hours. We didn't have lights. There were a few spectators that brought chairs and watched the games. Of course there was no charge. I believe my parents saw me play one game in the entire four years I played. I was really nervous and lacking in self-confidence when we played our first game. I was too conscious of what everyone in the crowd was yelling and saying to the players. After a few games I got over this and settled down. That first autumn I believe we won two games out of twelve.

We finally purchased for ourselves red basketball shirts and shorts.

I felt funny going out in public wearing shorts, probably because Mother said it was outlandish dressing that way in public. After the weather got cold we didn't have many sports at school. We did get boxing gloves and a few of us boys took turns wearing them and trying to box.

I liked and respected girls but was not going out with any when I was fifteen or sixteen years of age. At school I would go to the store across the road for a candy bar or drink and some of the girls would often come with me. I think they might have had more interested in the candy or drink than they did in me. I felt like I was awkward and unattractive.

Even when school was going on I still had to get up at four thirty in the morning and hurry to get my chores done and walk the mile to catch the bus. If the bus was late for some reason we had to stand and wait in the cold and rain with no shelter. When I got home more chores would be waiting for me to do.

When the weather got worse the roads did too. Seldom did we miss a day even if the buses required chains. Often the roads were so muddy the bus would get stuck and all the boys would have to get out and push. We would be late getting to school. During the winter months when we had snow my private road stayed blocked for a long time. The road was narrow and had a rail fence on either side.

The road would be drifted full and would be a long time melting. I would walk over and on top of the drifts for days until a warm rain would melt them out. During Christmas vacation we had snow and Dad had not been to see his mother for a while. He and I walked about four miles through the snow to see her. I had a cold and didn't feel very well. When we started home that afternoon I felt terrible and didn't feel like walking but had to anyway. I had no choice. I didn't think I would make it home I felt so sick and weak. I finally did get home and went to bed. That night and the next day I was running a high fever and really sick. They finally called Dr. Glenn Cox on the old telephone. He came late at night and said I had double pneumonia. He left a lot of pills for me. They were the first ones I had ever taken. I was scared for my Dad's brother, Dexter, and others in the community had died of pneumonia. There was not a lot you could do but let it run its course. I was sick for two weeks and when I recovered I came down with the flu and was sick for two more weeks. I did not get back to school until February. However I caught up on my subjects and made good grades in everything but Algebra. I got really behind on that but did manage to pass.

Frank Hylton failed algebra and had to repeat it. He always had a great sense of humor. When he finally did pass it he took his algebra book and sat down by the wood stove and burned it a few pages at the time.

Miss Essie Hopkins sent him out into the hall for talking one time. He got the croup and had to go home or so he said. He was a lot of fun.

Someone was always playing pranks. One boy dropped some poke berries down another ones shirt collar and then slapped him on the back. The shirt was white but not any more! The next day the boy returned the favor by dropping an egg down his collar and slapping him on the back. A couple of boys slipped a black crow with a broken wing into their desk. When the lady teacher had back turned they released it. The crow walked across the floor and was standing right behind the teacher. When she turned around the crow let out a squawk and the teacher let out a louder squawk. No one knew where the crow came from.

We played baseball in the spring. I was never very good at baseball, probably because I was never very interested in it. No one played any football. I was like one local citizen who said he didn't know any of the rules of football and he wondered why they were out there kicking a ball when so many butts needed kicking.

I had trouble with acne and the doctor told me not to wear a shirt that summer and to wear short pants. I got very brown but I always kept a shirt handy to slip on in case anyone came along. The doctor said stay out in the sun without any clothes. It did cure the acne but the doctor never said anything about skin cancer.

Roads were improving in this area due to the City of Danville W.P.A. Work Project. The road from Meadows of Dan to Mayberry had been topped. It was narrow and not wide enough for two cars to pass without getting off the pavement but it was an improvement. Men from out of the area were coming in to work, even from out of state. They were building a camp area near the lower dam, places for workers to stay and storage place for supplies. Much more than this was going on. They had started some grading on the Blue Ridge Parkway between Meadows of Dan and Floyd County. Some people, like my dad continued to farm full time while others went to public works.

The Triple A Program for farmers was started. This was extended help for the farmer, financial aid and educational. Local truckers were hired to haul the stones from off the farm to be crushed and put into the concrete for the dams. Arnold Banks hauled many loads from our farm. He got them from the piles we had made over the years as we had cleared them off the land. I believe he paid us fifty cents a ton. I don't know how much he got paid for them. We were glad to get the old flints and gray rocks out of the way.

Mother's health didn't improve. She had very high blood pressure and was on a strict diet and took lots of medicine. Medicine was beginning to change, there was lots more medicine to take now other than caster oil and Epsom salts.

Mother made a cough syrup by boiling wild cherry bark into a tea and adding honey. There was one tree and some smaller ones around it that grew on the banks of Squall Creek. I don't know the correct name for it but Mr. Radford called it a Babbigilla tree. They gathered the large buds from it and boiled them down in a small amount of water, added beef tallow to it and made a salve. It was used for healing and did seem to help on sores, cuts and scratches. The Watkins man still came around about once a month. Mother bought flavoring and food coloring. Dad bought liniment for whatever ails you, either horse or human. It had always been a thrill for me to see the Watkins man come as a small lad. He came in with his satchel and opened it up and showed his many different wares. At first they came by horse and buggy then by car.

I still didn't have much of a social life outside of school. There was a lot of square dancing going on but I never got into it and was discouraged from doing so. It always seemed to be work, work on the farm. That always came first.

I went to my first movie when Mr. Spanglar took a busload of students to Stuart from school. The movie was about India when the British owned it. I believe the movie was called Ghunga Din. It was very educational and I was much impressed.

My parents went to church almost every Sunday since they had a car and the roads were better in the summer.

They had not become members of the church at this time. They went to Bell Spur, Concord, Maple Shade and Dan River Primitive Churches. They, as did all Primitive Baptist churches, had services one Saturday and Sunday each month. The preachers were shared among all the congregations. There were lots of baptizings then. I can remember going to the Bell Spur baptizings on many occasions. They would leave the church and would walk about three hundred yards down the dirt road to the baptizing hole, singing all the way down there. The candidates would enter the water with the preachers. They would be baptized under the water one at the time. Sometimes one preacher would lower the candidate under the water and sometimes another preacher would help. There was singing, always "Shall we Gather at the River" and other songs, as they came out of the water There was much hugging, shaking hands and tears. Many of the people I know were baptized there including Mother and Dad later.

I went to the dentist at Stuart a Dr. Neal. He was a very good dentist, however I was shocked when I found out I had fourteen cavities. Dad and Mother took me three times to get all the work done. They would shop while I got the dental work done. then it was straight back to the farm and work. There was no time for me to shop. That summer wasn't very eventful for me, but a busy one and a very good one for the farm.

A tremendous amount of work was going on all around us. A lot of construction work, we could hear the dynamiting and heavy motors as we worked on the farm. I didn't go and watch the work much as my parents were afraid I might be hurt, besides there was too much work to be done at home.

We had to be on the lookout for snakes. The explosives had run them out of the mountains and a lot of copperheads and rattlesnakes were being killed.

I was still having trouble with acne and after having pneumonia the doctor said to get plenty of sunshine. One day I was hoeing potatoes by myself. It was a nice day and I had taken off my shirt and overalls and was getting a good tan. I heard someone yelling rattlesnake! They sounded desperate so I started running toward them carrying my hoe. It was a neighbor lady who was hoeing her potatoes and discovered a rattlesnake. I killed the snake and did not realize that I was standing there in my underwear until I noticed her staring at me instead of the snake. I could hear her laughing as I hurriedly left, running over the hill. She told my mother that I looked like an Indian.

I continued to read anything worthwhile every chance I got. I subscribed to the "Roanoke Times" and found out I could get books from the state library at Richmond. They would mail books on request and I could keep them for two weeks. It cost me only the return postage.

I got a list of books on fiction, educational, history, travel and such. I had good books to read any time farm work would allow and school work in the winter. I had read the few books they had at school.

Some of the girls encouraged me to read "Anthony Adverse" and then asked me what I thought of some of the passages. I was too embarrassed to discuss it. I think they enjoyed my embarrassment. When I returned to school Mr. Isaac Stanley was the principal. He taught geometry and I liked that much better than algebra. Mr. Spanglar taught Shakespeare, Twentieth Century Bookkeeping and Bible. I had not liked what I had read of Shakespeare but with his teaching I learned to love and understand it much better. I did well on it but not as well as I would have liked. Bookkeeping required a lot of work and time but I liked it and did well. I burned a lot of midnight oil. I learned much from bookkeeping that has been useful all of my adult life.

I had studied the bible much before that year but I found that my classmates that had attended Sunday school knew more about it than I did. Since my parents did not believe in Sunday school I did not get to attend. I got along very well in the study and made good grades. We studied the spiritual and historical side of the Bible.

It was one of the best subjects I studied in high school and has certainly been beneficial to me all my life. We did not get near through the Bible, covering only a part of the Old Testament. I wish we could have had another year.

The state gave full credit for Bible study at that time. How things were to change later when school were not to even allow prayer in school. All through grade school we would start the day with prayer and I feel it helped get the day off to a good start.

Our basketball season started off with a little more confidence this year since we'd had some experience. The outdoor dirt court was the same, out coach was the same, our red shorts were the same ones we had purchased the year before and our players were about the same. We had to replace out tennis shoes when they split or wore out. Our transportation was an open truck with a frame on it for hauling cattle. It was a bit cool at times, especially when we were returning from a game and it was getting almost dark. The fact that we were winning a few games was good for our morale. The girls were winning some too.

There were several couples that were dating and were always together when coming home from the games. One girl seemed to think I was all right and we did talk some and were friends. I never dated her though. In fact I did not really date anyone when I was in high school. My parents always said there was plenty of time for that later.

The high school had a box supper to raise money for library books. This was a big thing. All the girls brought pies. Some of the girls that were dating were surprised at the price their pies brought. When their boyfriends started bidding on them, boys like me started bidding against them just for fun. I ended up with two pies and did not know which girl to eat with. It was a bit awkward at first then I finally ate most of both of them so nobody's feelings would be hurt.

The high school put on a really good three-act play. I wasn't asked to take a part in it. I guess I did not appear to have any talent.

After basketball season was over all the high school boys began training for a countywide track meet. I believe it was a first for Meadows of Dan. I tried out for the one hundred yard dash but was not fast enough. I was better in the 440 yard run. I was not really good in the broad jump or the high jump. I was fair in the discus throw but I settled down on the shot put and started practicing on it a lot. The school did not have a shot put so we found a sixteen-pound cannon ball that I used for practice. Mr. Spanglar coached all of us in our best talent and saw that we practiced every chance we got. When the day for the track meet came we were ready. Our school did well and Mr. Spangler was quite pleased.

Ephraim Richardson, a cousin of mine, was first place in the hundred-yard dash, Willard Underwood was first in the broad jump. Edward Helms first in the discus throw and I came in first in the shot putt. The regulation shot put weighed only twelve and one half pounds and I had been training with a sixteen-pound cannon ball. Since we were the only school on top of the mountain the schools below the mountain thought we were backward and ignorant and often made fun of us. We felt good about how well we had done in the track meet. We were beginning to make a name for ourselves and earning a little more respect. We had good teachers and parents and we knew it.

Chapter Ten

We continued to sell cream and milked several cows. We were trying to improve our pastures. More lime was being used and more fertilizer, especially phosphate was being used. We had begun to have our soil tested. We would take several small soil samples to our county agent, a Mr. Price. He would meet us at Meadows of Dan and send our samples to V. P. I. in Blacksburg, Virginia. When we got the report we would know how much lime the soil needed. Most all our soil needed lime and was badly in need of phosphate.

Once when we carried our soil sampled one old farmer came up riding a mule with a burlap sack full of dirt. Fifty pounds or more. If all the farmers had brought that much Mr. Price would have had a time hauling it in his 1929 Model A Ford.

Some calves had blackleg in our area. Mr. Price would come around and vaccinate the calves for blackleg. The state and federal government had a man come out and checked all cows for tuberculosis. He went out in the field and lassoed them and the cows were nervous for a week afterward. I tried to learn to lasso but was never very good at it.

I did have a horse I rode to bring the cows in from the pasture. He was very good at it. He was just a workhorse but smart, and a good riding horse as well. I found, again, that a man could become very attached to an animal.

This horse while out playing with the other horses ran underneath a big low tree branch and broke his hip. He never recovered. It broke my heart when the vet said he could do nothing for him. I had some cats I thought a lot of. Mother had forbid me to touch cats when I was small. We now had cats at the barn and I usually had a favorite we would let come in the house. occasionally. I had one big Tom that went with me rabbit hunting. He would follow along like a dog. Sometimes I would carry him while I tried to jump a rabbit out of a thicket or brush pile. If one jumped out I would throw Tom down and he did catch a few. He was the only cat I ever knew of that would do that. Since my parents did not care for a dog, we did not have one.

Our Guernsey cows were very gentle and some of them were big pets. They all had names and many would come when you called their names.

The year 1937 was a very busy one on the farm. We had a lot of plans for the year, many of which didn't get carried out because of the wet weather. When it rained and the land didn't get dry we couldn't get the plowing done to put the crops in. There was plenty of work at the City of Danville Power project and other places. Anyone that had a truck could get a job hauling for them. Farmers could not compete with the wages. There was a good demand for farm produce and everyone was busy and buying more cars and trucks. Trucks were larger and more powerful.

Franklin D. Roosevelt was president and most people now had a radio on which to listen to his fireside chats. He was promoting his programs.

This year things happened that would affect me for the rest of my life. I did not know it at the time. The pretty little girl, now age ten that I had seen several years earlier came back into my life. Her widow mother married our widower next-door neighbor, Mr. Asa Shelor.

I saw Marie when we went to serenade the newly weds. In those days every one was serenaded. Mr. Shelor was in his early sixties, too old to ride a rail around the house. Cousin Harless Turman got two hay poles and put burlap bags around them to make a stretcher and carried him around the house in it. Some ladies carried Marie's mother around the house in a washtub. There were quiet a few people there marching around with them singing, yelling, making music, beating on pans and even shooting off fire crackers. It was quite a serenade compared to some in those days.

They got married on May 12, and a few days later it started raining and continued for two weeks. Every day was foggy, damp and dark. Most people could not plant their corn until June. Marie and her sister Opal were stuck at home in a strange new place with nothing to do, no friends to play with. nothing to read but the "Enterprise" and "Southern Planter."

I really did not know them or their mother and only went by when I had business with Mr. Shelor. Finally the weather did clear up and they ventured out. We began to get acquainted but we were both shy at first. Marie's sister Opal would talk with me more than Marie. I began to share the "Roanoke Times" with them. We received the Sunday paper on Monday, through the mail, and they would come down on Tuesday to borrow the Sunday paper. They would go back up the road reading as they walked. I laughed at Opal once as she ran into the rail fence as she was reading the funny papers.

At that time I was wishing that Marie were older, nearer my age. Sometimes I worked for Mr. Shelor and Marie would bring us water to the field from the spring. Occasionally they would come down to the house for something. This was all I saw of them that summer. One Saturday afternoon they and their mother visited with my Mother. Mother was working in her flower garden and I was going to take a bath while she was out. We had no bathroom or bathtub so I was taking a bath in a washtub of hot water I had warmed on the stove in the kitchen. I had been cultivating corn with the horse and plow and really needed a bath. I was undressed and ready to get in the tub when I heard the girls at the door. Not having any clothes near and having already put mine in the laundry bag I ran into the pantry and closed the door.

Mother came in from the garden with Ada and the girls. I'm sure Mother wondered where I was. She could see the tub of water in the floor. Something was said about the cookies Mother had baked and they were in the pantry. Mother opened the door and got the cookies.

I stayed behind the door as she opened it. She left the door ajar and I stayed behind it. The girls wanted more cookies and she told them to help themselves. They got more cookies while I held my breath. Finally the girls went outside to play. Their Mother and my Mother were still standing in the kitchen talking. they began to whisper and laughed. I then realized they could see me through the crack in the door. They went out laughing.

The rain finally stopped and we got up some late hay. With all the rain and poison snakes coming out of the mountain it was hard to make hay that year. They were escaping the blasting riot into the hayfields. We did have a good corn crop that year but the other crops weren't much. Many people had other jobs than the farm, so much public work was provided by the new administration in the White House. Not much work was provided for the women outside the home. They spent their time cooking, canning, preserving food in many ways as well as working in the fields and gardens. I never saw women cradling grain but just about every thing else, even plowing with horses and steers.

They didn't pitch up hay but they did tramp the stacks. I was doing all the pitching for my Dad as well as several of the neighbors. I was strong and fast, I believe some bragged on me just to get me to put out. I didn't mind the hard work. What bothered me most was to come home after a really hard days work, tired and hungry and I would have to chop Mother some wood before she could cook supper.

She would say, "Now you go milk the cows while I cook supper."

School time was here again and I was not ready. I had not had time to shop for new clothes. I had to order them from Montgomery Ward. Locals said Monkey Ward. I ordered the latest fad for boys in high school, leather knee boots, riding pants, a flannel shirt and a zippered jacket. I felt really dressed up when I put them on. It was a warm outfit in the cold weather walking to meet the bus. The boots were good in the snow, too.

Marie and Opal were going to Bell Spur School and I still had to walk by myself. Later that year they transferred to Mayberry School and walked out to the road with me. They rode the bus as far as Mayberry and got off the bus and got on it in the afternoon for the return trip home.

The school at Meadows of Dan was much the same, Mr. Spanglar was my homeroom teacher and basketball coach.

I did well in school this year and we were still improving in basketball. We now were winning some games.

I had begun to drive a little. I did not have a driving permit so my driving was in the fields and on our private road. It was rough and rutted out most of the time. I put in lots of hours hauling rocks and beating them in the ruts. There was always work to be done on the farm and at school. We lived in such a beautiful place, I never had time to sit and enjoy the scenery as much as I wanted to.

It was beautiful in the spring seeing the first buds appear, seeing the redbuds and sarvis blooms, smelling the fragrance in the air, seeing the fields covered with green grass and the return of hundreds of robins.

Everywhere, such beauty, God's green earth alive again. His wonderful plan. Later there would be dogwood blossoms, rhododendron, mountain laurel and then mountain ivy. They all bloomed in their turn, keeping something beautiful to look at all the time.

I loved the summer also, the tall grass ready for the mowing and hay season, the fields of grain waving in the wind. I loved seeing the corn tasseling and the smell of the corn. Then would come the fall with the leaves changing to all the colors of the rainbow. Then came the beauty of the early frost, although I hated to see the plants die.

Some days when the air was crisp , the sky so blue and we could see the distant mountains so very blue. It seemed we could see forever. Even the winter snows were beautiful although it did make the farm chores harder. We had different chores in the winter, keeping firewood cut and taking care of the farm animals. going through paths we had made in the snow and ice. I guess the hardest part about winter was the colds, flu, pneumonia and other illnesses that were more prevalent this time of year.

Marie was sick with pneumonia the June after she was became eleven and I was so worried about her. She recovered in about two weeks, an answer to many prayers on her behalf.

Many of our neighbors and relatives had bought new cars and trucks. Our car was getting old and the new ones were much more advanced, nice looking, more powerful motors, better upholstery and a lot more comfortable. Of course I wanted one. We needed a pick up on the farm and my Dad decided to buy one. I would have liked to have a new car but a new pick up was fine. He bought a new 1938 Ford V8 pickup. I drove it around the farm a little and went to Stuart and got my driving permit at age 18. That didn't mean I would drive a whole lot. I could drive to the store, to the mailbox and also when we went to church or to visit relatives. I could not drive it to school or off to town to a movie or anything like that.

Occasionally I could go to some school function or some community party that wasn't in school hours. Sometimes I would go by and get Marie and Opal and take them to some community outing. Their mother let them go with me if the little one sat next to me and Marie on the outside. Neither one of them were happy with the arrangement but their Mother said there was too much difference in mine and Marie's age, and she didn't want Marie interested in boys yet anyway. We didn't think there was too much difference in our ages. Marie seemed mature for her age. I had begun to date different girls a little but none seriously.

This summer was busier than ever on the farm. I had market for farm produce. The state was building and hard topped road, Route 103 in Patrick County. There was a convict camp near Claudeville. They were helping build the road. I got a contract to furnish them produce that summer. I had about one and a half acres of green beans. This took a lot of picking. In August I was going down there every week with a pickup load of green beans, onions, cabbage, potatoes, tomatoes and even some carrots. I did make some money that summer and added some to my saving account. We were milking more cows, which meant we needed more hay and grain. It was a very busy summer.

I continued to notice the little girl Marie. One summer day when I was helping Mr. Asa get up hay, Marie brought me a bucket of cold spring water.

She was wearing a pretty yellow dress and I thought she was getting more beautiful all the time. I wanted to tell her but I was too bashful. I knew I was in love with her then! I felt like grabbing her and kissing her and wondered what would have happened if I had. I was still wishing she was a little older and I could date her.

I did take time to go look at the dams that were being completed and visit the tunnels. Cousin Ephraim Richardson and I walked down the mountain to Kibler Valley to see the powerhouse under construction. We could run down quickly, but it took a while to climb back. Cousin Wilton and I went back again later to watch the steam engine that was based at the foot of the mountain. It pulled a cable car with a cable while it sat still. One car went up on a track while another come down on a second track. They hauled material for the big race that connected to the tunnel. Then the material for the surge tank that went 700 feet above the powerhouse. From the surge tank a steel pipe come down the mountain reducing in size as it reached the turbines with a lot of pressure. This was all new and very interesting to me. Mr. Loy Harris showed me through it later. I was always fascinated by the fact that he could smell a copperhead snake when it was neat before he saw it. Some boys I knew went to look at the race or pipeline before it was finished. They decided to walk inside of it.

Someone mentioned that if they turned the water in and about that time they heard a roaring sound and they finally started running in the dark. Finally when they were outside they found the noise they heard was someone walking on top of the pipeline. They were trespassing anyway. They should not have been in there.

Workers were grading the Blue Ridge Parkway area and I went once or twice to see the bulldozers at work. They opened a rock quarry about two and one half miles from our house. The rock was to be used for the road surface. That meant more dynamiting going on every day.

This school year 1938-39 would be my senior year. I loved basketball, and was getting a little better at the game. My coordination was better now that I had stopped growing. We had improved each year under Mr. Spangler's coaching. We could have been better if we'd had an indoor court on which to practice. Stuart got an indoor gym, which gave them an advantage along with a much larger school enrollment from which to pick players. Playing on their court was different for us when we played them and took us a little while to get use to. They had lights and we could have a tournament and play at nights in the finals down there. That year we didn't make it to the finals.

In the early spring the junior and senior classed took a day outing. We went to the Buffalo Mountain, about eight miles away.

The mountain was called the Buffalo because it was a large rounded mountain you could see from a long distance away. If you used your imagination you could believe it was the hump of a buffalo. This trip was our special party of the year. Proms were unheard of at this time. We drove to the foot of the buffalo in Frank Hylton's bus, which was a pickup with a cover. It was large enough to accommodate our two small classes. We'd used it in the fall for transportation to basketball games. It sure was an improvement over an open truck. We ate our picnic lunch on the Buffalo and that afternoon went to the Bear Rock section, which had numerous small caves. Most everyone coupled off as many of them were going steady. Several of them married a year or two later. There were two girls that were not with anyone so I divided my attention between them. That did not work very well! Everyone did enjoy the beautiful spring day.

I enjoyed school so much and liked my coach and teachers so well I decided to go an extra year in high school. I had the required amount of subjects to graduate and very good grades also. I just made this decision on my own and never regretted it. Other boys were giving Marie attention and I was not happy about this. Her mother let her go out a little and she always said she was too young to go out with me. Marie and her sister did go with me to some things like the Fourth of July celebration.

I decided that she just went to have a means of transportation, not that she was interested in me. I was dating some and even thought I might be in love once or twice but not really seriously.

The summer of '39 was nothing like the movie by that title, not for me at least. I did lots of truck farming and hauled it to Mount Airy and some to the convict camp.

I had started going to the movies some. Clifton Jessup and I went together part of the time. Sometimes we took a girl each, four of us in my pick up or in his car. We didn't mind being crowded a little! There were two movie theaters at Stuart at that time.

I was able to save a few hundred dollars. Not bad for a farm boy in those days. I didn't spend so much - 25 cents to see a movie and 24 cents for a gallon of gasoline.

We still produced our own pork, beef, poultry and eggs, and sold extra eggs and a few hogs. Our main income was from the cattle, cream and calves. I loved the farm and watching things grow and working with the animals.

I knew there were easier ways of making a living and also knew much more money could be made in other professions, industries and etc. I was trying to decide what to do with my life. My parents reminded me that they had taken me as a small baby and had taken good care of me.

According to their thinking I was obligated to stay here and take care of them. I agreed that was true and since Mothers health was not good and Dad wasn't well either I would quit thinking about doing anything else.

I was very interested in world affairs and was following the news and reading about Hitler and his Nazi party. I could see that Europe was headed for another war and wondered if the United States would be drawn into it. I was always interested in other parts of the world. I had corresponded with a boy student in Poland who sent me literature about his country. I was disturbed when the news came over the radio on September 1, 1939 that Hitler had attacked Poland. I never heard from the boy again.

When I returned to school that fall one of the subjects Mr. Spanglar taught was current events. I really enjoyed that subject and as the war went on in Europe I read and reported in class and we were tested. We learned all the towns and areas where there was action in and all the new weapons names and terms being used. With Mothers illness I had to take over more and more of the responsibilities at home and would have to miss a day of school now and then. I knew I would graduate anyway.

The basketball season was great. I had played center all the way through high school and never had a substitute. I would play the whole game and don't recall fouling out but once.

This last year we won over half our games and got to play in the tournament. In the tournament we played two games in one day. one in the afternoon, which we won and the night game three hours later. We were a bit tired when we played Ritz. They were a very tall team and were expected to win, and did. When they picked the All-Stars from the seven teams in the county I was picked as the center.

In February Dad broke his arm and I missed school much of the time. I did all of the plowing, milking, taking care of the cows and helping with the housework while Dad's arm healed. I took Dad to Dr. Thompson's office when he broke his arm. The Doctor had to have my help in setting his arm.

I plowed 25 acres that spring with the good team we had. We had our biggest and best corn crop we had ever grown prior to that year. We were using more fertilizer and a better variety of corn. The hay and oats were good and the cows had plenty to eat.

When I got my high school diploma I had completed more subjects than most students. I'd had one more year in the new Meadows of Dan High School. Everyone was so proud of the new building. We really took good care of the new building with its auditorium, inside bathrooms, and central heating system. How thankful we were! The teachers saw that no one so much as made a pencil mark anywhere they weren't supposed to.

At the time we would not have dreamed of playing basketball in the auditorium with the beautiful floors. There was no dancing in the school then. At a later time the permanently installed seats would be removed and portable ones put in and an indoor basketball court marked off and there would be dances, but not then. The bathrooms and showers were great. I knew of no one that had them in their home.

There was the library too! We had so many books I wished I were starting high school, not finishing it. All the one-room schools were closed and the students were bussed to Meadows of Dan. Each grade had its own room! The buses were much nicer and were heated.

Chapter Eleven

In the summer of 1939 before my nineteenth birthday I had an unusual and rare experience. It wad on a Sunday afternoon on July 18 when I was visiting the home of my uncle Joe Turman. My cousins and neighbors and I were playing a game of volleyball as we often did on a Sunday afternoon. My parents were visiting next door with aunt Rena, Dad's only sister. It was a warm humid day and it suddenly began to rain and we all ran for the porch. Everyone ran into the house except for myself. I stopped on the porch and got a drink of water from the buckets on the table. I then turned and walked to the edge of the porch and stood they're raising my right arm and placed my right hand on the plate above the porch. That was the last I remembered for a few minutes. When I came to I was laying on my back in the porch. I remembered of hearing something like a great explosion. My first thought was that someone had shot me. I couldn't get up and could only move my left arm and turn my head. My right arm was lifeless and very black, my legs were the same my clothes were torn, I could not hear. I picked up my right arm with my left hand. It felt like I was lifting someone else's arm. people were standing around me very excited. Slowly I realized I had been hit by lightning. I told those around me to rub my arm toward my body also to massage my legs toward my body. Some of them began working with me.

Some said later it was amazing that I could lie there calmly and tell them what to do for me. They said they had no idea what to do. After awhile I began to feel a tingle in my legs. Then the pain set in very intense as the blood began to circulate. It was like the dead coming back to life, which in fact it was. Uncle Cephus had gone somewhere else to call a doctor since the lightning had knocked their phone out. Mother and Dad came from Aunt Renee's very excited and mother was crying. I reassured her I would be all right and after about an hour they carried me inside and laid me on a bed. I could still hardly hear what anyone said.

I discovered there was a deep burn on my right side and red streaks on my arms and down both legs. I could smell an odor of burned flesh, mine. I could hear my own heart pounding at a fast rate. The only Doctor they could find on a Sunday afternoon was a Dr. Burnette from the Hillsville area. Some said he was a quack. He didn't do anything and was amazed that I was still living. I stayed there in the bed that night not sleeping much. The next morning I got up and found I could walk but was dizzy and weak. 1 saw how lightning had ripped up my shirt and pants. My shoes had the soles torn off. There were holes where the tacks had been in the shoe soles. My socks had been burned up.

The lightning had hit the metal roof and come down my right arm and down my body.

The wooden porch floor and even the wood sill beneath where I stood were ripped into splinters. The bolt of lightning had traveled through my body. The Lord for some unknown reason had spared my life, maybe for my wife, or my parents' sake or even my children of the future. Only He knows now. I reasoned my right arm being raised might have helped in that the lightning didn't strike me in the head. The current had gone down my right side missing my head and heart. The next day they took me to Dr. Thompson at Stuart. He said it was definitely a miracle I was living. My pulse rate was still 120. He dressed my side, where I was almost burned through to my stomach in the area where anyone having appendicitis would have been cut. I had to return a couple of times for more attention to the burn. After a few days I seemed to be better. My hearing gradually returned.

Marie came to see me and told me later how worried she was about me and how she could see my heart pounding as I lay on the bed. (Part of the pounding might have been because she was near.) I seemed to recover all right, however, for several years I would have a severe pain in the right side of my lower back, usually when I lay down to relax.

In the fall of 1940 I missed going back to school so I organized an outside basketball team. We would go back and play against the school team on the hill that fall. It was good practice for the school team.

We were better than the school team since most of the last year's team had graduated when I did. We also went to Floyd and other places to play. I was dating a girl still in high school at Meadows of Dan. She would send me letters by Marie, knowing that we were neighbors and not knowing how much I loved Marie. I still did not know if she cared for me or not. She would bring me the letters when she returned from school. Often I was out in the field working and we would talk and I would admire her beauty while I pretended to read the letter. Oh how I wished she were a little older. She was going out a little and getting a lot of attention and I was feeling a tinge of jealousy.

I kept very busy during the winter. We had more cows to milk by hand, and wood to cut. Mother had not been well and I helped her out doing house cleaning. I did have time to read and was following the news as Hitler was continuing to advance across Europe. One after another the countries Norway, Belgium, The Netherlands and finally France had fallen. After Dunkirk the British were weak and now were fighting for their lives. Roosevelt was slowly building our army and navy and had the beginning of an air force. He was still hoping to avoid being drawn into the war.

I subscribed to farm magazines and news magazines and listened to the radio at night. I got all the books I had not read from the county library.

I never had much of a social life. I was never bored and did not mind spending much of my time at work. I did some hunting though I was never an avid hunter. The spring and summer of 1941 were much the same , hard work on the farm and enjoying it, dating some, going on picnics to Rocky Knob. That was getting to be a popular place for picnics and meeting to play ball and visit on weekends. I had a means of transportation and quite a few would ride over with me. One Saturday night Marie went with me along with the usual group. I was riding with her through the park alone and I wanted to kiss her so much but I thought I would get my face slapped. Later when she was thirteen she went with me and another couple to a movie and I felt she was showing more interest in me.

That summer was a busy one on the farm. I helped some of the neighbors to get in their hay. Marie helped some as we got up Mr. Asa's hay and I enjoyed her presence as we got to talk some as we worked.

Everybody was talking about the war and I was wondering when the United States would become involved and what the outcome would be. I was surprised as anyone else on December 7 when Japan bombed Pearl Harbor. Japan then immediately declared war on the United States. We followed by declaring war on Japan. I say this because many people forgot or do not know that Japan declared war on us before we did on them.

They were talking to us about a peace treaty when they made the sneak attack. They had people in Washington right then talking peace. Later it was proved they had planned this for years and had all the plans to take everything in the Pacific before moving on the United States. We were just a paper tiger they said and would fall without a fight. They had spies in Hawaii for years watching every move of our navy and daily reporting back to Japan. They walked the beaches without pencil or paper, only using memory and reporting back to Japan every move that was made.

Germany and Italy quickly followed suit, declaring war on us before we declared war on them. Unless we forget, we were attacked and declared war on before we declared war on them in December 1941.

All young men, including myself had to register soon after that. The draft call began. It appeared my number would not come up for awhile. The war was not going well at all. Germany and Japan were advancing in their plan. At home tires were rationed. I could do no driving for fun or pleasure, not that I'd been doing much. Marie and I saw more of each other that year. She had developed into such a beautiful girl.

There were parties and dances in the community most every weekend.

There were games of spin the bottle and drop the handkerchief in which you sometimes got to kiss the girl.

Ah yes, it was at one of those parties that Marie and I first kissed. Our noses got in the way the first time and we tried a second time. From then on there was a different feeling between us. Many men were going to Norfolk to work in the shipyards, and were getting paid high wages. There were defense plants built everywhere. I knew I would soon be in service and I thought some skills would help me and began looking around. Meanwhile there was much work to be done on the farm. I was trying to leave things in good shape before I left. Fences and buildings in good repair and the house painted to name a few. I bought a motor generator and batteries and put lights in our house. It was a six-volt plant. Thee bulbs were made like 110 volt and gave a good light. I would crank the motor awhile each night and let it run. It was beneath the house with the exhaust leading outside. It would be several years before the power line came our way. I decided to go to Winston Salem to take a welding course that required six weeks. I boarded with the Crawford family in Winston and did very well with the course, however I never did put into practice what I learned.

By this time I decided I would not wait to be drafted. I went into all the different recruiting offices while I was in Winston, the Army, Navy, Cost Guard, and Air Force. I first decided on the Marines but changed my mind. I had always been interested in airplanes so I decided to try the Air Force.

I was told I would be accepted if I could pass all the exams. I signed up and was told to be back in two weeks. I came home and got ready to leave. Many were signing up, our country had been attacked, therefore young men were eager to serve their country. we were proud of our country and our leaders were determined to win the war. That was a hard two weeks that passed quickly. I bid Marie good-bye but we shared no promise at that time. Leaving my parents was hard, very hard especially for Mother who had seen Dad go away to World War I in 1918 some 25 years prior to that time. Also leaving the farm was not easy. Rounding up the cows and milking them the last day was painful.

I left home on October 4, 1942. Wilton Stanley drove me to Winston Salem. There I took several written examinations the first day. The second was the written exam, not a very strict one. Several men all volunteers were all taken to a large room and we were told to strip and leave our clothes. Two army doctors came in and looked us over to see if we had any ruptures or flat feet. The old doctor said to me, "You've had your appendix out."

I said, "No, I've not."

"You have, too. I see your scar."

I said, "No, that's the scar where I was struck by lightning."

He laughed aloud at that and repeated, "You did have your appendix out."

He thought I was lying. I was told I would not be leaving Winston until the next day. They took me out to the fair to work with a recruiting officer who had a booth out there far a few hours. I got to talk to other young men and to try to get them to join the Army Air Force. They put me on a bus the next day with thirty-four men, none of whom I knew. We went to Camp Croft South Carolina, near Spartanburg. That night we went to a barracks where an old army sergeant was in charge of us all. He said lights out at nine o'clock and he didn't want to hear a peep out of anybody.

After lights were off for a few minutes some guy said "He He Haw I am a Ba-a-a-ad Man!" The old sergeant turned the lights back on but could not find out who it was. The next morning we marched out in single file to turn in our blankets.

While the sergeant conversed with someone this same guy gave the order "Forward March". We were going across the field when he caught up with us.

Later they were interviewing us and asking where we were from and etc. They asked one guy where he was born when he said Cowpens, South Carolina. There is actually a place by that name but they made fun of him and asked why he was born in a place like that. He told them he wanted to be near his mother. That day we got a real physical examination. I felt like a part of a herd of cattle or a flock of sheep.

We stood naked for what seemed like hours as we went from room to room. They checked us for flat feet, hemorrhoids, and any sign we had been injured in a car wreck or injured otherwise. We also had a chest x-ray, kidney specimen and an eye exam. They didn't miss anything. They still didn't believe my scar was from being struck by lightning. They even talked hateful to me for suggesting such a thing and put on my records that I'd had my appendix removed. Finally they were through with us. We had moved through so many rooms I was beginning to think I wouldn't find my clothes again.

The next day, just before we were loaded on a train, our names were called out and we were lined up. One man, a Cherokee Indian was told he had failed the physical and could go home. He never said a word, just turned and headed for the camp entrance gate, never bothering to look back. The rest of us were sworn into the United States Army and put on the train to Fort Jackson, near Columbia, S.C.

We were up very early the next morning, marched to chow and then to a huge building for written exams. If you passed you went on to another. We started out with a group of about three hundred, finally there were only sixteen of us left as the ones that failed the test were weeded out. After about ten hours we went back to quarters for a few hours rest. We were told we would be there until we received orders as where we were going.

I still didn't know whether I had made it into the Air Force or not. The next day I got my uniform. We went into a big supply building and they advised us to give our civilian clothes to the Salvation Army, rather than shipping them home. We threw our clothes into a barrel and were given a barracks bag to put our clothes in. Then we walked naked down a long counter. The men behind the counter asked your shirt size, underwear size, pants and jacket sizes. They grabbed a garment and threw it at you while urging you to move, move along. There was no time to get dressed or try anything on. You just dropped each garment into the barracks bag and moved on. Your heavy overcoat was last. Finally, we could put something on. We all looked alike, a bunch of sad sacks, nothing fit very well. After we dressed they did fit us carefully with shoes. They fit everyone with a size larger shoes than we normally wore. I had been wearing tens so I got elevens.

After this we awaited orders. Some were being called every few hours. Some would stay at Fort Jackson. I saw one boy who had been there for two weeks waiting for shoes. He wore a size seventeen. The next day they took me to a large kitchen where I scrubbed pots and pans all day. About midnight that night I was awakened and told to get ready to go, my orders were ready. All sixteen of us lined up and were marched out to a truck.

An officer was in charge of us as he hurried us to the railroad station. We boarded a nice passenger train, my second ride on a train. The officer in charge finally revealed to us on the train that we were headed to an Air Force base. I still didn't know any of the men but I began to get acquainted with one from North Carolina. Most of them were from Pennsylvania. We got off the train in Savanna, Georgia and were served breakfast in the station, eggs and grits.

The boys from Pennsylvania looked at the grits and asked, "What in the Hell is that?" We then boarded another train. Wow the railroad car was a far cry from the stream liner we had been on. It must have been left over from the Civil War. It had a coal stove bolted down in the center. It was hooked to a slow train and headed inland to Georgia. We were on the car all day, going mostly through swamps and stopping at small towns. We were once parked on a sidetrack and left for two hours until another train picked us up. The car in front of us on the second train had a few passengers on it. Two pretty girls were looking back smiling at us. The officer in charge allowed them to come back and -join us. One of them sat with me for a while. This helped to pass the time. I don't remember her name.

We didn't get anything to eat all day. When we finally stopped we were in Moultrie, Georgia. There a truck was waiting for us and took us to what we learned was Spence Field.

We knew we were at an air base by the constant roar of the airplanes. We were in tent city and were greeted by a sergeant who said he was a former marine and would give us our basic training. The commander of the basic training unit looked us over. He said we would be up at four in the morning for breakfast and a days training in the field. We hadn't eaten all day but since it was nine o'clock we were ordered to bed. The next morning we were woke by a bugle and told to be dressed and ready to march to the mess hall in ten minutes.

Outside we lined up quickly and were told to learn to move faster and look sharper, the old marine said we looked like a bunch of slobs. We had been the last to arrive the day before. There were already some three hundred men in tent city. We started off marching to a cadence and then were given double time to march to the mess hall. There we were given ten minutes to eat and get back in formation. Back at tent city we were chewed out. we had not left our tent in proper order, we were not clean-shaven and needed haircuts. I'd just had a haircut at Fort Jackson. We marched all day and learned to take orders and carry them out properly. I was moved to front rank pivot position. I got chewed out a lot for mistakes in the command given. I began to wonder would I ever have anything to do with airplanes? I was just seeing and hearing them in the distance. I hardly had time to get a letter off to my parents during the first six weeks.

I did learn to march, make a bunk bed-tightly and do everything quickly, salute and take orders and other things that go, with basic training.

Finally the six weeks were up and I was told what squadron I was assigned to. There I met my Commanding officer and first sergeant. The first thing I was told to do was to go to the supply room and get new and better fitting uniforms. I felt and looked a lot better after that. Then I was told I was going to Link Trainer School. The school was a very intensive training period. If I thought I had studied hard in high school, I was wrong. I got up at four o'clock, stood revelry and roll call, put my bunk and footlocker in order, made sure my area was clean and went to breakfast, then to school. At twelve I went to lunch.

From twelve thirty to one I had fast calisthenics, then I ran in formation for thirty minutes, after that I went back to school until four thirty. In this time we had to pick up mail and do drill practice. Lights were out at nine o'clock. We could go to the day room to write letters after nine if we wished. I did this and wrote several friends back home but mostly Marie and Mother. Their letters cheered me up. Finally I was told I could have a pass into town for six hours on a Saturday evening, from six until midnight. So for the big trip I went into town and looked around a little, rode in on the bus, went in a restaurant and enjoyed a hamburger and a milk shake.

Boy was that a treat! On the air base was a movie theater, but I never had time to go. This was a special treat too.

I was up against more competition than I had ever been before so I really had to work. After two weeks we were going to Link Trainer building at night. We were beginning to learn what the Link Trainer was like and how it worked.

In a Link Trainer the pilot sat in the cockpit with controls and instruments like those in a real plane. The cockpit was closed and the pilot had to operate it as he would a plane at night or in heavy clouds and he would concentrate on the instruments. A synchronized recorder was placed on a map on top of a desk. On it was an inking wheel, and it drew a line on the map showing the path the pilot flew. The instructor at the desk talked to the pilot by microphone much the same as a pilot contacts the tower operator. When the pilot came out he could see his mistakes on the map.

As a Link Trainer I had to learn all about instruments and how they worked and how the pilot was to use them. I also had to learn how to read maps and how to use a radio signal to find your way to a certain point when flying. A part of our job was to maintain the Link Trainer and keep it in good condition. After I completed the course I began my work as a link Trainer instructor. My students were mostly advanced aviation cadets who would soon receive their wings.

Then they would be commissioned fighter pilots. Officers also had to get a required number of hours to keep their status as a pilot. At that time in late 1942 and early '43 pilots were badly needed so they were training night and day seven days a week. They were running them through, cutting all the corners they could and moving them into combat. Our schedule gave no time for rest or leisure.

There was time to continue my training though. I was marching in parades, learning how to fire the M-l rifle, the 45 caliber, the side arm carbine, the Thompson sub-machine gun and the little machine gun called the grease gun. Later I would learn how to fire and maintain the 30 and 50 caliber machine gun.

I learned about chemical warfare. We went through gas chambers and learned to identify the different poison gases, how to protect ourselves from them and of course how to use the gas mask. Sometimes we were required to wear them for long periods of time.

We had all kinds of obstacle courses to go through. I was in top shape physically and had no problem with any of them except swimming. I had never learned to swim as a young boy and never could meet the standards required. I did find time at night to play basketball.

I went to town on pass when I could on weekends when I could. However there wasn't much to do in this small town. We were warned by our superiors and usually an army medic not to have anything to do with women that we didn't know. We were shown films on venereal disease that would scare you to death and told that women in South Georgia were worse than anywhere else. Later I learned that wherever you went you were told the same thing about the local women.

I wrote girl's back home, but mostly just Marie and telling her how much I loved her. She was writing sweet letters regularly, but she had not said the words I wanted to hear, I LOVE YOU. One day I did receive a letter from her and when I read the bottom line on the first page it said I love you, then I turned the page and it continued on and said, like a brother. That was NOT what I wanted to hear.

In those days we didn't make much money. They took money out for life insurance every month, then there was money for dry cleaning and laundry. I did do some of my own laundry and that helped some, but there was no way I could keep the dress uniforms good enough for the dress parades and big inspections.

Our squadron was tops at the base and our uniforms had to be creased and spotless. I even had my shirts, pants and dress jackets altered for a perfect fit.

The cooks were very good and it was amazing they did as well as they did with having to prepare so much food at the time.

The pilots and cadet pilots were fed in a different mess hall. Their food was of better quality and better prepared than ours.

I continued to write several friends back home but mostly Mother and Marie. Mother's health continued to get worse and I worried about her. Marie was writing me regularly now and I wrote her every chance I got. Most of our courting was done by letters because we had never dated much when I was home. Since Christmas was coming I decided to buy her a wristwatch and went into town for that purpose. We had a P. X. but everything was higher there. I tried to pick out a watch I thought she would like, the sales girl was very helpful and friendly and I finally decided on one. We got a conversation going and ended up going to a movie in town. She insisted on getting her Dad's car and driving me back to the base so I wouldn't have to take the bus. On the way back I apologized about my messy hair. My hair had grown out some after the G.I. and I went to a barber there on the base. I was expecting a nice trim but he hurriedly cut it leaving it a mess, all gaped up. I said some rather unkind things about him to her. She did not say anything and was rather quite after that.

I learned from my friend David Monk that the barber was her Dad. I was too embarrassed to go back to apologize after having been driven back to the base in his car.

One boy I knew wanted out of the service and talked about it all the time. He continued trying to find a way out. Finally he wrote President Roosevelt a letter that was a court martial offense going over your immediate commanding officers head. He was called to headquarters and I never find out what happened to him. Another boy went off his rocker or pretended to. He was given a section eight discharge. Any young man not in service was labeled 4-F which was a term given one that did not pass- the physical. Of course there were exceptions called hardship cases where the parents were unable to care for themselves and they had to stay home and run the farm. A boy from West Virginia went over the hill every time he got a pass. He would be brought back by the M.P.'s and put in the guardhouse for a while. When he got out he eventually got another pass and did the same thing again. Some days or weeks later he would be brought back and the cycle began again.

Everyone had to pull K.P., kitchen police, duty and guard duty. I once in awhile got these duties at night. They would not pull me off my regular line of duty though. I did not mind K.P.

It was hard work but early in the morning when I came off K.P. before leaving for my regular work, the mess sergeant would say, "Fix your own breakfast, whatever you want."

I found some eggs and toast which we seldom had, then some corn flakes and some milk that we never had. I really enjoyed that. It was worth the nights work. I could eat a box of corn flakes and a quart of milk. One boy I knew that we called steel wool, I never knew his name, was assigned to the kitchen regularly and he cleaned so many pots and pans they called him steel wool.

January of 1943 I suppose was like any other January in South Georgia as far as the weather was concerned. It seemed like late spring to me with quite a bit of rain, some thunderstorms, and some nice days. March was filled with blooming azaleas on every lawn. They were so well kept and the sweet aroma of spring filled the air. When we went to town we enjoyed walking up and down the streets and enjoying the beautiful sights. There was never a day when we did not go out for an hour or more of exercise, so we kept in good shape.

Chapter Twelve

Once when they took us out to a swamp and told us to run a mile or two across the swamp, and make it as fast as we could. Some officers were waiting for us on the other side to time us as we came out. It was a sunny winter day with a pleasant temperature. I ran at a good clip and was near the front. I saw a big rabbit asleep in a bunch of grass and I reached down and grabbed him as I ran. I carried him by his hind legs, and handed it to the first officer that I came to and told him I overtook the rabbit and my way across the swamp. We were always pulling some prank or another.

Very often on going to bed at night you found you had been short sheeted. Sometimes you would find a balloon full of water left in your shoe and when you got up hurriedly and jumped into them early in the morning you would be in for a surprise. The list of tricks went on and on. One Saturday evening a guy who had been a judge in civilian life opened up his laundry expecting to find a clean uniform to go into town when out fell a W.A.C.'s uniform. The look on his face and the words he said would probably have got him thrown out of any court in the land.

Tent city was soon done away with. I was near the last group of recruits brought to Spence Field and now the base was fully manned. Of course aviation cadets were always coming and going.

The cadets were advanced as they had already been through pre flight and basic training. Spence Field was for advanced training. When they left there they had their wings and their commission. Their graduation day was very special after their intense training. They were ready to be assigned to a fighter wing and on to combat in a foreign field of operations. The planes used at Spence Field were advanced trainees called A.T.6's. They had twin cockpits with dual controls. A single engine plane with front and rear cockpits. Its cruising speed was 160 m.p.h.

Before the pilots received their wings they went to Elgin Field, Florida for gunnery school. There they learned to aim their plane and fire the machine guns mounted in the wings. They fired at ground targets in the swamp. They also fired at targets towed by another plane and reeled out from the plane on a cable. This had to be done in a non-populated area.

I went on flights to see how the instruments really worked on a plane in flight compared to a Link Trainer. I was given a parachute. You never went out without one. I had some instructions on how to wear and use one.

Getting out on an A.T.6 would have been much different from bailing out of a regular paratrooper transport. I am thankful I never had to bail out of one.

I flew the plane from the back cockpit after the captain in the front took off and flew to 5000 ft. altitude. I watched the instruments instead of the horizon. He tried to get me to watch the horizon. We communicated with the headset and mike. I didn't do so well on that first flight. Getting the feel of the rudder and stick takes time and practice. I'd had no primary or basic instruction. On another flight when we came into land, our wheel would not lower, then one came down and the other stayed up. The captain remarked that I might have to bail out. I was glad when both wheels finally came down. When the flying weather was good we got a break in Link Training. All the cadets wore out flying that there were planed for and we did not have many in link trainers. On the other hand when the weather was bad we had a house fill waiting. Each student had an hour with the instructor. On occasions his flight instructor would sit by his student to see how he was doing in link trainer.

The war wasn't going well and we were pushing faster and harder to get more planes and pilots into action. Some of the flight instructors were really exhausted flying night and day. There were a few accidents in landing mishaps or midair collisions. There were so many planes in the air at the same time. They were taking off and landing so every one had to be alert at all times.

They practiced taking off side by side , two racing down the runway as two in front of them left the ground seeing how quick a whole squadron could get on the air and then merging to fly in formation. The linemen worked day and night too. Two shifts keeping the planes serviced and gassed up. All kinds of mechanics, radiomen, technicians, everyone was putting in long hours.

These were desperate days. We had to turn the war around. It was hard for me to find time to read the daily paper or listen to the news on the radio. I wanted to keep up with all the news that was happening daily. All kinds of papers and magazines were available at the base library. If I had time at night I went to the library to read and write letters. Letters came first and I tried to write Marie and Mother often.

I did not go to the beer parlor like many of the boys did at night or to town. Once in a while I would go to see a movie when a good one was showing. Every month or so a USO show came to Spence Field. I tried to see all of them. At these shows we could laugh and forget all about the war for a little while.

We carried a little record book in our pocket that listed all our shots and immunizations shots and dates they were received. Malaria or Yellow Fever always gave me a bad headache.

They were experimenting with a flu vaccine, first in a pill form. We all had to swallow a pill about the size of a dime. I don't think it helped.

I had been in service a long time and a lot had happened. It seemed like a long time. I missed my home and my home back in the mountains. I get a lot of mail from back home from friends, and sometimes it piles up and I get three letters in one day from Marie. Mother sent me a cake and of course I shared it. Sister Maude sent a cake and a bottle of Vitalis hair dressing. The bottle broke and soaked the cake. That sure made me unhappy. Vernon Knight and I went into town and made pictures. We were not allowed to make any here on the base.

The last of the month was payday. This was January 31. 1943. You lined up in single file and went by your commanding officer and gave your name, rank and serial number, saluted and received your money. Then after payday that night was the big night for some of the boys. Those that drank went to town or to a beer parlor and partied. Many of them went to the recreation room to gamble. Some blew all their money on girls. Some drank it up some lost it all in gambling, many were flat broke the next day.

Me? I looked for a good meal in town or on base, something that was tastier than the army food. Even a hamburger was a treat. I received a nice box of fried chicken from home; it was really good after coming through the mail.

Mother was feeling better and I was so glad for I had really been worried about her. I was greedy with the chicken and did not share it. We had been served stewed chicken a few times at the mess hall. It was chopped up with a meat cleaver and was full of bone slivers. I never was a lover of coffee and that was the main drink served, sometimes unsweetened cool aid, very seldom any milk.

Most every one smoked when they had the opportunity. Most buildings had no smoking signs and of course there was no smoking allowed around the planes.

Those working on the line where the planes were gassed up wore cork bottom shoes with no tacks to cause sparks on the hardtop and ignite the gasoline that might be spilled on the ground, especially on a hot sunny day.

I bought valentines and sent out a nice one to Marie. I received a sweet one from her and a box of candy. I love her more all the time and keep telling her so.

The 444th squadron that I had been assigned since my basic training broke up and I was assigned to the 443rd Squadron.

I never get to go to church since I always have to work on Sunday. There is a nice chapel here and I have met the chaplain.

March is finally here and the azaleas are beautiful and the lawns are pretty. By being here I've missed all the snows and ice of the winters at home. That is not really what I miss.

I miss my family and Marie, the beautiful mountains and the farm animals, the horses and the cows, and my cats. I really miss the good mountain water. The water here has a bad taste. The chlorine does not cover it up, it still taste like a swamp smells.

I keep writing Marie every day and she writes me every day. I know that she is the only girl for me, and it is so good to know that she really loves me.

I had been told that I might get a furlough in May and was really looking forward to that. On March 31, I received a telegram from Dr. Cox saying Mother was really sick and I should come home if possible. On April 1, the headquarters granted me a furlough to go home and see Mother. I was glad to be going home but would rather have been going home on a happy occasion. I wondered if she would be alive when I got home. I caught a train to Atlanta, and from Atlanta to Greensboro N.C. Then I caught a bus to Mount Airy, N.C. Mother was so glad to see me and was a little improved. I still wondered how she lived. She had a large blood clot near her heart. Her left shoulder was really black and a big knot rose up about the size of a grapefruit. She had to lie perfectly still for weeks. The doctor was afraid to move her to a hospital. I still think it had to be a miracle that she lived.

Marie and I got to be together some here at my home. One day we were sitting together in the front living room and were looking at picture albums. Our heads touched and an electric current seemed to flow between us. We looked at each other in great surprise. We both were very shy. We kissed and embarrassed knowing what we meant to each other. I had never felt that great a love or magnetism before. I knew I wanted to be with her always and I knew we must soon part. Oh, how the thoughts of leaving and saying good-bye hurt. The days were so uncertain, Mother was so ill, I loved Marie so much and she loved me, yet the war was going on and I must go back to my duty.

On my second evening home my brother Arthur brought two girls to see me. I guess he thought I needed company. I had a date with Marie who was preparing supper for me. I hated to be rude but they were hard to brush off, however, I finally succeed in getting them to go. I was two hours late, my supper was cold and Marie was hot with anger. She did forgive me though.

The five days home passed quickly. I did all I could for Mother and Dad, spent some time with Marie and enjoyed seeing the mountains and the farm animals. It was so good to be home. This trip made me realize what a beautiful place I live in and how much more I appreciated it.

I will always be forever grateful to God for this beautiful, peaceful spot on His earth that I am privileged to live. My prayers were that I would someday be able to return to live here again.

I told Marie good-bye the night before I left as she would be in school the next day. How good it was to hear her say she loved me. Her love would give me strength to carry me through the hard days ahead. Leaving Mother was difficult especially since she took it so hard. The trip back was long and tiresome but I made it back on time. I had a new out look on life and I prayed that I would see my Mother again. Little did I know that I would be seeing her very soon.

I got back to Spence Field and had just gotten back into the routine of everything when again I received another telegram. Daddy Mont (my birth father) had died with a sudden heart attack. I received the message April 15, 1943. The next day I again received an emergency furlough of seven days to go home. I could not leave until midnight that night. At twelve o'clock I picked up my furlough papers and could find no transportation until two A.M. I caught a bus out of Moultrie and it was a slow one stopping at every little town. I finally arrived in Hillsville at three A. M. the next day after many delays. Hillsville that didn't have much going on in the daytime was dead at 3 A. M. so I started walking down highway 58.

I walked about two miles before I saw a house with a light on and found a farmer up early. I hired him to take me to Laurel Fork where I phoned Dad to come and get me. Then I found out that Daddy Montague's funeral had been the afternoon before. They had not waited for me to get home.

It was good to see Mother looking so much better, although she was far from well. I was glad to have a few days with Marie again. We were so happy to have some time just to be together no matter how brief it was. I got to see several of my relatives and almost before I knew it, it was time to leave again. It was oust perfect spring weather at home but when I got back to Spence Field it was really hot and felt like summertime. The barracks were so hot at night it was hard to sleep. At least the link trainer building where I worked was cool and I was thankful for that.

We worked out every day in midday and this sure got one sweating. I was in good shape weighing 175 pounds with my six feet two inch height.

By summer the war effort seemed to be improving but I wondered if it would ever end and I would get to go home again.

We had lots of cockroaches and water bugs in the barracks, which I'd never seen. They were so bad that one night they gassed the barracks and we had to leave wearing our raincoats.

On returning the next morning we found dead cockroaches laying everywhere. This took cars of them for a long time.

I saw a lot of soldiers I knew who had their wives come and live nearby and they could be together at night. I thought how great it would be to have Marie down here with me. I wondered how long I would be stationed here. Someone was always getting shipped out unexpectedly.

I was always meeting someone new, soldiers from almost every state in the country. There were a lot of northern boys that liked to make fun of the south and our accent. Some of them called me a coal miner. They didn't know I had never seen a coalmine. I thought it was amusing when someone from New Jersey made fun of the southern boys. They would say, "You's guys sound so funny when you say you all."

One guy making fun of us said he was from "Pittsboigh" and the south was for the "boids". It was all in fun and we liked kidding each other.

I liked the air force better than at first. I did not mind the hard work as long as it was accomplishing something. I felt we were doing our part for our country and wished I could do more to keep our freedom.

I remembered our Fourth of July celebrations at home and wished I could be home for this one. I was remembering seeing my first airplane at Laurel Fork on the Fourth of July.

Now I was seeing airplanes all day long and hearing them continually anytime I was awake. At first it had been hard to sleep hearing the roar of planes taking off constantly. After awhile I became accustomed to it and it was just a part of life and it didn't bother me any more.

The heat did bother me though and most everyone else. So on this Fourth of July the public was allowed to have an open house at Spence Field. It was a workday as usual for me most of the day. No one was allowed in the Link Trainer building and many of the other buildings were off limits. The visitors could watch the planes taking off and landing from a distance and some of the planes went through maneuvers. In the afternoon we went out on the field in full dress parade and marched in review. That was fun in the 100-degree temperature. Later that weekend we went into town for a parade down Main Street. I always enjoyed a parade, but I enjoyed watching more than being in the parade.

Being a pivot man in the front ranks was not easy, you had to be sure you made the correct move when the command was given since everyone follows you. At one time we had a commanding officer that would get mixed up on his left and right. He gave a to the right column march, when I knew he meant column left. If we had gone right it would have ran us into a wall instead of the street.

One day I went up with a flight commander and he did a lot of dives, loops and acrobatics that I had not experienced before. We also landed on a dirt airstrip and took off again. He was watching the student pilots that were flying all around us. He would come up underneath them where they could not see them and buzz them, giving them a scare. This was just a part of their training to teach them to be alert so the enemy would not slip up on them and shoot them down. When we came back to the field a plane had cracked up on the runway. We had to circle the field with lots of other planes while the wreckage could be cleared. The commander got on his radio demanding that the wreckage be removed. It was amusing to see everything go into action as vehicles and men removed the wreckage in a hurry. As we watched from the air we could see every movement. We were not far, as the plane flies, from Okefenokee Swamp. A few of the trainers had gotten lost at night and ran out of gas and bailed out over the swamp. I knew of one that was lost for three days before he walked out on a roadway. I never talked with him personally, however he had many adventures with quicksand, cottonmouth moccasins, alligators, and all kinds of bugs.

One boy I heard of was busted, or washed out, they called it. This meant he went back to buck private and could not fly anymore. He had been caught diving at some of the local country people out working in their gardens.

He would come so close to them before he would pull up that they would run into the woods or their homes. He thought he was having fun but he was putting their lives in danger.

Chapter Thirteen

There was always being something being developed every day. In my work, there were new instruments to learn about and to teach, with something being added to the planes or Link Trainers. This as well as new things coming out in weapons or chemical warfare, always new orders to be carried out. We had to be careful and read the bulletin boards where we worked and in the orderly room. You never knew when your name would be on the bulletin board for a special duty, and failure to see and carry it out could mean real trouble.

One day the order was posted that everyone would wear shorts for physical training the following day. Many did not have any shorts or any time to purchase them. The supply room either did not have any or would not issue any. A lot of the boys sewed up the fly on their G.I. underwear and wore them. You could not always get what you needed from the Air Force supply. I bought pants more than on one occasion because they did not have my size. I also bought dress low cut slippers to wear because the Air Force did not issue them. I could wear a brown dress slipper with a plain toe and keep them polished to a spit shine. Our regular high top shoes were polished, too. We had two pair and one pair was always left by our footlocker and bunk for inspection.

The inspecting officer one day picked up my shoes to see if he could see himself in the shine on them. Footlockers had to be opened and correctly arranged. Beds were made with white collar, sheets turned down over the blankets, and blankets were to be tight enough that a fifty-cent coin tossed on it would bounce off. Windows were to be spotless. Our C.O. got us up once at 2 A.M. to clean them. The latrines were to be cleaned thoroughly every morning.

There were beer parties almost every weekend. I took no part in them for I needed that time to write letters. Most of my letter writing was to Mother and Marie. Marie wrote me almost every day and I loved her more all the time. She was great at writing letters. In fact she was great at anything.

I was glad when fall came and the weather was a little cooler. It was October and I had been in the Air Force one year now. This was also a beautiful month back home with all the lovely fall colors and a great time to walk in the mountains.

Thanksgiving dinner was a big thing with lots of turkey and everything to go with it. This was one day when the food was good and there was plenty of it. They gave us free cigarettes, which I took and gave to some of my buddies who smoked. I did not smoke the first one.

Christmas came and went with nothing special.

Just another day and a time to be homesick for family and loved ones back home. I did send Marie a small gift and she sent me one through the mail. There was a rumor that someone would be going to school for training in something new. There were written test given to see who was qualified. I took the written exams and how different they were. I did not think I had done well and just forgot about it. One night after Christmas the charge of quarters came to tell me I had a telephone call. I knew I wasn't getting a call from home since the phone service was so bad there. I was happy when a sweet voice said they wanted to congratulate me. A W.A.C. from headquarters said my name had just come out to attend a school. How I loved to go to school. I really did. She invited me to come on down to headquarters to read it. I hurried on over and sure enough, there it was with two other names from Spence Field. We would be going to Navy school in Washington, D. C.

The W.A.C. was a very pretty girl from California. Many of the boys had tried to date her. She asked me to walk her to headquarters and we talked awhile in her recreation hall. She told me about California.

Eugene Cone and Ike Croft were going with me to Washington. Ike was from Atlanta and Eugene was from Baltimore. We would be leaving in a couple of days. I packed my barracks bag and included my heavy winter coat.

I went to the store and bought a suitcase to put my uniforms in. I could not keep the press and wrinkles out of them when they were in a barracks bag. I did want to look nice when I got there. We were told we would be there six weeks. We were individually given our papers and were to be sure we kept up with them. We had the address of the school we would attend from 6 A.M. to 6 P.M. six days a week. Sunday would be ours to do with as we pleased. We must find our own lodging and meals. Each of us was given four hundred and fifty dollars. Imagine trying to live in D.C. today on $450.

On New Year's Eve we left Spence Field and caught a train out of Moultrie. We barely made connections with a streamliner out of Tallahassee. This took us to Savannah where we caught another fast train. This was my first ride on a Pullman. It was New Year's Eve and everybody was in a party mood and there was lots of drinking.

I was surprised to see how quickly the seats could be made into bunks. I took an upper berth. Since I didn't drink or take part in the partying I climbed into my berth about ten o'clock. There was a lot of noise over the roar of the train as the hour of midnight approached. There were both service men and women on the train and more women than men. I was really surprised to see women drinking so much. I had not seen this back home.

When I peeped from my curtained bunk around midnight I saw men and women in various stages of undress going up and down the aisle. I was glad to keep quiet in my upper berth behind the curtains. Things finally quieted down some and I went to sleep.

When I woke up it was quiet except for the roar of the train. I lay still for a while and then decided to get up. No one was in the little rest room and no one was stirring. I found the dining car, only three or four were having breakfast. Everyone was sleeping off the party of the night before. It was getting daylight outside when the train stopped and I found we were in Richmond, Virginia. This meant we would soon be in Washington, D.C. I went to my car and found Ike. He didn't look too well. he'd had too much to drink the night before. Cone was planning to stay with his mother and commuting back and forth to school in Washington. I thought, how nice, how lucky to be able to stay home with his Mother and still be able to go to the school.

Before noon we were in Union Station. Ike and I found our bags and got off the train and were greeted by M.P.'s demanding to see our furlough papers. We showed them our papers and asked them where to find lodging. They couldn't help so we went outside and talked to a taxi driver. He suggested the Soldiers, Sailors and Marine's club. We asked him to take us there and after paying him we knew we would have to find a cheaper place to stay. After checking further we decided this would be fine.

We could get an army bunk like we were use to sleeping in for $1 a night. We could get breakfast and an evening meal for fifty cents each. We could catch a streetcar two blocks from there on New York Avenue. That would take us all the way to the Naval Air Station where we would take out training. It was a pleasant surprise to find we could get a pass that was good for a whole week. They cost service men a dollar and a half. We could ride as much as we liked, change cars and go anywhere in the city twenty-four hours a day. We had it made as far as money was concerned. The meals were good and girl volunteers waited on the tables.

The next morning we walked to the corner and caught the New York Ave. Streetcar. Even at 5:30 it was crowded. We found the address we were looking for, the Anacostia Naval Air Station was a laboratory for testing new equipment during World War II.

We met our instructors and were told that we were not to reveal anything we saw or heard there only to the proper military authorities we were to teach later. We found our instructors to be very thorough. They covered so much so fast it was hard to keep up. I wished I had taken short hand. I did get most of it. However when they showed me the Gun Air Instructor I felt panic. How could I learn to learn to operate and maintain anything so complicated in just six weeks. How to use the gun sight in itself was not hard; it was mounted in front of the pilot's eye level.

It was a lighted circle a little like looking through a scope sight, only you could see a much larger area in front of you. The fighter plane on spotting the enemy would approach it and try to get the enemy inside the circle. He could tell by reading the gun sight how far he was from the enemy. While controlling the plane, he tried to get the center dot fixed on his enemy. When he accomplished this and was in range he would fire his guns by pressing a button on the firing control stick. The machine guns mounted in each wing were aligned with the gun sight. The gun was fixed solid so you could not aim them except by aiming the plane.

The Gun Air Instructor was about thirty feet long and it had two sets of controls like the trainer plane. It was housed in a Quonset hut and there was no outside light that came in. It was dark like a movie theater. When you were seated there was a movie screen in front of you. The pilot sat above you in the back cockpit. When you were both seated the instructor turned off the lights and numerous switches were turned and the projector showed a horizon, land, ocean, fields, streams, clouds and blue sky just as you would see from a plane in flight. The horizon moved according to the throttle and controls the pilot maneuvered. The sound came on and it felt as if you were actually in flight. A second projector was turned on which showed a small plane as it in the distance on the screen. This was the enemy.

The instructor with his controls controlled this plane as if he were flying, diving, climbing, turning and trying to out maneuver the pilot. When the pilot was allowed to catch and thought he had the plane in his gunfights he would push the button just like on the plane. The sound over the speakers sounded very real as he fired. The sound of the motor and roar of the propeller was very real. If he hit the plane it turned red an electric counter counted the rounds he fired and also the hits. The flight would last ten minutes. It was so real to the pilots that often they came out sweating and shaky. The instructors took turns. After three or four hours the instructors were tired and a little dizzy with a headache from all the noise.

One did tend to get use to it though. So with all the cables, micro switches, sound devices, controls and hundreds of parts imagine what it was like to repair this monster. We had to assemble it when it was first sent to the base, a package deal. I studied all the maintenance books and notes I had taken with great diligence.

There were other boys there from air bases all over the U.S. as well as Mexico. There was a great rush to complete this program so all we did for lunch was to send out for a sandwich and a drink.

There were so many high-ranking officers in Washington that you did not salute because everyone's arm would have been worn out. At school that was a different matter.

In Washington I got to wear my heavy overcoat that I had been issued in Georgia and never needed. We went sightseeing and saw the Lincoln Memorial, Washington Monument, foreign embassies. The Capitol, White House and many other places. I spent a whole day in the Smithsonian.

Everywhere I went I met girls. They would throw snowballs. whistle or do anything to get your attention. So many of- them were working as secretaries and were lonesome and far from home. There was a great need for many secretaries to keep the many war records. They lived anywhere they could find a room for rent. I did not know there were so many pretty girls in the world and I did my best to ignore them.

I just had one girl on my mind and I was writing to her a few lines every day and wishing I could write more and I wanted to see her very much. I was thinking of giving her a diamond if I just got to see her. I was saving my money for it and not spending foolishly as were so many of the other boys here in school. Ike was going out every night and having fun.

I decided after the first week I could go out one night a week and get my studying done.

I went to a stage show one night, another night I went to a nightclub for a good meal but did not drink. I really did enjoy looking through all the government buildings I had access to. There were not a lot of tourists in Washington at this time because of the war and security. There was also not much gas or tires for people to do much traveling. Lots of service men were in and out of Washington all the time as well as a lot going over seas. One night two Air Force buddies that I had met at the school and was staying at the club went to a supper club and saw a floor show. Later some girls joined us and we hired a taxi to take everyone home. A girl from Pennsylvania and I were seated in front with the driver and the other two couples were seated in the back seat. The couples in the back asked the driver if he would take us someplace dark and park for a while. He said he would for a price and they agreed to it.

The girl with me said she wanted no part of that and I said I didn't either. We asked the driver to take us to a location near where she lived, which also happened not to be far from my club. He did and we got out and they went on their way. I walked her to her apartment and she said she was glad to meet someone that was nice and treated her like a lady, and would like to see me again. I told her I was promised to a girl I hoped to marry. and did not wish to get involved. I returned to the soldiers, sailors and marines club and did not see her again.

She did call the club several times and asked me to call her, however I did not have time for things like that. So on one Sunday I went alone to the Smithsonian and really enjoyed looking around. As I was on my way walking through the snow, after I got off the streetcar, three girls started throwing snowballs at me. I tried to ignore them and got inside my building and there were only a few people in there. The girls followed me in and continued making conversation and were hard to ignore. One girl was especially beautiful and I did end up going out with her a few times. I told her I had a friend back home that I intended to marry and nothing serious developed. She did seem like a nice lady and was from Michigan. She did write me letters later before I was married.

Each day became more hectic in school and after three weeks we were given a written exam on what we had covered. I did well on it. Some of the guys from the other bases did not make it and were sent back to their home base. So I began to work and study harder. I did not want to fail. I was really concerned about the maintenance of the Gun Air Structure. I felt I could pass the written part all right and the operation and instruction exams which we observed while we actually did them I felt very confident about this. Doing the maintenance work while being observed was another matter. There was so much to cover.

I had been able to save much of the money they gave me on living expenses and the time for the final exam was drawing near. I reviewed all my notes and got ready for it. I tried to get a good nights rest and prayed that I would make good. We were given four hours for the written test that consisted of two hundred questions and problems. I worked through it leaving a few time consuming ones until the last. I got through in plenty of time and felt pretty good about it. That afternoon was the instructors test and manual test. I was relieved at the end of the day when they told me I did well on the manual test. The written test I would find out about later.

It was time to return to Spence Field and I asked for a delay in route on my way back so I could see my parents and, especially, Marie. I loved her so much and it had been months since I had seen her. I wired my company commander about my request. Ike did the same.

Ike thought we should celebrate so we went to a nice supper club and floorshow. It was in the basement of a big building. Ike did drink but I did not. When we were ready to go we went by the hatcheck office where we had left our overcoats and caps as we came in. Ike was pretty tipsy. He got his coat ahead of me and went staggering off. When the girl gave me my coat and cap I noticed they had switched them and he was wearing my coat and cap. Ha-Ha.

I ran to catch him and he was nearing the top of the long flight of steps when I caught him just as he emerged on the street. He was much shorter than I and smaller, so my coat reached the ground and his hands were inside the sleeves and the cap was dropping over his eyes. He was a funny sight, however an M.P. would not have laughed. We would both have been picked up. So I managed to get him back to the club and into his bunk.

The next day I was elated to get a telegram from my CO. My delay was granted. I was going home! I went to the bus station and found I could make connections to Roanoke and on to Floyd that night. I would be leaving Washington at midnight. Ike would be catching a train to Atlanta. I finally got a call through to my parents and told Dad to meet me in Floyd the next day. I had a meal that evening with Betty, the girl from Michigan and told her good-by. I never saw her again.

Most of the buses were crowded in those days so was this bus coming in from Baltimore in route to Roanoke. There was one seat left beside a nice looking middle age lady. She talked all night and I had planned to sleep on the bus and be rested when I got home. She was lonesome and had been to see her husband in Baltimore for a week. She lived in Roanoke in a big house all alone while he was away. She told me all about her life. I was shocked when we got near Roanoke about daylight.

She invited me to go home with her and she would treat me to a big breakfast of ham and biscuits. She said we would be all alone and she would give me a big time. I thanked her and told her I had to be on my way and catch another bus.

Living in the country as I had and stationed in Southern Georgia I had not seen what the world was really like until I went to Washington.

Now I boarded the old bus to Floyd and there was hardly anyone on it. I wondered if Dad would be able to meet me. It was February and the weather was pretty cold but no snow was on the ground. While riding the bus was thinking I would soon see Marie and get to hold her close and tell her how much I loved her. We had been writing and courting in the mail and we were promised to one another. I had been thinking I would give her a diamond while I was home it she would accept one and we would be engaged.

The diamond would be proof to others that we were engaged. I did not know at this point when I would be out of service or where I might go and she had not yet finished high school. She was planning to take nurses training when she finished school.

When I arrived in Floyd no one was there so I got my barracks bag and suitcase and started walking down highway number 8. I felt sure I soon would meet Dad. I had been walking only about ten minutes when I saw his pick up coming. There were no other vehicles on the road.

I was really surprised and overjoyed when he got near. Marie was with him! We soon made the trip home across Rocky Knob by the Parkway, so very beautiful in the wintertime. Mother was so glad to see me and she seemed in better health. Marie and I talked and planned. She was pleased that I was giving her a diamond. The next day we drove to Floyd and took the bus to Roanoke. We looked in jewelry stores down Jefferson Street and other places. We finally decided on one. She was pleased with what I could afford. Afterwards we went to visit my Aunt Vergie Goad for a short while before returning to Floyd on the bus.

When we arrived back in Floyd I found I had done a very stupid thing. In all the excitement of our being together I had locked the keys inside the pickup. The weather was cold and we didn't know how we would get into the pickup. Finally a man came along to help us and he and I, together, finally managed to unlock the door and we headed home. I had been able to get a few gas stamps that were allotted to servicemen and gave them to Dad. There sure wasn't much driving done in those days. Gas, tires, coffee, sugar, and other things were rationed. Some people worried a lot about sugar. Dad said he knew one man that had three hundred pounds saved up when the war ended.

Marie and I made the most of every moment in those three days. However time passed and we were saying good-by again.

I boarded the bus at Mount Airy on my way back to Spence Field. I knew I would really be busy when I returned. The Gun Air Structure had already been shipped and men would be they're setting it up when I arrived. The trip back was tiresome.

I got to Moultrie and went to the laundry and dry cleaners and had my uniforms all pressed and ready to wear. When I got to the main gate I was stopped by the M.P. and told to report to headquarters. I wondered why, I was not late. When I got to headquarters I found that my C 0. had not gone through the correct channels in granting me a delay en route. I got all this straightened out without having any real problems. When I got back to my squadron I found I had made an average of 94 at the school.

There was a lot of catching up to do at Spence Field. There was six weeks of letters to friends and relatives that needed replies. There were new orders to comply with that I was behind on as well as work on my new assignment. I'd been instructing men with high ranks for a long time as a Link Trainer instructor. This was one on one and I had gotten accustomed to that. This was a new experience because I had to go into a room with dozens of high-ranking pilots and stand before them and explain how to use the new Gun Sight. I was nervous and worried, however, I found they were eager to learn and glad to hear what I had to say.

They knew nothing about the new Gun Air Sight and they also knew that learning how to use it could save their lives, as well as win the war in the air. I felt more confident after the first session. After that we took them one at a time into the Gun Air Instructor, ten minutes for each pilot.

All of the instructors and all of the cadets were very eager to get their turn. Each morning there was a group waiting to take their turn and it seemed we would never catch up. We took turns teaching outside and operating the Gun Air Instructor inside. It was interesting and rewarding work. It was also tiring at. times doing the same things over and over, hearing the noise over and over and watching the action on the screen. However I was thankful that I was teaching instead of in the action. Sometimes you got a real headache. The pilots reacted differently, some did really well, and others had a difficult time. Some remained calm while others got very excited and after ten minutes were sweating and anxious.

Then we had the maintenance of the Gun Air Instructor, almost every night after a hard days use we had to replace parts and make adjustments. This took lots of time and patience. At times we would be working until the wee hours of the morning. It was hard to find time to even write Marie. I loved her so much and I wanted her to know I did.

She was such a wonderful person and was so beautiful I was afraid I might lose her to someone else. I wondered what she saw in me and why I was so lucky to be engaged to her. She was very busy also in her senior year at school, but she found time to write me long sweet letters every day. We often wrote about our future and when we could get married.

It was impossible to really make plans, not knowing what the next day held. One thing we did know was that we were in love and we wrote about that constantly. It is true that absence makes the heart grow fonder and you miss each other so....

Chapter Fourteen

Sometimes Ike's wife drove down from Atlanta to be with him. How great it would be if Marie could come and be with me!

One Sunday we were off and I rode down to Apalachicola Florida, just a ride down there and back with a quick look at the beach. How nice it was to get away from the constant roar of the planes and see something different for a few hours.

This spring was extremely hot for me and even the local people were complaining and the papers were carrying articles about the heat.

By now the war was going better. Germany was being constantly bombed night and day and was showing signs of weakening. I hardly found time to read the "Atlanta Journal". From what I did read I knew we would soon be invading France.

Marie and I decided we would get married this summer and she could live off the base and we could be together some of the time. As we did not know how long the war would last or what the outcome would be, we felt if we could have a few days or weeks together it would be better than none. We wrote and planned a lot about it. I knew that some of her relatives did not want her to marry me. We had friends and relatives that were getting married and were together, maybe a few days or weeks, and then the guy would be shipped overseas.

Some returned later and some never returned. How our hearts ached for them! So we wanted a little time together.

Marie was graduating the last of May and her uncle was taking her and her sister to Richmond and Petersburg, Virginia to visit his children and their cousins. I knew he was hoping she would meet someone there and forget about me. I was worried. I knew how beautiful she was and I knew something could happen. She might meet some charming young man and she might prefer him. I was sure she could have any man she chose. I was really blue. Would I loose the only one I loved? She did continue to write though, however her letters were delayed and that kept me worried. Since she was visiting from one place to another my letters could not reach her.

June 6, 1944...D-Day- We was awakened early on the morning of June 6. The invasion of France was underway. There was much praying that day but otherwise it was a day as usual at the base. Many were Praying and trying to hear some news.

Marie wrote me about her experiences in Petersburg on this day. They awoke to the sounds of church bells ringing all over town. All day people were going to church to pray for our country and the safety of our service men in action. She said it was a very unusual feeling of grief and anxiety, knowing that at the very best there would come forth heartache and sorrow for many families.

I was really glad when Marie got home and let me know she was still coming to Georgia and marry me. It sure had been a long month for me. I began to look for us a place to live in the town of Moultrie. It was already crowded with so many wives living there. I went into town every chance I got to search for us a place to live. It seemed every room and apartment was full. I was about to the point of giving up when I found one room I could rent. I had to pay in advance to get and hold it.

Then the big day came. I wrote Marie's mother a letter asking for her daughter's hand in marriage. I then waited several days for an answer. I prayed and hoped she would say yes- Marie was seventeen and I must have her consent before I could get the Georgia State marriage license. I knew it would be hard for her to let her seventeen-year-old daughter go off to marry a soldier.

At last my prayers were answered. She gave her consent. I was so happy. That was the best letter I ever got. I told Ike the big news and he wanted us to go out and celebrate. I said no for I knew he wanted to go out and drink. I went to the Colquitt County Courthouse and obtained the marriage license. Now the next problem was to get the day off. I knew a three-day pass would be all I could get at this time. I finally managed this. I could leave Spence Field on July 11 and be back by midnight of the thirteenth of July. Marie would leave Mount Airy on the morning of the eleventh of July and travel by Greyhound bus to Atlanta.

I would leave Moultrie that day and arrive before her to Atlanta and be waiting for her at the bus station. On the tenth I found I was scheduled for a dental appointment to have two wisdom teeth removed. They would not cancel it. I went and had the two lower wisdom teeth pulled and I never thought of them anymore. They never bothered me much and I didn't have time to be bothered with them. I had too many other important things to think about.

On the 11th I made sure I had all the papers in order, uniforms clean and pressed. With my three-day leave in hand I was one happy man. I was really praying everything would go according to our plans. The weather was very hot and it had been one of the hottest months on record in South Georgia. The month of June had recorded twenty days of over 100 degrees. One day it had been 114 degrees.

So what was Marie doing back home in the mountains of Virginia to get ready for the wedding? She had purchased a piece of white satin fabric while in Richmond from Miller and Rhodes Department store to make her a dress, also some light blue fabric to make a traveling suit. Her mother was helping her make them. She had a very difficult time finding white pumps (high heel dress shoes). It was wartime and many things just were not being made. She also purchased a stylish light blue hat to match her suit. It was impossible to find luggage but her uncle gave her a piece of his.

When I got to Atlanta I found a hotel room and got two adjoining rooms. I told them we were getting married the next day and wanted nice rooms. Then I hurried to the bus station where Marie was supposed to arrive at midnight. The bus station was very busy even at this hour. Many service people and others were coming and going. I waited anxiously wondering if Marie would back out at the last minute. Would her relatives talk her out of marrying me? I didn't think they could but I kept having doubts. Would she be safe on the bus? It was her first time out in the world all alone and she was so attractive.

Finally the bus pulled into the station at 2 A.M. So many people were getting off the bus, but I did not have to wait long. there she was! My heart was racing, she was so beautiful! I breathed a prayer of thanks for her safe keeping. Finally she saw me and we hurried to each other. We clung to one another forgetting about the crowd all around. We hurried to the hotel only a few blocks away. She was tired from the long ride, having left Mount Airy at seven o'clock Tuesday morning. The bellboy took us to our rooms and smiled as he unlocked the door between our adjoining rooms.

The next morning we were up early. Marie dressed in her street length wedding dress, she had made, and I in a fresh uniform. I knew then, and still know she was the most beautiful bride that I have ever seen. I was so proud and happy.

When we went down to the lobby the clerks and everyone starred at Marie and commented on how lucky I was. We then had breakfast. I don't remember what we ate. Then we went to the jewelry stores on Peach Tree Street and purchased matching wedding rings.

The next step was to find a minister as I did not know anyone. I decided to look in the phone book and saw a Rev. Harris. That sounded like a good old familiar name from back home. I phoned him and asked if he would perform a wedding ceremony. He agreed and was setting up where we would meet and then he asked, "Is you all a white couple?"

I said, "Yes."

He said, "I am a colored minister."

I thanked him and hung up and Marie and I decided we had better find a different way to find a minister. It was so hot. We walked and walked and finally came to a U.S.O. The first person we met was the well-known minister Rev. J.C. Daniels. He took us out to his lovely country home. His wife and sister were there and they witnessed our ceremony. So we were married in their lovely front lawn surrounded by flowers. The two ladies shed tears. Some people always cry at weddings.

I thought maybe they were looking at the beauty of the bride and the happiness they saw in our eyes. Perhaps at my uniform and the compassion they had for us. The Reverend Daniels then drove us back to Atlanta and I tried to pay him and he would not accept anything.

Now we were man and wife and were so happy to be enjoying the moment, the day and hours we had together. We tried at the hotel to get a message through all the party lines and the operators back to Mother to let her know we were married and every thing was fine.

Marie was not used to the hot temperatures of the south and she really was tired from all the excitement of the past few days. The day we had looked forward for so long had come and gone and would be forever much cherished in our memories. The next morning we caught the early bus out of Atlanta and headed back to Moultrie. The bus was so crowded and hot even with the windows down we got very uncomfortable. It was one that stopped at every little town.

The wedding was over and the marriage was beginning. We were so happy but I would know jealousy at times although she never really gave me any reason to be. When we were in a crowd waiting to get on a bus the driver would see my beautiful wife and reach over lots of people to take her ticket. He would usually give her a seat behind him.

She would save me a seat and when I finally got on the bus and sat beside her he would seem quiet disappointed. I guess he meant to talk to her as he drove.

We would talk about many things as we rode. She was seeing it all for the first time. There were the large pecan orchards near Albany where the rows of trees seemed to go on forever.

When we reached Moultrie in mid afternoon we headed to the room I had rented. Mrs. McArthur who was anxious to meet the new bride greeted us. Mrs. McArthur was a typical southern lady. She had a cleaning lady and a cook. These were two black ladies that had been with her for years and helped raise her children.

Marie was experiencing several things she was not use to such as living in town after living in the country for several years. She was among strangers but would soon meet and made friends with other service men's wives. I hated to leave her alone in one little room in a strange house in a strange town with strangers, and so far from her home back in Virginia. I had to go back to the base that first night we got into Moultrie. Two nights a week I had to stay at the base, other nights I could come in on the Spence Field bus and be with her. Some evenings I would be in by six, other evenings I would be much later. I had to leave at 4:30 in the morning to be at the base on time.

How wonderful our few hours together were! It made the days more bearable and gave me something to look forward to.

The days were long for Marie until she made friends with other ladies and had someone with whom she could talk. She enjoyed meeting people from other parts of the country but the long days were tiring. She then rode the Spence Field bus to look for work as so many others were doing. I told Marie to meet me in the cafeteria. She got there before I did and wasn't prepared for all the attention she got from service men flirting with her. Two of my buddies that had seen her picture spotted her in the cafeteria and were enjoying talking to her. When I came in they moved away.

One evening as I came into town on the bus she was waiting on the corner for me at the bus stop. I was talking with an Air Force friend who did not know I was married. When he saw Marie he started making remarks.

He said, "Oh my, look at that girl, how would you like to get hold of that?"

I got off the bus and hugged Marie. The bus went on and when I saw him the next day he apologized to me.

We did not have nearly enough time together so when we could be together we did not go anywhere. Late in the cool of the evening we would walk through town and see the pretty flowers and rose gardens.

How sweet they smelled late in the evening at sunset after the sun had bathed them all day. Moultrie had such beautiful well-kept lawns. We would walk and hold hands and daydream about our home in the future after the war, and how maybe someday we would have pretty flowers.

Marie finally found some work with a real estate man. He was different, to say the least. I guess Marie's talent for listening to other people's problems began with him. He talked to her about his problems. One weekend he gave her a considerable amount of money to hold for him until Monday. We knew this was some kind of trick and carefully guarded it until she could give it back to him on Monday.

When she returned all of it he asked her, "Where in the world did your husband find you?"

She did not work for him long; he was too dangerous. Later Marie found work at a department store and it gave her something to do. She was a sales clerk and they made a point of putting her in a prominent place. The Air Force guys would come in and buy something they didn't need just to get to talk with her. Some of them that knew me liked to pick at me by telling me they had seen my pretty wife in town and had flirted with her. One officer who had a nice sports car said he was going to see if she would go out with him. I don't believe he ever asked her. Our love was a deep love the kind that last forever.

Our love was a strong physical love and much more than that. It was a spiritual love that goes much deeper. We had the same interest and caring hearts. Our love was all we had and we lived just one day at the time. We truly appreciated the precious times just being together.

I received a call for Aerial gunner that I had received before but I was too tall for the gun turret on the B-17. Now they were flying the B-29 to bomb Japan and they needed more gunners. I was examined and passed but I was still turned down. They wanted men under six feet tall.

Marie and I went shopping and bought us a hot plate so we could cook a little in our one room. The landlady did not want us to cook because it would run up the electric bill. We had dry cereal for breakfast and had milk delivered which we kept on a shelf in her refrigerator. One night we cooked some vegetables in our one cooking pot. We put everything in together and cooked it. We locked our hot plate in our trunk in the daytime so she wouldn't know we had one. Dad mailed us a whole cured ham and one night we were cooking some and it smelled so good. The landlady knocked on the door. Quickly we unplugged the hot plate and shoved it under the bed.

In she came saying, "I smell ham cooking." We said we did too and asked if she was having some for dinner. She said "Humph" and went out.

We pulled the hot plate out from under the bed and finished cooking our ham, after we locked the door.

Marie did not have a sewing machine, however that did not stop her from making a pretty yellow dress all by hand. There was one problem, every time she wore it the seams would rip out and she would have to sew it again.

We played cards, just Marie and I. Marie won most of the time because she knew how to distract me, and outthink me.

We were friends with Willie Taylor and his wife from Tennessee. I had met him in Link Trainer. We were playing cards one evening with them in their apartment. I dropped a card and bent over to pick it up and the whole seat of my pants split out- Well they all died laughing and I had to go into the bathroom and hand out my pants and wait for them to be sewn up. I stood in there for a long time listening to them laughs. Marie finally brought my pants in to me and I wondered if she had clipped the seams so they would split. She was always pulling some prank on me.

Sometimes when we were alone we would wrestle and I was amazed at her strength and how she could tie me in knots and pin me down. We were never bored with one another and never at a loss of something to do. We just never had enough time together.

One Sunday we went to Tallahassee, Florida. We enjoyed looking over the capitol and other buildings there.

The gardens were especially beautiful and we went to Wakulla Springs.

There wasn't time to go far from the Air Base.

Since we never had time for a honeymoon trip when we were married we were now planning one. In November we caught a bus to Jacksonville, Florida and stayed in a hotel. We were delighted at all the interesting sights we saw at the state fair. This was the first time we had been to a state fair. Then we went to St. Augustine the next day. It was very interesting, the oldest city in the United States. It was there we saw the old fort used in the Revolutionary war, an alligator farm, the first schoolhouse and the first church in our country. We always enjoyed seeing new things. These three days of honeymoon we will never forget.

There was a nice old black man that drove us all over town in his buggy. The horse and buggy maneuvered the narrow streets well and we were happy to have the day together. It was amazing to see the old Indian cemetery. We picked our first orange off a tree, what a thrill! The food was also good. Marie ate her first shrimp. What a wonderful honeymoon! We were so much in love and how we valued the precious time together. The more we were together we realized we were meant for each other and we never had arguments. Being away from friends and family we learned to trust and depend on each other more.

I believe this one-year we had together helped our marriage to survive these many years. I had not had a furlough and Marie was homesick for the mountains and her family. Once one is raised in the mountains we are always homesick for them when we are away from them very long. My request was granted and I could pick up my furlough papers at midnight.

When I arrived at Moultrie from the base the door was locked and I had to go to the window and awake Marie to let me in the front door. We caught the bus out of Moultrie at 2 A.M. It was a long ride home by Atlanta, Greenville, Charlotte, Winston Salem, and finally on to Mount Airy, N.C early the next morning. Dad met us and we were so glad to be home. The weather was hot when we left Georgia but it was cool here in the Blue Ridge Mountains of Virginia. Marie spent some time with her mother and sister Opal while I helped Dad cut the winters supply of wood. Mother seemed to be feeling better and they all seemed to be pleased with our marriage. They asked Marie to stay and not go back with me, and that did not interest her at all. We did not like leaving our parents to return as they seemed to be getting old. Our parents asked us not to have any babies until we got out of service and could be back home.

We did not fully agree as we had already discussed the matter and had not made up our minds. We wanted a boy and a girl, in that order, but the Lord had other pains.

We were very busy when we got back to the base and Marie was busy in the store as a clerk with the holidays coming up. Soon it would be Thanksgiving and the big meal at the base. I was really looking forward to taking Marie. I had seen other boys with their wives and now I could take mine. The day came with all the trimmings and we really enjoyed it. That night I had to sleep at the base and Marie went back to town. That night I heard sirens several times and early the next morning. I learned that several of the boys had been quite sick with food poison from the turkey dressing. I tried to phone Marie and she did not answer so I guessed she was sleeping. Later I was to learn that she was very sick and heard the phone but was not able to answer it.

We tried to go to church and did go to different denominations but we never fit in or feel welcome. We learned the South was still fighting the civil war verbally and they considered us Yankees from the north. We felt resentment. They knew we were just passing through and would not contribute much to the church. But, oh, how we needed the church! I am sure the sudden buildup of the town was quite a shock to the people and it must have been a letdown when we left. The base provided many good paying jobs for the civilian community.

When Christmas came it was my third one away from home, and my first one with a wife.

We just enjoyed it together, no party or anything special just being together, and thanking God we were together. We sure didn't have any extra money. We had a good lunch at Spence Field and sent Christmas cards and received several. We didn't attend any New Year's eve parties because we knew there would be drinking. We were just happy to be together.

The year 1945 was here now and the war was going well in both Europe and in the Pacific. Our work began to slow down. We had all the pilots trained we needed and just needed to retrain some on gunnery. Marie and I had a little more time together and we sure did appreciate that. The weather was so mild there in South Georgia that in February there were already signs of spring.

Now more of the regular personnel were being shipped out of Spence Field. There were hopes the war would soon be over. The Battle of the Bulge had been a set back and my cousin was missing in action. Later we learned he was a prisoner of war. When he was released at the end of the war he was in a poor condition weighing only 68 pounds. He had been a prisoner for several months.

The German prisoners that were sent to Spence Field were treated and fed well and spent most of the day playing soccer and living a life of leisure. At times they kept the grounds mowed and well groomed.

It was evident I would not stay at Spence Field long since training had almost stopped. Ike and I soon received orders to go to Napier Field in Alabama. It did not take Marie and I long to pack. We had two suitcases and a footlocker. We could pack everything we owned in them, including our hot plate and we were ready to travel.

We boarded a Trailway bus for the short journey from Moultrie to Dothan Alabama. It was a cool day in March when we left Moultrie, just when all the beautiful azaleas were blooming.

We arrived in Dothan not knowing anyone and it was hard to find a place to live. At first we had to stay in a hotel and I had to leave Marie there while I reported to the base. She was really afraid since there seemed to be lots going on at the hotel.

At the base I was assigned to a squadron and found I could live off base every night and day when I was not on duty. Ike and I went to the gunnery building and found it in poor condition. We could see it would take us days to get everything in working condition. Most of the instructors there would be advanced pilots with much experience in the European war. However only a few had arrived and we had time to get the equipment ready. I was given money for meals and could eat at the local mess hall or in town. I paid less at the mess hall and the food was good. The physical training was much the same as at Spence Field.

Marie found a room in town after walking the streets for days and reading the signs on the lawns, "No dogs and no service men wanted."

We stayed in the room a few days and I could catch a Napier Field bus to the base. She did not like it there for she had nowhere to cook and felt like the landlord was watching her and she were afraid. As soon as I left she went to the USO and stayed there all day. There she met other service wives and they played cards and kept from being bored. She continued to look for a place and soon found a two-room apartment out in the country. We had a bedroom and a small kitchen with a small kerosene stove.

We were moving up and we could share a bathroom with two other families! She liked this place. A camp Rucker bus ran by the house into Dothan regularly and she could catch this into town when she wanted to go. The one problem was that it did not run early in the morning and I had to get up at four o'clock and walk two miles in the dark, into town to get a bus to Napier Field. In the late afternoon I could get a Camp Rucker bus for the ride back.

When Marie rode the bus she had to endure the stares and flirting of the Camp Rucker soldiers. She looked for work but there was none to be had.

We became good friends with Russell and Vicki Drews who lived in the adjoining apartment. Marie and Vicki enjoyed being together. The Drews had a car.

I had Sundays off and we could sleep late and sometimes I got home early in the afternoons. We took long walks in the late afternoons, in the beautiful countryside and the woods. There was an airport nearby and the planes would go over the house at all hours, the vibrations would rattle the windows. They would be flying so low at night their lights would shine in our windows.

While there we were having more spare time so we learned to play chess quite well. We both played to win and one time we were having a really close game and Marie saw I was about to win so she "accidently" tipped the board and all the chessmen fell into the floor. I wasn't about to loose either so we wrestled and I turned her across my knee and paddled her, just playing, not mean but did she make me remember it later!

A Dothan banker lived in a nice mansion near us and he got us started playing chess. They were really a nice friendly couple to us. Since Marie could not find work she decided to enroll in a business college. She took Shorthand, Typing and Business English and did well. The banker would give her a ride into town each day and told her he would have a job for her when she graduated.

Marie was always full of fun and pranks. The bathroom we shared in the house where we lived had been converted into a big bath from a regular room. It had an outside door and a small back porch. One afternoon after we had taken a shower she opened the back door and asked me to get her a mop and she would mop the floor. I looked and no one was anywhere in sight so I stepped outside and was going to grab the mop and step back in. She slammed the door together and locked it. I could hear her laughing as I stood outside naked so I hid beneath the edge of the porch. I could hear her and Vicki talking as they sat on the porch on the front side of the house. I had to stay out there for several minutes with the mosquitoes biting me and I was thinking, "I sure won't paddle her any more." She let me know she was getting even with me. Finally she let me back in and helped me doctor the bites.

Cousin Gene Barnard was stationed at Camp Rucker and came by to see us one Sunday afternoon.

Marie was more beautiful than ever this spring of 1945 and I was made aware of this wherever we went. All eyes were on her when we rode the Camp Rucker bus as well as when she came out to Napier Field. The war was ending in Europe and it was evident the war in Japan wouldn't last much longer. We were told I would be stationed at Napier until the war was over so we thought it would be a good time to start a family. We both wanted a baby.

One week end Russell, Vicki, Marie and I went to Panama City, Florida.

We went with them and spent the day at the beach and came back the same day. What fun we had walking on the sandy beach and playing in the water. We took a picnic lunch and ate on the beach in the warm sun.

On the 12th of April we were saddened by the news that our president had died suddenly in Warm Springs Georgia. The war was not over and we wondered what would happen. Franklin Roosevelt had done much to get our country back into production and out of an awful depression. He had been a great leader. I wish he could have lived to see the war end as he had put forth such great effort and accomplished much. He was greatly mourned, and as his body was carried by train back to Washington, the roads were lined with mourners.

After the fighting was over in Europe, our work really slowed down and I knew we would not stay at this base. Some got discharges and some were sent to other bases.

Marie decided she would go to the base doctor to see if she was pregnant. He said she was and we were very happy. We were hoping we would stay at the base until after the baby was born. She felt good and decided to continue with her schooling.

Chapter Fifteen

Ike had his car at the base and he continued to drink heavily. One Sunday Morning Marie and I were enjoying sleeping when a knock came at the door before daylight. It was Ike and he wanted to borrow some gas money to get home to his wife who was sick. We could tell he had been drinking. I didn't have the money so I knocked on Russell's door and borrowed ten dollars from him.

The next week orders came out that Ike and I would be leaving Napier Field for Spokane, Washington. Marie lacked one week finishing her business course. I called her at school and told her I was shipping out. She fainted at the phone and fell to the floor. She had never fainted before. She left all her books and came back to the apartment and waited for me to return that night. I got in about nine o'clock. We made a difficult decision: she would go home and stay with my parents until the baby was born. I was given a week to report in at Spokane. We packed up again and rode with Ike to Atlanta. On the way to Atlanta he blew a tire. We sat in the hot car while he went to get it repaired. He was gone over an hour. Finally arriving at the Atlanta bus station we caught a bus to the mountains. It was late in the day when we arrived in Winston-Salem and Marie was very tired. We could not get a bus to Mount Airy for several hours so we called her uncle in Mount Airy and he came and picked us up.

He took us to his home and it sure was good to get a bath and rest awhile before we went on home. Mother seemed to be in a little better health. The time quickly passed at home and then I was on my way to Christiansburg to catch the train west. I told Mother good-by at home and Dad and Marie took me to Christiansburg where I caught the Norfolk and Western Pocahontas train. It was very heartbreaking to tell my bride of one year good-bye and ride away knowing she was carrying my baby. I didn't when I would ever get to see her again. I left with a heavy heart and Marie cried all the way home.

As I rode through the mountains of Kentucky that night I noticed a soldier guarded by two M.P.'s. We were going up a long winding grade and the train slowed down. The soldier suddenly jumped up and ran out of the car and jumped off the train. They stopped the train but never found him.

At Cincinnati I changed trains boarding a New York Central to Chicago. At Chicago I had hoped to get a Pullman but there was not one available. So I went from the New York Central to the Union Pacific Station. I rode all the way on day coach, two days and two nights. We went through Omaha, Nebraska and Cheyenne Wyoming. At Pocatello, Idaho I changed trains for Spokane, Washington. The ride through part of Idaho, Eastern Oregon and

Washington was very beautiful.

When I arrived at Spokane I did not have to be at Geiger Air Base for a while so I got a hotel room and had a good hot bath and a rest in a comfortable bed for a few hours. I put on a clean uniform and boarded a bus for Geiger field. I had mailed Marie cards along the way and a letter from Spokane. Of course upon arriving at Geiger I had to meet and make new friends. It would be quite a while before I heard from Marie.

She had to get my address before she could mail me a letter. Soon I met lots of people and made new friends. My best friend was Gene Llammond from Nashville, Tennessee.

The barracks at Geiger were about the same as I had been use to except they had upper and lower bunks. I took the top bunk and Gent the bottom one. The only problem was that he would sometimes talk in his sleep and keep me awake.

Geiger was where the Air Force engineers trained. In two-month time I would be trained in many different things. I would learn how to use heavy equipment such as bulldozers, draglines and etc. Then I had a course in demolition and rigging, also how to use explosives for construction and destruction. There were courses in bridge building, road building, and how to build a temporary landing strip in a few hours time. We put in long days and learned a lot of new things. It was all very interesting.

On weekends Gene and I went into Spokane and visited the parks and other areas around Spokane.

The country out there is beautiful in the summer. The people were friendly much like people in Virginia.

One man I met invited Gene and I to have a picnic lunch with him and his family at the park. He said his Dad had moved out there from The Shenandoah Valley of Virginia to produce apples. Gene was bald headed and only twenty-four. Someone had poured house paint on his head in a college initiation and it removed his hair.

They had dances at Geiger Field recreation center every Saturday night, but neither Gene nor I took part in it. There were many who did enjoy it as many girls from town came to the dances. We spent our time writing letters home to our wives.

I went to Spokane and bought Marie a lovely green suit and mailed it to her. I was sure glad to get mail from her and know that she was all right. I was really missing being with her.

Gene and I went to a good restaurant in Spokane every weekend for a good meal, usually Sunday lunch. One day the waitress patted his baldhead and said it felt just like a baby's butt. He sure did blush and I laughed.

I never saw Ike but once while I was out there. He was in a different outfit. Sergeant Agar was stationed there and he and Shirley Temple were married while I was there. I saw them together on several occasions. They were divorced after a few years.

Anytime we were not in school we were out on the drill field. They always saw that we were busy. We went on the gunnery range one day and rode several miles on a large bus. The road was very narrow and we had to dodge an oncoming truck and slid off the road. We were hanging right on the edge of a canyon wall. Everyone quickly piled out and waited for the bus to be pulled back into the road.

In the test we took while there, I made high scores with the Ml, 45 and other firearms.

In August 1945 the Atomic bomb was dropped on Japan and they surrendered. Everybody was celebrating and most of my outfit had gone into town that night. Gene, I and a few others stayed in the barracks giving thanks and praising God that the war was over. After most of us had gone to bed some girls who were plainly intoxicated came through the barracks kissing everybody and talking about spending the night with us. The M.P.'s were right behind them and hurried them out.

We had no idea how long we would be in service now that the war was over. There was an army of occupation in Germany, already, and probably would be one in Japan. We were told we would be going overseas, somewhere. Time passed and school was soon over. We were told to report to Kerns Air Force base at Salt Lake City to await orders. We had a week to be there.

I wanted to go home but a week wasn't long to travel twice, almost, across the country and have any time at all to stay. Most every one was going home Gene was going to Nashville. I checked and found I would have three day at home with two days going and two days returning to Salt Lake City. I decided to try it, I wanted so much to see Marie and she wanted to see me. Gene and I packed up and went into Spokane to buy tickets. We bought tickets on the Milwaukee road train. We found that the next train would be at 2 a.m. and that would be day coach but a fast train. It was only 8 p.m. then so we went to a near-by hotel and got a room to rest awhile. I was so excited about going I could not go to sleep. Gene went to sleep and when a freight train came through he had one of his nightmares and jumped up hollering, "Hold that train for me."

I laughed at him and we just spent the rest of the time talking until time to catch the train.

The Milwaukee Road train was the northern route and when we went through Butte Montana the ground was covered with snow. I had not seen snow in mid-September before. We made good time through North Dakota and on into Minneapolis, St. Paul and into Chicago. I got directly onto the New York Central for Cincinnati and only had an hour to wait for the Norfolk and Western back to Virginia.

I had sent Marie a telegram when to meet me in Christiansburg and hoped she would get it. As the train slowed down I saw Marie and Dad waiting for me. It was so good to see them. Marie being pregnant had changed a little in the two and one half months.

I thought she was more beautiful than ever. We were so glad to be together again for the short time and made the most of every moment. Mother seemed to be doing pretty well. She had her usual pretty dahlias in full bloom. She had sixty-seven different colors. She sold bulbs every spring by advertising them in the Virginia Bulletin. She received orders from people all over the state of Virginia. She did a very thorough job of wrapping and mailing them for $1. per dozen. She also had many other flowers.

This time at home passed so fast and the three days were gone. Marie and I just drank in every moment of it. Leaving was difficult for us both knowing I would probably not be there when our first baby was born. Telling her good-bye was harder than usual and hard for my parents also.

I took the usual route to Chicago, leaving Christiansburg and on to Cincinnati. When I arrived there I saw the train just ready to leave for Chicago. I rushed to the gate just before they closed it and got on board. It was a really fancy train and when the conductor came to get my ticket he said, "You were not supposed to be on this train, but it is too late now."

I learned that some congressmen were on it from Washington, also Military officials on their way to a big meeting in Chicago. There was a club car on the train and a fine dining car. It didn't stop until it reached Chicago. On reaching there I was ahead of schedule and had six hours to wait so I decided to look around a little in Chicago. Now it was time to catch the Union Pacific out of Chicago for Salt Lake City. This was my third trip across the country in less than three months. I was on a day coach but I could walk around and go to the dining car for meals and made it fine. I didn't see Gene anywhere on the return trio or anyone else I knew. A lady sat by me and told of going to visit her husband in Illinois and was returning to California. She was a great talker and I was really tired. After awhile I leaned back and went to sleep. When I awoke a few hours later that night as we rode through the level plains she was sleeping with her head on my shoulder. I would not disturb her and sat quietly for a while as she continued to sleep. I felt rather embarrassed with a stranger sleeping with her head on my shoulder.

I had seen most of the scenery on my first trip out west. When we began to get into Utah the scenery was different though. We were going through a colorful section of a rocky canyon. When I arrived in Salt Lake City I went immediately to the Kearns Air Force Base.

It was a base used primarily to form groups of men bound for overseas. The barracks were tar paper and very poorly constructed. Not much better than a tent. We did have an indoor latrine and outdoor showers. They were right out in the open, but we did not use them at that time. They had probably been used in the warm months. Here the weather in late September and early October was already cool. I would not have liked it there in the wintertime. Kerns was called Pneumonia Hill by the news media back then because so many men had contacted pneumonia there. You could see the snow already on top of the mountains in the distance in the early fall. The base was in the edge of the desert and it was dry and cold at night and usually windy.

Gene and I were not in the same outfit but we soon discovered one another and got together whenever we could. Letters were slaw in coming from home to the new address, but finally after two weeks I got a whole bundle of letters. I had been writing every day.

Salt Lake City is a well-planned city with wide, strait streets that run North, South, East and West. We visited the impressive State Capitol and the Mormon Tabernacle and the Sea Gull monument.

I appreciated the story of how the crickets were destroying the crops of the early Mormon settlers and when they prayed for deliverance.

Sea gulls came in great flocks and destroyed the crickets and saved their crops. Salt Lake City was more than one thousand miles from the ocean and the gulls had come all the way from the ocean. This is the reason they built statues to the Sea Gull thanking God for their deliverance.

I was interested in Mormon religion and went to libraries and read much about them and their struggles to go west. I was not convinced in their belief, but was impressed by how they helped one another and those in need. If some one's house burned down there in the Salt Lake City area, the Mormons put a house right back up for them in a few days. If someone was sick and could not pay their bills they took care of their bills.

The farmland in the valley was very pretty and productive. Much of it was irrigated and they raised vegetables, fruits, and lots of grains, corn, wheat, and barley. There were beef cattle and dairying around the Ogden area and lots of sheep in the mountains. There were also large poultry farms. The main crop was sugar beets. I visited a sugar beet factory where the sugar was being re-fined.

Gene and I went out to the Salt Lake and noted how very salty the water was. It is more than twenty percent salt. They pump it out in the desert sand near the lake and allow it to evaporate in a shallow pool. Then the salt is scooped up.

We visited the world's largest open pit copper mine at Bingham. This was a town with one street through a narrow canyon that was just wide for a narrow street with a row of buildings on either side between the canyon walls. From Bingham the bus went through a tunnel to the copper mine. The copper mine was shaped like an ice cream cone. The railroad track goes around and around it to the bottom to haul out the ore. The top of the cone is several miles wide.

Near Bingham was a place called Copper Town where several homes and buildings were constructed of pure copper outside. I did not see them inside. Utah is rich in gold, silver, lead, zinc and many other minerals.

I was in a barracks where there was much grumbling. Many of the boys had friends who were being discharged and going home. Some of them had been service for a shorter time than they had.

We had no idea where we were going or when, and I did not worry about it. I was more concerned about my wife back home than anything else. I hoped our baby would be all right. I wrote her every day and received a letter from her every day.

In the time Gene and I were together he witnessed more to me than anyone ever had and made me realize how important salvation was. He was a great guy.

I finally met up with Ike there on the base so he and I went into town and talked a lot.

That was the last time I ever saw him. When I looked for him again his outfit was gone.

Our last weekend at Kerns Gene and I visited some of the colorful and interesting canyons around Salt Lake City area. We did not know it would be our last weekend together there.

The next morning I received orders we were leaving and I did not see him until years later, when he brought his family to visit us from Nashville, Tennessee.

I had never really got acquainted with any of the boys I was leaving with. They were all griping and complaining. I did find one little guy who was fun to be with. He was from a place called Castle on the Hudson in New York. We tried to have some fun instead of complaining all the time.

That Monday afternoon in late October we marched up the long hill from Kerns to board the train with heavy packs and a barracks bag. This little guy that I called Shorty was marching behind me and he could hardly carry the load. He held onto my pack to keep up. At the top of the grade was a big arch and on it was printed *BENEATH THIS ARCH PASS THE BEST*

DAMN SOLDIERS IN THE WORLD. Shorty turned loose of my pack and walked around it. Someone yelled, "Get back into ranks." He did not feel he was so good since he'd had to hold on to me to make it up the hill. We carried about 130 pounds and he only weighed about 135 pounds.

Now we were on a train and I was put in charge of part of the train. I had to post guards on each car and see that every one obeyed orders. We did not know where we were going but I knew the train was heading west toward California over the mountains by Lake Tahoe.

We were not fed anything on the train and I could not sleep with the responsibility I felt. It was not a comfortable train anyway. but I was not complaining. The war was over and wherever I went I felt I would be all right. I did worry about Marie.

Everywhere I went I saw written on the walls KILROY WAS HERE, but I never saw anyone writing it. I did see a corporal drawing and writing in different places. He drew two little hands holding onto the top wall or board. Two little eyes peeped over the board and he wrote LUKE THE SPUKE. I saw these in different places but I didn't believe he wrote them all. Lots of songs were composed and sung during the war. When we left the train we were at the point of embarkation in California in the Bay area near the town of Pittsburgh, California. We were given an A.P.O. address and told our mail would be censored.

Chapter Sixteen

Hurry and Wait, these were words we had learned quite well, so this was what we were doing now.

I read all the papers and got acquainted with new friends. We were not allowed a pass and there were no movies there. I wrote lots of letters to folks back home and sure did miss hearing from them. It would take awhile for my mail to catch up with me. I tried to stay away from the lots of complaining that was going on around me.

We were issued new clothing, shoes and such. From the types of clothing we were issued we knew we were going to a cold climate. We were told our ship was being readied for sailing. I had not been paid for a while. When I received orders to go to the office to be paid I went and was handed my money by a lady. When I returned to my quarters and counted it I found two one hundred dollar bills stuck together and I had one hundred dollars too much. Some of the boys said, "Keep it." I knew that was wrong so I went back to the office and found the lady in tears. She had come up a hundred dollars short and would have to replace it out of her own pocket. She sure thanked me.

I read in the daily paper that anyone having over thirty-six points would be discharged, and not sent overseas.

You received a point for every month of service and two points for overseas duty. I had thirty-six points and wondered what would happen to me. Congress had started the point system to have a fair way to reduce the size of the armed services. We continued to wait and everyday saw numbers of men leaving. They sailed out of the Bay and underneath the Golden Gate Bridge.

Finally one morning a list of names came out it read, "Men with over 36 paints not eligible for overseas duty unless they so desire." My name was on that list. Praise the Lord.

I learned that Ike had already left a week earlier. Years later when I corresponded with him he wrote that he had been turned around in the Pacific and not know it until they came back in sight of the Golden Gate Bridge.

The news that I would not be going overseas was a great relief and I wondered where I would be going and when I would be getting out of service.

A few days later some of us were loaded on a truck and went to Mather Air Force Base near Sacramento California.

I wrote Marie the good news and gave her my new address and hoped I would soon be hearing from her. At Mather my records had been miss printed arid they spelled my name Truman instead of Turman, like President Truman. Many asked me if I was related to him. It took awhile to get my name straightened out.

I was not there very long, just long enough for some of my mail to catch up. It sure was good to hear from Marie and know she was all right. I was not assigned to any regular work while I was there. I only went into town once and saw the Capital Sacramento, a very beautiful city.

They kept us busy in parades going through several small towns. It was near Thanksgiving and we were celebrating. On Thanksgiving Day we had the usual good meal of turkey and all the trimmings. When we sat down to eat I noticed a nice plate of butter on the table and I had not seen any for a long while. We had the blessings and found the butter was gone when we raised our heads.

That very evening we received orders to move out. We loaded on a truck and rode in the rain in an open truck for several hours. We were soaking wet and our entire luggage was wet. We did not have any dry clothes to put on. We went to Hamilton Air Force Base near San Rafael California. There we were housed in a nice permanent building. More comfortable than any I had been in since I had been in service. The kitchen was near by and the mess hall was a small one. The food was very good and well prepared. There was always fruit on the table and milk to drink. I had not seen this before.

I started working on something I knew nothing about. I was issued parts for the C-54—four engine planes which were in a large building. The mechanics lined up as I and others found the parts for the plane they worked on. It took much paper work and I had so much to learn. There were hundreds of parts to learn the name and number of. I never learned them all in the three months I was there. Shorty was still with me but no one else I knew. I got acquainted with others that I worked with but we never became close. We worked different shifts as the parts supply was always open. The big planes flew continually bringing the boys home from the Pacific. Mostly the sick and wounded were coming home on the first planes. Most of the rest would be coming home by ship.

I saw men every day coming in and leaving on their way to be discharged and going home. My mail was coming on a regular basis and it was good to hear from Marie. She thought I had gone overseas because my mail to her was censored for at least six weeks.

When she found out I wasn't going overseas we thought of her coming to stay with me and wished that she could. Her mother and my parents thought this would never do since she was pregnant. They thought it would be too difficult a trip for her.

I liked California and really wanted her to see it also. There was a bus running every thirty minutes to San Francisco from Hamilton Field.

It was only a thirty-minute ride across the Golden Gate Bridge. I had the weekends off and could pick up a pass any time. The whole bay area was full of all branches of the service at this time, especially sailors and so many army men coming home every day. There was no place to house or feed all the men coming in. Same of them had to stay on the ships docked in the harbor for days. The trains could not move the men out East as fast as they were coming in. Most were happy to be going home. I saw a few who did not want to leave the service. Others who left came back trying to reenlist. It was difficult for them to adjust to civilian life. Some returned to find a wife who had found someone else while they were gone. I saw some who just wanted to return to the Pacific to one of the islands.

The Del Monte canning company was badly in need of workers to take care of the harvest out there. Once when I had a three-day pass I went with one of their employees to Oakland and worked three nights on a twelve-hour shift. It was at a Del Monte Catsup plant. My job was to pour the sugar and salt into the huge boilers. They would call out sugar, and salt in number one, three or five which ever it might be. I was busy pouring 1000 pounds of sugar and 100 pounds of salt into each boiler, the boilers were two stories high.

A lady mixed a big pan full of several ingredients together and poured it into each one as I poured in the sugar and salt. It was interesting to see the big truckloads of tomatoes coming into the plant. They were so pretty and ripe. Down on the first floor was where the bottling was going on, most of it was by machine, like a coca cola battling plant. They were really turning out the catsup. I enjoyed the work and learned a lot in a short while. I also made some money that I sent to Marie.

I really liked the beautiful farmlands of California. The farms were very productive and produced so many things. I thought it would be nice to have land and farm out there. I learned the land was very expensive and it would take a bundle of money to get into any kind of farming.

The cities were nice to visit, but I don't think I would like living there, they were too crowded and there was much rushing about. People drove like mad, ran to catch a bus or train and always seemed in a hurry.

I rode the electric tram or train across the Oakland Bay Bridge several times. It shuttled back and forth every few minutes and was always full. The people got on running and left running. The double deck bridge was always full of traffic, as were the ferries that kept busy going back and forth.

There were a lot of people in the Bay area. San Francisco with a population of nearly one million. Oakland with almost half a million, as well as Berkeley and Richmond being good size cities. There were many mare smaller towns and many army, navy and air force bases as well as the whole area being overrun with returning service men from the Pacific.

I saw lots of U.S.O. girls and entertainers who would go aboard the ships to entertain the men who were sometimes stuck on board the ships for days because there was no place to house them and no transportation back east for them. We were trying to return men much faster than we sent then out. I heard from Marie that many from my home area were already home. I saw many interesting things in San Francisco. I toured much of the area, Market Street, Knob Hill, the library and spent one day on Fisherman's Wharf. I saw the stage shows on Powell Street, rode the cable car and visited China Town several times. China Town was interesting, but I never cultivated a great taste for Chinese food. I walked up and down the beaches and through Golden Gate Park and toured the international settlement. San Francisco was full of bars, saloons and nightclubs. Since I did not drink I passed most of these places. Most of the nightclubs seemed too expensive to me but they seemed crowded all the time.

Crossing the Golden Gate Bridge toward San Francisco on a clear afternoon was a beautiful sight, seeing the colorful city in front of you, the ships on the water below and in the distance Alcatraz prison. How I wished to have Marie by my side to see it with me and had hopes of bringing her there sometime to see the sights.

There was lots of rain this time of year and we could hear the foghorns all night if the planes were quiet long enough. Many times I could feel the earth shaking when I lay in my bunk. Occasionally it was slight earthquake -tremors but it was hard to tell the difference with the planes leaving the nearby runway constantly.

I worked five days a week, twelve hours a day and the noise did keep me awake at night. I was in close touch with Marie by letter but sure did wish we could have talked. The letters were five days getting to me. We sent them airmail but that didn't help much.

Our baby was due in February and we talked about the possibility of her being blocked in by snow on the mountain. We decided she should go and stay with her Uncle Edgar in Mount Airy to be near the hospital. It looked like I would not be home for the event.

I finally learned that we would have gone to Korea if we had gone overseas, because the United Stated wanted to stop the communist advance. I don't know if it would have prevented the Korean War, or the subsequent buildup of Communism in that part of the world.

The Christmas of 1945 I celebrated in California. This was my fourth Christmas away from home. I would surely be home for the next one in 1946 and have our new baby to enjoy. The New Year was going to be one big celebration out there. I stayed at the base not wanting to be a part of the drinking and wild partying. San Francisco was noted for its celebration. There were numerous ads of the entertainment that would be featured at all the nightclubs.

When the war ended their celebration had out paced other cities. The many men had filled the streets and took their wine and liquor from the A.B.C. stores and bars. The police could not control the crowds, girls stood in hotel windows and threw their clothes down to them. Other girls swam nude in the swimming pools. The police rode horseback trying to keep order.

There was also much gambling going on in this big city. One guy from St. Lewis that I knew and worked some with was a big time gambler. I saw him in San Francisco one night with a girl and flashing money around and drinking.

I took him aside and told him I was going back to the base and didn't he want me to carry some of his money back and hold it for him. He had seventeen hundred dollars and gave me one thousand and kept seven hundred. The next day when he came for the money he was a sad looking sight. The girl had disappeared and so had his money. He thanked me for looking after him.

The rainy season continued and some of the roads were blocked by mudslides. The fog and rain was a little like many times back home in the mountains except the weather was warmer and the fog was not as thick.

I was longing for the day I would be back in the Blue Ridge Mountains of Virginia. I began to think of what I would do to support my family. I knew my parents were expecting me to return and take care of them and run the farm and I was duty bound to do so. I was reading and studying in the library about agriculture and was trying to decide what I would do when I got home. I still had no hint as to when that might be and Marie's time was getting nearer. She would be going to stay with Uncle Edgar. The doctor was saying she and the baby were fine. The Air Force offered me a three-year sign up for continued service. I had enlisted for three years plus the duration of the war. My three years had been up the first of October 1945. Now it was January 1946 and the war was over. They were sending men home as fast as they could and replacing them with volunteers.

How I wanted to be home with Marie, also our parents were not young and I felt they needed me. I heard some of the Air lines who were going to hire Link Trainer Instructors there in California and it would pay well, so if Marie had been there it would have been interesting to have stayed out there.

There were seven women Army Air Core (W.A.A.C.S.) at Hamilton Field. Some of the service men and women had married and many had become good friends. I saw a lot of them kissing good-by as one of them were discharged, leaving the other behind. I knew how they felt. I saw many of them leaving everyday.

When I went to San Francisco or Oakland I saw the big ships docking and the troops waiting for the train to carry them back East. The docks were always busy both day and night and the trains were always loaded. Some who were not getting out of service were being shipped out of Hamilton Field to New Mexico. They were going there where the atomic bomb would be studied. I did not volunteer for that.

Hamilton Field held an open house on Field Day. Civilians were allowed to tour the base. This was a big day and the base was crowded with people from the Bay area. I watched the crowds and looked at the big planes. They were not allowed in the planes and stood behind roped off areas. Some of the B-29 bombers were there. They had been brought back and were being taken out and parked in the desert.

It was always interesting to see the artwork and paintings on them. The crew gave them a name like, Memphis Bell. Most of the pictures were of scantily clad girls with curvy figures. There had to be some good artist in the Air Force crews that flew them. The fighters and bombers passed through there but the C- 54's were based there. The day of the tour I saw the crowd watching from behind a rope as a C-54 was brought and parked. The plane came forward toward them and then turned with its tail toward them to stop. They had not realized they would get a strong draft of wind from the rear propellers with the big four engines going as it turned around. The women were trying to hold onto their children and grabbing their skirts.

When I saw all the service men returning from overseas and knowing that I had not been overseas really bothered me. They called me a stateside man. I decided not to let this bother me. I had volunteered to go anywhere I was asked to go and my superiors had made the decisions, not me.

I had trained pilots how to use their instruments and rely on them to get them through night flights and rough weather. I feel sure this training saved some of the fighter pilots lives. I had trained many fighter pilots how to use the gun sight and their guns in a dogfight with the enemy. I feel sure many pilots came out the winner because of this training and lived to tell the story.

Also, I am sure some of the enemy fighter pilots lost their lives and planes because of this training, someone had to do this job and it was all hard work and no glory or ribbons or awards for it. Now here at Hamilton Field it had been my work to keep the C-54's flying, bringing the boys back home. McArthur came through one day on his way to Washington. Eisenhower also landed and attended a meeting in San Francisco.

Our work slowed down though and the planes flew less as the big influx of the return was over and more men were leaving the base.

Back in Virginia Marie's time was getting nearer. We understood the baby would be born on her birthday, February 15.

I often went to the library and there I could read the daily papers and read the Teletype, which printed the news on the Teletype twenty-four hours a day. I saw it there hours ahead of the daily paper.

I enjoyed visiting many places in the bay area, like the zoo and walking through the many beautiful parks, also the shopping centers, the art museums and many historical sights. I was usually by myself as I had no close friends at that time. I made friends and they went home, and others came and went. I was brought up and learned to be alone so that did not bother me except, I sure did wish Marie could be with me and enjoy these things with me.

I never went into the water on the beach and never out of uniform. I enjoyed seeing others enjoy the water.

One day on the beach as I was having lunch at a small restaurant near the beach and being served at a side table. I would see people change from street clothes to bathing suits while someone held a blanket in front of them. Others would whistle at them from the distance. I saw two ladies holding a blanket up while a third changed behind it. All of a sudden they took the blanket away and ran with it and also her clothes, leaving her standing naked. The beach patrol rushed to cover her with a blanket.

Chapter Seventeen

There was always something going on in San Francisco. One night as I was riding a city bus back to Market Street from Fisherman's Wharf I saw two young women helping a middle-aged man who was well dressed on to the bus. He seemed to be too intoxicated to stand alone. They went to the back of the bus and I sat in front. As we neared the bus terminal where I would catch another bus to Hamilton Field, I saw the two ladies get off carrying something. They got off about two blocks from the terminal. When we stopped at the terminal the driver turned on the lights. I heard laughing and snickering behind me and the bus driver picked up his coat and started to the back of the bus. The drunk man I had seen getting on the bus with the two ladies was laying in the back seat naked. The two women had taken all his clothes, even his shoes. The bus driver covered him with his raincoat.

I was always amazed at the cable cars as they went up and down the steep streets from Market Street to China Town. Small boys and girls clung to them and they were always full. They didn't look that safe to me, especially for the children. I never heard of any accidents though.

I was worried about Marie and the weather in Virginia and hoped the snow would not block her in.

We decided it was time for her to go to Uncle Edgar's and stay with them until the baby was born.

I watched the list every day hoping my name would be on the list to go home so I could be there when the baby arrived. New names were being listed every day and I sure kept watching for mine.

After Marie went to Mount Airy so she could be near the hospital I felt better about her. I could tell by her letters she was feeling very lonely away from home. I prayed every day and night for her and our baby and that I could be with her. She wrote that it could be any day now. We had both a boys and girls name picked out for the baby. We would be happy with either. In my heart I felt that all would go well for her. Now February was here and I would not go far from the base for I might get a message from home.

I did enjoy the redwood forest. I liked this area more all the time. I was thinking what beautiful farmlands, how fertile and flat the fields were, seems they would grow most any vegetable or fruit. How I would love to farm here if Marie and my family could be here. It would have taken a lot of money but I knew I could take a loan and really make a go of it. Yet I knew I must return home and try to farm there in the mountains. I had such a deep longing to see Marie, to hold her close, to comfort her and tell her how much I loved her.

On the morning of February 9, 1946 I had a feeling that today would be the day our baby would be born. I went to work and thought maybe I would get a message or some word from home. I told those with whom I worked how I felt and they just laughed at me. As the day wore on I felt more anxious. Somehow I felt that the Lord was telling me today was the day. After lunch I could stand it no longer and went to the telephone and called Mount Airy Hospital.

I asked if Marie Turman was there and they said she was, but could not talk to me just now.

They put her Uncle on the phone and I asked about Marie. He said she was all right and had just had a little girl and both were fine. OH how I thanked God! It was good to hear all was well. How I wanted to hear her voice.

When I returned to work the guys could not believe what I was telling them. How could I possibly know my baby girl was being born when I had not heard from my wife for a few days and the doctor had not given us any date to expect her early? She was born at 5 P.M. on Saturday and I called five minutes later! This shows how the great love for one another and God's love reaches his children regardless of the distance apart. We were 3000 miles apart.

Oh how I prayed that I would soon be going home. Marie was in the hospital for fourteen days as was the rules back then. Laying in the bed so long left the mother weak. I would not be getting a letter from Marie for a few days, however, three days later I got a telegram from the Red Cross informing me of the birth. It scared me at first when I got it, I was afraid something had happened to Marie. It read your wife Marie has a baby girl, Dana Antoinette Turman. What a relief, but how much quicker had been the message I had received three days earlier. I thanked the Red Cross anyway.

I continued to work and wait until the time came I could go home. I worked with a skeleton crew and different ones all the time.

I finally received a letter from Marie stating she was home with our new baby. She had been through quite an experience all by herself. Uncle Edgar had taken her to the hospital at seven o'clock that morning and left her all alone. She sat in a very crowded waiting room with many others until after twelve, having pains all the while. She was treated like an unwed mother, which at time was considered trash. They could see she had no one with her so they thought she was abandoned. It really hurt me to think she was treated this way when I was on duty defending my country.

At last my name was posted for discharge from service. I would be leaving for Fort Mead Maryland the next day.

There I would go through the final process for discharge. I sent Marie a telegram to let her know I would be home in a week or so. I got ready to go and waited for my papers and orders.

There were only ten men leaving Hamilton Field with me, but I was not acquainted with any of them. I left a happy man to be going home and with good feelings about my base. It had been the nicest place I had been stationed.

We left Hamilton Field on a truck and went to the Ferry Dock at San Francisco. I looked at the scene as we crossed the Golden Gate Bridge. It was a clear afternoon and anyone who has come to San Francisco across the bridge can remember what I am talking about. It is such a beautiful sight. When we sit on the ferry and crossed the bay it was breath taking to see, as the sun was setting and we were looking back at San Francisco and Treasure Island, the large ships going up and down the bay and other ships at anchor. Of all of the cities I had seen from the air or on foot I liked San Francisco the best. I wondered if I would ever see it again and secretly hoped I might bring my family back to see it some day.

I was realizing that when I thought of my Marie now that I must think not just of her but my little girl too. Life would be different now with a child in the picture. Things would be different than when I left home.

I knew that I would have a big adjustment to make. Just going from military to the civilian life would be a big change.

The ferry docked at the railroad station and we walked to a long line of Pullman cars already hitched together.

We loaded into one of the Pullman coaches. I was finally going to get a Pullman. I had crossed the United States three times on coach but had not been able to get a Pullman. There were already a lot of servicemen on the coaches, men from every branch of service headed East for home and a discharge.

Everyone was all loaded and ready to go but there was no engine to pull our cars. We waited for three hours. A beautiful streamliner called "The City San Francisco" loaded upon the track beside us and pulled out for Chicago. We were all wishing we could have been on it. About three hours after it pulled out a big diesel freight engine came and hooked to us.

Some of the boys said, "Oh no, a freight engine, we'll never get anywhere." I was not a railroad man and didn't know what to expect. When we moved out and reached the mountains we were making good time and the mountains didn't seem to slow it down any.

I went to sleep thinking of how it was going to be when I got home.

When I woke up it was getting light and I was surprised to see things I recognized. We were going through Salt Lake City. We sure had made good time and were not stopping at all. I found the dining car and enjoyed a good breakfast. I talked to different ones as we rode along and found everyone to be in a happy and joyful mood as they were going home. They lived in all the different states along the East coast. One boy had his guitar and was playing and singing as we rode along. We were really moving now as we arrived in the Great Plains away from the mountains. Somewhere out there we were passing another train going the same way we were. It was a streamliner and I was surprised to see it was "The City of San Francisco" the same train that had left three hours ahead of us. Another night of rest on the Pullman and we were nearing our destination. We had breakfast once more on the train just before we reached Fort Mead Maryland.

At Fort Mead it was just waiting for your turn. Nothing to do but talk with someone you did not know or listen to a radio. So I spent some of my time thinking of what it would really be like when I first saw my new daughter and family. I was going back a family man now. What difference four years can make. Now there was a wife and baby to support, parents to care for and trying to make a living on the farm was not going to be easy to say the least. I was thankful to be going home to a wife whom I could trust and one who loved me.

This was not the case of many of the guys who I heard talking while they waited to return home. I heard them talking of wives who had been unfaithful while they were away and not being happy going back to them. I heard two guys joking about it. One said he was going to knock on the front door when he got home and run around to the back door and catch the rascal.

The other one said, "You better not; you might get run over."

After two days my name came up and I was given a physical. The word was a laugh. They just took a quick look and if you had two arms and legs and no large hernias they could see from twenty feet, then you received your discharge. They gave you your discharge after asking once more if you wished to reenlist for three years.

While waiting I had come in contact with some guys who had got their discharge and gone into bars in Washington or Baltimore and got drunk and lost them. They had been picked up by police and brought back in so they were waiting to be reprocessed and get another discharge. Some had been waiting for over a week. I think they were the ones in no hurry to return home and maybe had nothing to go home to.

When I got my discharge in hand I headed out at 6 P.M. going to Washington Greyhound Station and heading for home. At the bus station I waited two hours to get a bus to Roanoke. The night ride was uneventful and we pulled into Roanoke before daybreak.

There I had another two hours wait before I could get a bus for Floyd. I had time to get some breakfast and after awhile boarded the old bus for Floyd along with two nice passengers. When we reached Floyd I started looking for a way to get home. I was getting home a few days sooner than I expected. I found one man who had a taxi service and he said he would take me home for ten dollars. We rode down the familiar parkway by way of Rocky Knob. There were still snowdrifts around the first of March and it was quite cold but not weathering. I wondered if we would be able to get down our private road, or if I would have to walk in and carry my suitcase and barracks bag that I was bringing home. I brought home a lot of wool clothing I would never wear again. I did wear the khaki as work clothes later and the army shoes as work shoes. At last we arrived at out private road and we could get to the house. There was snow piled along the old rail fence all the way home. It was hard to believe I was really coming home after being away for so long. Here I was at last as I looked at the old rail fences on both sides of the road, at home.

I saw Dad outside of the house. He was smiling as he recognized me. I know he must have known how I felt as he saw me coming home because he, too, had come home from war some twenty plus years earlier from World War I. I greeted him and went into the house. Mother was surprised and delighted. They had not expected me so soon.

Then I went into Marie's room. She was almost in a state of shock she was so surprised and delighted and not expecting me until a couple of days later. It was 9 A.M. and she was wearing the pretty long yellow wool robe I'd sent her before the baby was born. It was so good to see her and after we had hugged and kissed my attention turned to our baby who was three weeks old. Antoinette was such a pretty and I thought a tiny baby. She was not actually a small baby, I was just not use to babies. I felt so awkward when Marie handed her to me to hold. I don't recall ever having held a baby before. I had to learn how to hold her. I was so afraid I might hurt her. She was so pretty and so precious. How rich I felt.

Everything at home was much as I had left it three and one half years earlier. The difference was that now I had a wife and little girl.

It seemed so strange to light up the old kerosene lamps. I had been use to the electric lights for three and a half years now. It seemed strange for it to be so dark outside now. There were always so many lights around the air base. It was going to be a big change for me.

I was so glad to be home and hold my wife close at night in our own bed. The first day home when I went into the dining room to eat lunch I ask Marie if it was alright to leave the baby in bed while we were in the next room.

She assured me it was, however in those short hours I was already feeling like the protective father. I didn't know much about caring for a baby, but I would soon learn. Antoinette was such a sweet little baby I loved to cuddle her close and love her. It was such a blessing to be home with my dear little family. Mother was such a help in teaching us how to care for a little baby.

The next day I was up early and looking over the farm and pondering where to start and just what to do. Dad had only one horse. He and Mr. Asa had been putting their horses together for a team, to do the little teamwork that they were able to do. Many of the old rail fences were down. It was going to be difficult, there was so much work to be done. Dad and I went looking for another horse and it took awhile to find one. Farm machinery was hard to come by and you could not buy a new car or pickup. Marie and I wanted a new pickup because Dad's was getting old and needed new tires. We talked to a dealer and he put us on a waiting list with a one hundred dollar deposit for a Chevrolet pickup. We would be lucky to get one in a year. I think we were 48th on the list.

Finally we got a horse and I started plowing some. I decided to plant about three acres of potatoes and plowed what we called the mountain field. It had rich black soil suitable for potatoes. I plowed it with the hillside turning plow.

I turned the field that Dad had in corn the previous year for oats and grass, and plowed some for corn.

I quit wearing my uniforms and went back to my old bib overalls. Marie did not like that. She had married a soldier in a fitted uniform and she never did like me wearing bib overalls. I wore them because they were more comfortable doing the farm work. Marie learned that she could unbutton my suspenders and trip me up with my overalls around my feet so quickly I hardly knew what she was doing. I was surprised at her strength and how quick she was in playing tricks on me.

I planted a large garden and Dad and Mother enjoyed having me help them. We planted the field of potatoes, the most I had ever planted. We drilled the oats and grass, and a few days later, the last of April it came a rough thunderstorm and rained three inches or more in a few minutes. It also hailed enough to cover the ground. The potato field had washed badly and the oats and grass were badly eroded. I was really discouraged and saw I would have to make some changes in my farming practices. I had forgotten how bad the storms could be here on the mountainside. In all the places I had been I had never seen it rain as hard as it does here on the edge of the mountain. I have not seen the wind blow as hard or the lightning and thunder be as bad anywhere else.

I contacted the soil conservation service and Mr. Dickerson, the technician, came and surveyed strips out on the farm for strip cropping. This meant changing the fences and doing lots of work. It sure did help though and if I had not done this I would not have been able to farm our mountain land.

I then had some logs sawed and built a chicken house, and we bought lots of baby chickens. They were shipped earlier than expected and the house was not yet ready, so we put all 800-baby chicks in one of our unfinished bedrooms of the house we were just building. This turned out to be interesting, or that's one word we could use.

We raised broilers that first year and after raising two batches of broilers, of about 800 in each, we cleared only 36 dollars. We never tried that again. We did raise pullets and kept layers for several years and made some money on them. I liked working with hens and we had eggs to sell and eat.

The potatoes did all right and we had several hundred bushel. I plowed them out with the horse, but picking them all up by hand, a hauling them out of the mountain field was a big job. Marie and I picked them up and we hired Garcie to help. Dad did a lot of the work with the horse. We sold a lot of them that fall for a dollar and fifty cents a bushel. We put about three hundred in the concrete basement we built before I went into service.

We held them over till spring expecting to get more money per bushel but they still sold for one dollar and fifty cents per bushel. I never planted that many any more.

Dad still had a cow and some heifers all Guernseys and we were selling milk now. The Carnation Milk Company had a plant at Stuart. Milk looked like the best way for us to go here at the farm. This would be a year round income. Marie and I had talked about beef cattle but thought we did not have enough land.

We talked about working in a factory but none were really nearby and it would mean driving to Mount Airy every day, up and down the mountain road in all kinds of weather. I did not like working inside and Marie wanted to be with her baby and most of all we enjoyed being together and working together.

We were carrying water from the spring and taking the milk on a wheelbarrow to the spring to cool it. Pushing it back up a steep hill was not easy. We put up a lot of hay, about thirty stacks that summer and with the oats and corn, had food for the cows and heifers. We had to cut wood for the heater in Mother and Dad's room and stove wood for the kitchen stove. This took a lot of work with a crosscut saw and axes. I also used a bow saw by myself much of the time. I helped Mr. Asa with his wood. That winter Marie and I started talking about building a house of our own. We had enough money to begin building. My parents didn't think we needed one.

Building material was hard to find and mostly it was of poor quality. Most of those who were building were talking about getting a loan. My parents were strictly against us getting a loan. This was almost a sin in their eyes.

We did not buy plans or blue prints. We couldn't afford it. I started drawing plans and expanding them, Marie added her ideas to them. And all the time we had to keep in mind our limited means since we couldn't borrow money. We planned how to make good use of all the space and get as much under roof for as little money as possible.

Antoinette was growing and developing as a healthy child should. She got plenty of attention from Marie and I as well as her grandparents. We loved her so much.

Dad and I cut some of the large pines on the lower end of our farm. Uncle Earnest, Martin Marshall and Carl Jessup sawed them. Uncle Earnest hauled the sawed lumber out by the old Dock house and by the Jake Radford place up to route 614 with his truck. We cut all the timber with the cross cut saw. We cut a few large oaks and Uncle Earnest used them in building his barn.

The steep field, which we had buckwheat in before I went into service, now was thick with little white pines that had come up. so we allowed them to grow there.

Jake Radford and others had cleared all of this land and it was too steep for farming.

In 1947 when Antoinette was a year old, and began walking Marie and I could leave her with Mother and Dad for a few hours to go shopping, however we seldom went shopping because we did not have the time or money. We were saving all we could toward our house. We had finally decided on the house we would try to build. I had the plans all drawn out and Marie was desperate to have a home of her own. We looked all over the farm and tried to decide on a building site. We looked at different places where we would be near a spring as we did not consider drilling a well. There were no wells near us at that time, everyone was still using spring water. We even thought of building on the lower end of the farm where we would have plenty of water by gravity. Then we knew it would be too hard to build a road in there so we decided to build near our parents and be near them. So we decided on a site near Dad's house next to the road.

I would put in a new hydraulic ram to pump water for both houses. The old one had worn out years before.

In August 1947 we began staking our house off in the middle of a hay-field.

We could not afford a bulldozer for digging the basement so we used a scoop and horse to dig it. I would hold down on the handles while Marie drove the horses. I would load the scoop and that took mighty strength, and wait to hold the two heavy handles down while Kate and Nell, the two big horses pulled.

They then drug the loaded scoop out of the hole where I would dump it by flipping it over. We did this over and over and over hundreds of times. After a few days of very hard work we made good progress. I then used the maddox and shovel to square up the banks after digging the dirt down. We used Kate, the pretty black horse and Nell a dapple-grey to dig the dirt out with the scoop. When I reached the depth I had planned to go I began to hit a grey rock that required a pick to break it up. It took hard digging to dig the footer to pour the concrete in for setting the blocks on. I finally finished the digging and borrowed a cement mixer to pour the footer.

Now I began to look for someone to do a good job of laying blocks. It was hard to find anyone that wasn't already busy. Barney Shelor promised to start on them before too long. I purchased the blocks and had them delivered and covered them up so they wouldn't soak up so much rainwater.

In the meanwhile I was trying to keep up with the farm work and was beginning to cut timber. I was planning to have most of the house sawed out of our own trees. Lazarus Light helped me cut the trees. We cut mostly oak and other hardwoods. Some were pine and poplar. Uncle Everett Stanley agreed to do the sawing. Glenn Stanley would help him. Ebb Stanley was a careful hand at sawing and he sawed boards and framing very carefully. It was almost as good as sized framing.

I pulled the logs in to the sawmill with Kate and Nell. I worked in all kinds of weather, cold, wet, muddy and even when they were not sawing I packed boards near the mill on the creek. Aries Quessenberry helped me pack the high stacks of lumber. I hauled all the building material out with Kate and Nell and a long sled that I had built. I worked all the daylight hours and after dark when the moon was up.

Barney worked a day now and then, laying the blocks and when he worked I waited on him. I was carrying the blocks to him and mixing the mortar by hand in a box, stirring it with a hoe. We finally got the blocks laid before cold weather set in.

Waymon Banks started to build a house and then changed his mind when he bought the Columbus Stanley farm and house. I bought the boards and framing he had cut for his house. I hired Calvin Willard to haul them to Coy

Thomas at Stuart to have them sized. After the weather got rough I continued to log and finish cutting timber and packing the lumber that I would sell. We had a few warm days in December before Christmas. Barney and I put the sleepers down and got the sub floor down. Then the weather got rough and we could do no more to the house that winter. I was busy with the feeding and milking the cows and cutting wood.

However, on the really rough cold days I had time to enjoy playing with the baby and reading some. Marie enjoyed me being in the house and seeing me playing with the baby.

I finished cutting the timber and logging by the time spring came. Every chance I had I was looking at material, windows, doors, and all kinds of material was really hard to find in those days following the war. We wanted paneling for our living room but none was available. Also I had finally found the roofing and asbestos siding. I bought the hydraulic ram and pipes to put in a water system.

This year I would concentrate on making feed for the cattle and not do much truck farming. I had to have time to work on the house I wanted to get it under roof as quickly as possible. The sawing was finished and I sold the lumber to Johnny Alderman. It was difficult to get the lumber out from the lower place on the creek I had to pull most every load out with the horses in front of the truck. Everyone was surprised how much the horses could pull and how well they worked pulling the truck up the hill. The money for the lumber would help to get the house under roof.

I received a card in the mail saying the pickup I had ordered a year earlier had finally arrived. I could not really afford it now since I was building a house. We sure did need it.

Robert Foley who was working in Stuart every day and commuting back and forth from Meadows of Dan was in bad need of something to drive. I decided to let him have it and maybe we could get something later. Mother and Dad went somewhere most weekends and that left Marie and I home without any transportation.

Sometimes we drove Marie's mother and stepfather, Mr. Asa to church in his old car, which was sixteen years old. Lots of people made fun of us for driving in such an old car. Pride did not bother me very much. So many people judge you by the car you drive and the fine clothes you wear. I learned early in life that outside appearances could be very deceiving in many ways.

Chapter Eighteen

We did not get to go to church very much and our parents warned us against going to Sunday school or any other church but theirs, which was Primitive Baptist. My parents had not yet been baptized but Marie's mother and Mr. Asa were members at Bell Spur Church, which had been their family church for many years.

Barney still only worked a day now and then on our house. He had five other houses going. We were in such a hurry to see progress on our house. I was busy on the farm so I hired Jim Bowman and Aries Quesinberry to help get the house under roof. They got it all framed and under roof and siding on by the end of June. In July and August I helped Barney frame in the windows and outside doors and get the windows in. We also built the flue in the kitchen. I was planning for a wood or coal-burning furnace in the basement with a large register in the living room to heat the house. We sealed the kitchen and dining room with sheet rock. Most of the walls were first sealed with dressed boards, which Uncle Ebb had sawed and I had hauled to Stuart to be sized.

I bought a second grade hardwood flooring for the kitchen and dining room. I could not buy first grade because there was such a demand for it. There were many other people building homes. After laying this floor which I did myself I bought inlaid linoleum for both rooms and pasted it down

I had hand dug the ditch from the spring to Dad's house and our house and installed a hydraulic ram. It was a busy summer trying to do this whenever I could get a spare hour.

Mr. Asa and Dad had helped me pour a concrete tank for the ram and we made it large enough to put the milk cans in to cool the ten-gallon cans of milk we were selling. The milkman came to pick it up before daylight so I had to be out early and have it rolled up to the road.

Troy Terry delivered me a load of sand with which to pour the cement. When he dumped the sand he got out of the truck and left the dump bed raised and the truck out of gear. The wind caught in the bed started the truck rolling. It struck a tree or it would have gone down the mountain. It did only a little damage to the truck.

I had to carry the sand by wheelbarrow to the spring along with the cement and we mixed it by hand. I put a kitchen sink in Dad's house and one in mine. I installed a one hundred gallon tank in my attic with an overflow pipe coming back outside the house. This gave us a little pressure in our kitchen sink and plenty of pressure down in Mother's kitchen. Their house was some forty feet lower in elevation than ours.

A few friends dropped by to see our house and their first question was, "Where did you get the blueprint?" They had never seen one like it.

Some said I had put good material into it, some said it was too large, some said it looked O.K., most offered constructive criticism.

So I received much advice, some had laughed and made fun of my mistakes. I was not a carpenter or a builder so I welcomed advice from those who were talented and experienced. I did take some of their advice and made some changes from my original plans, which I found later was a mistake. I had spent hours and days and nights planning and thinking and they had given me advice off the top of their head. Everyone said the room I had set aside for a bathroom was much too large. Much later when we finally finished it and put all the fixtures in along with a washer and dryer it was just right.

I learned that when building your house do not try to build it to please some one else because you are the one that will live in it. So don't worry what everyone else thinks. If two people, a man and wife can build a house that the two of them are satisfied with, they have accomplished more than most couples. Really every couple should build a house together before the wedding, and if they can agree on it and build it together and can still stand each other there would not be nearly so many divorces.

Building a house on the farm is even for difficult for the farmer who sees the farm and all the surroundings and not just the house. It was difficult for me as a farmer to decide when I got a few dollars whether to put it into finishing another room in the house or to improve the farm. I was putting much into fertilizer and investment into the future for maybe more money later, however putting it in the house would mean more comfort for my family. I tried to strike a happy medium and divide it both ways. This was not always easy for Marie to see when I spent money on the farm.

Now we had the kitchen sink and water coming into the house. We had one bed and one old table and two or three chairs. We bought a kerosene kitchen range and decided to move into our new home on Sunday October 8, 1948.

Antoinette did not want to move out from Grandma and Grandpa, it was her home. She was two and one half years old. We moved her little rocking chair and she cried and we had to take it back. As a little girl she spent a lot of time going back and forth and moving her little red rocking chair her Grandpa had made her.

We slept in what would later be our dinning room and cooked in the kitchen and ate at our little table. The back door of this house had no steps and was locked all the time.

The kerosene range was a mistake, it did not work at all and we could not use it. It tried my patience as much as any thing ever had and I threatened to throw it out the back door. We did ship it back to Sears Roebuck.

Barney and I then built an outside flue to the kitchen so we could have a wood stove. The roof was high so we had to build the flue high so it would draw. Now we went shopping for a wood stove and bought the best one we could find. It cost $105. We used it for six months and sold it for $35. I sure did look forward to coming in after dark and having a good supper cooked on our new wood stove.

Marie would say, "Honey as soon as you cut me some wood I'll cook us some supper."

I'd been busy with the farming and forgot to cut the wood. Some women did cut wood. Marie had other talents. Meanwhile the farm work had to be done, the many chores and fencing to be done. The corn was cut and stood in big shocks waiting to be shucked.

I kept doing things to the house. Finally I got to the front steps and poured concrete ones to replace the wooden ones before cold weather and poured the concrete porch. We were busy shucking corn and cutting the winter wood for our and Dad's house. We had a wood heater in our living room on the sub floor for heat. When the weather was too rough to work outside Dad and I began to lay the beautiful hardwood floor in the living room.

We also put up the sheet rock and Barney hung some of the inside doors. This way we had heat in three rooms of our house, which was warmer than the old house had been.

Marie and I put rock wool batting insulation in the outside walls as we sealed them and insulate overhead. Not many houses built before World War II, in this area, had been insulated.

We prepared to celebrate our first Christmas in our new home. We put up our first Christmas tree in 1948. We did not have any money for gifts for one another but just being in our new home was gift enough. Antoinette received some gifts that included a little tricycle she loved very much. One day after Christmas when she was misbehaved I told her Santa Clause was coming back and get her tricycle if she didn't straighten out. She promised she would be better if he would let her keep it and she did behave after that.

On New Year's Eve of '49 we had very high winds and zero temperatures. After midnight I heard a loud cracking noise. I told Marie that the tall kitchen flue was rocking in the wind. Sure enough in a few minutes it was blown down across the lawn. Fifteen feet of it had blown across the roof. The structure of the house was not hurt. We had just put the sheet rock in a small room we called the den on the north side of the house. We had to move the cook stove in there and the kitchen sink was in the south end of the house.

Meanwhile I continued to work inside the house when the weather was too rough to work outside and when I could afford any material for the house. We did buy a couch and one easy chair and a metal kitchen table and four cheap chairs. The chairs were made of a hollow tubing and one day I was sitting in one and Marie sat down in my lap and the chair folded up with us. I got up off the floor and straightened it out and we continued to use it. We really did need more seats so Marie covered some of our many nail kegs with fabric from the chicken feed bags and put a feather pillow on top of them. The feathers were saved from the chickens we had butchered.

One Sunday my sister Viola was visiting and she sat in one of our kitchen chairs and it folded up with her. She did not realize it had already collapsed and was really a hazard. She wasn't hurt but was embarrassed. She had four boys all close together in age. Larry the oldest then Lynwood and then Carl and Clyde the twins. She had three in diapers and on bottles at the same time. Sometimes one of the little boys would stay with us for a week in the summer. Once when Clyde was here, Marie sent him to the field with ice water on a hot day where Dad and I were working. She put the water in a glass jar and the jar in a cloth bag so if he broke it he wouldn't get cut. He bumped the bag over the ground as he walked along and broke it. When he arrived where we were working he had a wet bag full of ice and glass.

Sometimes when Sister Viola and her husband were visiting us I would like to play with her and put her on my shoulder. That really amused her boys and they asked their Daddy why he didn't do that. Taylor was much smaller than I was, and Viola weighed as much as he did.

Marie wanted to show me up and grabbed my suspenders and I lost my bib overalls and that gave Taylor a laugh. "See," he would say to Viola, "He is not so powerful after all."

So they all laughed at my expense. Marie knew my weak points and how to get the best of me.

Building the house took most of my time in the winter months. When winter started breaking I started thinking more about farming and making plans for the coming growing season. It seemed like milk and the sale of cattle would be our chief income from the farm. I started early in the spring spreading fertilizer on the pastures and meadows. I was using more fertilizer now on the grass lands than had been previously been used. After testing the soil I found that most fields needed phosphate, and many were low on potash, also nitrogen increased the yield too. I was liming the fields also with about two tons per acre.

I bought a spreader, twelve feet long, which was mounted on rubber tires with a tongue in front. I pulled it with the team of horses. Lime was brought in by trucks and dumped into a pile.

I shoveled it into the spreader and took a good hour to put out a ton of lime with the horses.

Fertilizer was delivered in 100 pound and sometimes 200-pound bags and poured into the spreader. I began using 2-12-12 and 10-10-10 but later switched to 0-30-30 with a mixture of 33%. nitrogen.

I still thought about going back to school and would have loved to have gone to college and got a degree to be a veterinarian. I loved to work with animals and did do all that I could for sick animals. I knew I could not leave my parents that were not well and no one to look after them. I could have gotten financial aid to go to college under the G.I. bill. I did sign up for on the farm training and went to night classes under the guidance of Howard Underwood. I learned some new things about agriculture. I tried to learn all I could to improve my farming and make a living for my family. It was with the help of Elmen Quesinberry, Tyler's son, that I wired our house for electricity. We worked days when it was raining and soon completed the job. I appreciated working with Elmen. When we had finished his Dad inspected it and it passed his approval.

I had worked hard and met with the power company officials to try to get power to our area.

I had stirred up interest with my neighbors and persuaded them to give a right of way for the power line to come through their property. Finally it looked like we would be getting power. I was really excited about getting power for the house and farm. It would make things easier for Marie and me. The cooking, hot water and laundry would be easier for her and my Mother.

Elmen and I wired Dad and Mother's house ready for power and then went and wired Mr. Asa's house. Elmen was paid for his work of course, but I was just glad to do it for them.

Early in the spring before the weather warmed I took the team and hillside plow and plowed the steep hillside near Squall Creek as it was growing up in broom sage, which was of no value. Early in the spring I sowed it in fescue, clover and lespedeza and orchard grasses as well as ladino clover. I limed and fertilized it good. I used forty per cent phosphate, fifty percent potash and thirty three percent nitrogen on it. Soon it came up, grew well and made a lush pasture for the cows.

Mr. P.H. Bowman asked me to serve on the board of directors for the Farm Home Loan and I accepted. We met at least once a month to approve or disapprove loans mostly for veterans. Many veterans were building new homes with a loan. Others were buying farms and buying equipment and putting up farm buildings.

I thought of doing this, however my parents were strictly against me taking out any kind of loan.

So I continued to build a little at the time on what little I could make. We did build a flue to our kitchen and moved our stove back to the kitchen. Some young farmers were buying tractors but I didn't have the money at that time to pay cash and was still driving Dad's thirty eight ford pick up when he wasn't using it.

Many new things were being developed on the farm. We began to spray weeds with 2-4-D in the corn. Hybrid corn was beginning to be planted and I planted a test plot for V.P. I. There were twelve different kinds of hybrids. I was one of the first in the county to plant hybrid field corn and I had some high yields.

Construction was beginning on the power lines and the workers were looking for boarding places. Marie and I decided to keep three of the linemen. Early Light was one of them. We put beds for them in our newly finished bedroom and we slept in another room in a twin bed. The two of us in a small bed was real cozy. Of course every one had to use the outhouse. We did have running water thanks to the ram.

Marie cooked on the wood stove for the boarders, packing their lunches and taking all the milk and butter back to the spring way down the hill below Dad's house after each meal to keep it cool. She was also helping me on the farm and working in the garden. She still went to the spring to heat water and wash clothes with the old gas washing machine.

She would often fill the cast iron pots with water, heat it with a wood fire she would build and get everything ready to wash only not to be able to crank the gas engine of the washing machine. She would have to come out to the field where I was working to get me to crank it for her. She would be angry because she could not crank it and I would be angry because I would have to leave work. One day I remember well, I was planting corn when she came after me. I reluctantly went with her. Mother was waiting to do her laundry also. The motor was very stubborn and I lost my temper and said some words I should not have said. My mother said she would have whipped me when I was a boy for talking like that. Marie said I might still get it. The motor finally cranked and I started to leave when Marie grabbed me from behind. She had a way of flipping my suspenders quicker than a bolt of lightning could strike and dropped my bib overalls around my feet. I tripped and fell. She grabbed them off my feet before I could recover from the fall spanked my bottom and grabbed the rest of my clothes and threw everything into the washing machine. I very humbly walked naked to the house to get more clothes.

Marie and Mother were laughing as I walked up the hill. I was embarrassed and humbled and my bottom was stinging from the spanking and two or three cuts from a switch my mother had given me.

I was very careful after that with my language when I lost my temper. At least I looked around to see if they were within hearing when I lost my temper over a piece of machinery. Today I am most thankful that Marie can wash by pushing one button.

If I got angry about anything when Mother was around she would say, "You better be careful; I will call Marie to take care of you."

I guess Marie was good for me she helped me to get rid of bad habits.

Antoinette continued to grow and seemed healthy. She was small for her age and only weighed sixteen pounds when she was one year old. She was a very busy and active little girl and went back and forth now on her own from our house to her grandparents house. She also went up the hill with Marie to see the other Grandma often. She was blessed to have two sets of grandparents so close by.

We had not been to a movie in ages and decided to go to Stuart one Sunday afternoon. We took Antoinette and as we were watching the movie she slid down out of the seat and crawled under the seat. We kept trying to get her and she came out way down in the front of the theater. After crawling under the seats she was so dirty and sticky that we had to bring our little black girl home. We did not try that anymore for a long while.

Everything was growing and doing well on the farm. The cows were milking good and we were milking enough now to wear your hands out milking both morning and night. The power line was progressing and we were really busy. With the farming and keeping boarders I could not find time or money to work on the house. I did buy an electric radio to be ready for the power. We decided an electric range would be our third item to buy. The churn came first since Marie did not like to churn butter.

Sometimes I would still be so busy I would forget to cut the stove wood and when I came home hungry I would still have to get Marie some wood before she could make supper. One of our neighbors said he would not get an electric stove because it was the only reason the women kept him around was to cut wood for them.

Chapter Nineteen

The line was complete and I had bought light fixtures for some of the rooms and was ready for the power. This was a great day when they turned on the power. We had lights and my new radio worked. It was great to have good lights now. I could read more at night and we could work inside of the house later at night and see how to do the painting and finishing work.

We went to Tom Agee's Store and bought a Westinghouse Kitchen range, It was the fifteenth stove he had sold that month. Many people in our area were just getting power and buying appliances as were we. Marie's special prize was her new electric churn, which she used in making butter and buttermilk, which we liked. Then we bought an electric iron.

Marie was now pregnant again and we were very happy as we had been hoping for another child. We did not tell our parents because they said that we did not need another child, especially now, as usual.

I was learning that I really should have gone to college and became a veterinarian. I learned to give our cows shots and to give them medicine in their veins. Many cows had milk fever then and neighbors were always calling on me. Dr. Witt, the local Vet. would come when he could but it was a long way from Stuart.

When he was so busy and out on a call sometimes it was too late when he got to the sick cow. I would drop whatever I was doing and go get the cow back on her feet, most of the time. Of course I didn't charge anything and often paid for the medication. If I had been a Vet I probably would not have made any money. I always felt sorry for the animal and the farmer and would not have charged enough to make a living.

I was blessed to have an extra abundance in the garden, all kinds of good vegetables we shared with those in need.

That fall of 1950, about the tenth of August, I sowed my first acre of alfalfa. I had been reading about it and was convinced I could grow it. Most everyone said it would not grow in the mountain. I studied everything I could find concerning the seeding, fertilizer and every phase of growing it. I plowed and worked the soil over and over with the horses until I had a good seedbed. I sowed the seed with a cyclone seeder and harrowed it in. I got a good stand and it got a good growth that fall. I was strip cropping and working closely with the soil conservation service and the extension service. My topsoil was not being eroded anymore and the crops and pastures were looking much better with the heavy fertilization I was using now.

The Tennessee Valley Authority was selling fertilizer at a discount to those who would experiment with it and I decided to try it on a three-year basis.

It was a high analysis fertilizer, 10-20-20- and 0-30-30- and 33% nitrogen. I had to get it hauled from Bristol, Tennessee. I really got good results from it.

That winter we worked on the inside of the house every chance I had when we could buy a small amount of material. We bought a refrigerator, which sure helped to take care of our food. It was great not to have to take the butter and milk and other things to the springhouse. I bought a water-cooled milk cooler that I could put up to eight- ten gallon cans of milk in to cool. We put it in our basement. This sure did help so I didn't have to haul it up from the spring in the wheelbarrow and our milk was so good and cool. It sure was a good place to cool watermelons in the summer time too.

We continued to increase our herd and were beginning to get a few hailstones to go with our Guernseys. I was thinking about corn ensilage for another year and was wondering how to go about it. Ensilage is a way of preserving the green corn. I decided to plant more hybrid corn the next year also. The trial plots I had grown looked very promising.

Marie was progressing very well with her pregnancy and always looked so pretty when she was pregnant and I told her so. She didn't believe me though. She was going to Dr. Thompson at Stuart.

The winter had been pretty cold and I got a furnace and installed it in our basement myself. It really warmed up our house so nicely we had to be careful not to over heat. I also bought a Maytag electric washing machine, which we put in the basement also. It was a wringer type and was a good machine. I moved the cast iron pot up from the spring and set it below the house to heat the water. We still didn't have a water heater. We heated the water on the kitchen range for dish washing and bathing. We took our baths in the kitchen where we could pour the water down the drain.

Doing the laundry and ironing was easier for Marie and Mother now. My Mother brought her laundry up to our basement so they would have a warm place in the winter and a cool place in the summer. I put up a good clothesline in the back yard.

Marie would go to the old Stuart Hospital to have the baby this time. It was in January before the baby was born that we bought our first television set. It was the first set in the community. It was on this television that the neighbors came to watch the inauguration of President Eisenhower.

It was a very cold February sixteenth, a day after Marie's birthday that I took her to the hospital for our second baby to be born. They would not let me stay in the delivery room so I stayed close by and prayed. I was very nervous.

Marie's cousin Marjorie Ayers was in a room with her baby girl near the delivery room. In fact there were no delivery rooms. Just regular rooms with very poor worn out mattresses. Marie's back hurt for years after having her baby in such poor surroundings.

I tried to see inside as the nurses came and went. The hours went on and on and I thought the baby had been born and I had not heard my baby cry. What could be wrong? My heart was in my throat. How the tension built up. Finally I peeped through the door and saw the Doctor holding the baby by the heels and I could hear him spanking her. The baby girl was all right but the cord had been wound around her neck three times and it had been a difficult birth. Finally I heard the baby scream. What a relief.

Oh what a beautiful baby! She had lots of black hair that the nurse soon tied a ribbon in. We had already decided to name her Bonita Ruth.

Antoinette was so thrilled with her baby sister and when I took her to see her the next day she said, "Oh mama, where did she come from?"

Marie did not know what to say but in a moment Antoinette said, "I know, she came from heaven". To this day we know this is true. She has been such a blessing to our whole family.

While in the hospital the nurse brought Marie the wrong baby at the 2 A.M. feeding.

The nurse left immediately to attend to others. She had taken Bonita upstairs and Marie could hear her crying. It was forty-five minutes before the nurse realized her mistake and switched the babies. She asked Marie not to tell the doctor about this mistake and she didn't.

Both mother and daughter got along fine and came home in the customary two weeks. It was still the custom that mothers stay in bed for the whole two weeks. The weather was cold and Dad's old pickup had no heat in it so I borrowed Arnold Bank's car with a warm heater to bring them home. Marie breast-fed all our babies and they did well with no allergies.

Bonita was a quiet baby and never cried very much and was such a pretty baby. We would wake up at night and look to see if she was all right and she would be laying there in her bed with those big eyes open just looking around as of she were thinking of something important. Now we had two little girls and our family was growing wonderfully. Our family had doubled now and we sure needed better transportation.

Marie was prettier than ever as the mother of two. One day when we were in Mount Airy I was on one side of Main Street and she was walking down the other side I heard two men commenting to one another what a beautiful woman she was. They did not know me. It made me feel proud that she was my wife.

The year 1951 was an eventful year for Marie and me. We had two daughters and now we were a family of four. It was so sweet to see Antoinette's love for her little sister and see her tender play with her.

We had much responsibility looking after our four parents. We had to take my Mother and Dad to the doctor quite often. Marie's Mother and stepfather, Mr. Asa was getting quite old and needed much care. I tried to get Mr. Asa to put in a water system and even offered to pay for it but he would not agree to do it. I really thought this would help Marie as much as anyone. She went most every day and carried water from the spring and brought in stove wood. They still made a garden and I did most of the plowing for them.

I sowed more alfalfa and I knew that if we must build a barn to store it in if were to get full benefit from it. Too much was lost storing it outside in the rainy weather.

Early in the spring I cut some timber from which to have the barn framing sawed. Gene Barnard helped me cut it with an old maul chain saw. We had some big trees to cut below my Dad's house. There were oak, poplar and a few pines for rafters. The maul chain saw was hard to crank but we cut the timber in a few days. Earnest Stanley sawed it and we sold the poplar. Thomas Smith hauled it to Galax. I logged it with the horses.

Everybody said I would have to get someone with a Caterpillar to pull some of the big logs in. I pulled them all in with the horses. Some of the largest I pulled in one morning when we had two inches of snow on the ground.

It was with the horses I graded out and scooped for the barn and dug the footer by hand. After pouring the footer it was farming time.

I hired Lloyd Banks to lay the blocks and frame the barn. Harless Turman sheeted and roofed it. We put a track and hayfork in the top of it and it was ready to put hay in by mowing time. We were still mowing with the horses and hauled the hay in and pulled it up with the hayfork. I worked the side with one horse. Now we were putting in some good hay that would stay in good condition.

Carnation was still buying our milk. A few farmers were selling Grade A milk around Meadows of Dan and Laurel Fork and there was a demand for more. We decided milking by hand, as we increased our herd, was getting to be just too much, so we began thinking of building a milking parlor. This was what we wanted and needed so we began making plans. This meant borrowing money, which my parents had not changed their minds about. I might have been better off if I had not listened to them. I started buying blocks for the milking parlor and was not able to do anymore on our house or buy any more furnishings that year.

Every dollar went into the milking parlor. Lloyd and Harless began laying the blocks on the milking parlor late that summer. I put an electric pump down at the spring. The ram would not furnish enough water or pressure for the parlor.

I continued to buy material and Lloyd continued to work and by fall the milking parlor was finished. I had really worked hard trying to keep up with the farming, working on the barns and helping when I could to build the milking parlor. We had to put a hot water in the milking parlor before we put one in the house. We had to have hot water to wash up the milk utensils.

We did have to buy a few groceries even with all the canning Marie was doing. She had worked hard taking care of the girls, helping with the milking, working in the garden and helping with the hay. We still helped out lots with all four of our parents. Looking back I don't know how we did it all.

Neither Marie nor I had many clothes and did not dress as nicely as many of our neighbors. This did not bother me for myself but I always wanted to give Marie pretty clothes to wear. She always looked so good in a new dress and she really appreciated one. It made me feel good to give her something pretty. Marie made all the clothes for herself and our daughters. She was very talented to create pretty clothes. Her mother had taught her how to sew as well as taking home economics in school.

We had very little time for ourselves or to visit and only went to church occasionally. Vacation was a foreign word to us that we heard other people talk about. We wanted to go to church regularly but still did not have transportation. Dad and I decided to buy a car together. Dad would pay the top half and I would finance our part. We bought a fifty-one Ford. It was an automatic V-8. We found out this was a mistake.

We did get to go get groceries in the car and business trips during the week. On the weekend we either went to church with them or stayed home. We wanted to go to the Missionary Baptist church so our girls would have an opportunity to be in Sunday school. Our parents said that would never do. Sometimes I took them to church or someplace where Dad did not want to drive and Marie and the girls stayed home. The parents liked to go to all day meetings and it was difficult to keep the little ones out that long especially with no provisions being made for children at church.

Thanksgiving came in with a bang. The weather was rough! I was putting the finishing touches on the barns and on Thanksgiving Eve the weather was nice and warm. Suddenly a thunderstorm rolled in. It rained for a while and after dark it turned to snow. Marie's sister Opal and her husband Bill had come to spend the week end with us. They had been married in June of 1948 and did not have any children at this time.

They were living in Ridgeway, about sixty miles away and working at Du Pont. The next morning when we got up the weather had really turned cold overnight. It was below zero and the snow was piled high with drifts in every direction. They had to go through fields and cut wire fences to get out to the road and go home.

It had been a warm fall and the sudden cold killed the north side of pines and evergreens. The weather warmed up, though, and I was able to get the corn shucked and some wood cut before the next cold spell.

The hybrid corn I was planting was producing really well and giving high yields. I belonged to the Hundred Bushel Club. The extension service and the F.F.A. had gone into the county measuring corn and said that my corn was the top yield in the county at that time, one hundred and forty bushel per acre. I made better corn in years after that. I had been too busy to raise very much in truck crops. I always planted more garden produce than we needed like beans and corn so we could share with those in need. We also canned much and gave lots away as well.

I was so busy during the week I got in the habit of doing little things like picking beans on Sunday afternoons. Marie did not like this at all. She had been brought up by a good Christian Mother who taught her to keep the Lord's day holy and to not do any work.

One Sunday afternoon I said I was going to pick some October beans. She said, "Fine, I will help you."

I should have been warned by her change in attitude but I was surprised and pleased by her change. I did wonder if something was wrong and if I should really go. She had never offered to help on a Sunday before. The patch of beans was a long way from the house. I carried some baskets and some buckets and we walked across the fields. When we reached the bean patch she said she was tired and wanted to sit down. I sat down and she sat across my legs. The weather was very hot and she asked me if I wanted to take my shirt off. I said it would feel good and she unhooked the suspenders of my bib over-alls and took off my shirt. She was talking and rubbing my back with one hand, and that felt good. It made me relax and I did not even notice she had untied my shoes with her other hand. By now she was pulling off my shoes.

"What are you doing?" I asked too late. She began laughing that mischievous laugh that always bewildered me and I couldn't think who I was. She started tickling me in the ribs, which I could not tolerate and just drove me crazy. I struggled and tried to get up. It was too late! With one flip she grabbed my overalls, shirt, shoes and underwear.

Over the hill she ran yelling, "Catch me." I tried to run after but my feet were too tender.

I never could stand to go barefoot. She just ran off and left me. I thought surely she would stop and turn back. No way, she went out of sight to the house.

I could not believe she had done that. Here I was barefoot and naked on a Sunday afternoon and a long way from the house. I wondered whose idea this was to plant the beans so far away anyway.

I made my way carefully with my tender bare feet across the meadow and into the cornfield and worked my way to the house. I was wondering who might have seen me and who might be visiting on a Sunday afternoon at the house. I finally slipped in back of the house through the pines and made a fast pass into the basement. Whee, I'm safe!

She was watching me all the while, and as soon as I entered the basement she called, "Honey, did you finish picking the beans?" and threw me some clothes. I guess she thought I might be cold.

Many times after this she would ask me on a Sunday afternoon if I had any beans that needed picking, and laughed that incredible laugh. No, I never had any more beans that needed picking on a Sunday afternoon. She was always full of pranks and I was always was on the lookout for them.

Nevertheless I would fall for some of her traps now and then and find myself in an embarrassing situation on the farm. It was usually when she wanted to teach me a lesson.

Coble Milk Company had paid Grade A prices for our milk through the winter, but when spring came they cut the price back to grade B. I was getting the same price as Carnation paid and I still had to meet Grade A standards. Federal inspectors from Virginia and North Carolina were always dropping by unexpectedly. How nice to farm and be your own boss or so many people say. They just didn't know!

Coble had cut my butterfat back and I would have been better off selling to carnation. The Coble Milk Company made promises they did not keep.

The year 1951 was a bad crop year. First it was dry through the month of June and July and the hay was short and the pasture was low. On the last day of July there came a severe thunderstorm and hailed like I had never seen before or since. The hail was large as baseballs and some of it was long shaped and up to four inches long. It lasted for twenty minutes. The ground was covered several inches deep and it took three hours for it to melt in the hot weather. It sounded like rocks falling on the roof. The tin barn roofs were dented by it.

We did not get one tomato that year.

Not a blade of corn was left on the stalks and the ears did not fill out. We cut it all for silage. The storm came from the edge of the mountain facing Kibler Valley.

Not a one of our neighbors had any hail out of the storm. Aunt Alma Stanley and Tyler Quesinberry shared some tomatoes with us. We had made a little hay and some beans before the storm. I put silage in wire pins lined with heavy tarpaper. It did all right and we had enough feed to make out, but I did not make any money that year.

We did have a big blessing on the way. Marie was pregnant again and of course we were hoping for a boy. As usual our parents let their feelings be known, which was disapproval that we were going to have another mouth to feed so soon. They thought that we would soon be in the poor house. Dr. Thompson was Marie's doctor again.

Our dear friend Tom Agee died suddenly in the month of August that year. What a blow to the community as well as to his church and family. He was dearly loved by every one. He was only forty-two years old. He and I had been good friends and I had done a lot of business with him. You could always depend on his word. I had bought building material for my barns, feed, fertilizer, farm supplies and household appliances from him.

I was a board member for Southern States and he and I went to meetings in Richmond together on several occasions.

We stayed in the John Marshall Hotel and enjoyed some good meals together. I missed him very much as did the whole Meadows of Dan community. I bought one of the first T.V.'s that he sold and his partner Arnold Banks ask him later of I could pay part down on it and the rest a month later. He said, "Of course; it's Silas isn't it." He knew me too.

We did enjoy the T.V. very much. We use to listen to the radio and think, oh, if we could only see them, never believing that one day we would.

On November 9, 1951 our first son was born at Stuart hospital just before noon. He was hungry when he arrived. I had taken Marie to the hospital before day and had come back home to milk, Of course. I had returned to be there when the baby was born. So again there was a long wait, or it seemed so to me. I was nervous but I'm sure that was mild compared to what Marie was experiencing. Finally the doctor came out and told me I had a son and I could go in and see them. Marie said that was the first time she had ever seen me with tears in my eyes when I came into the room. She was sleeping but I kept waking her up and telling her we had a son. She would say tell me again what we have. We named him Theodore Clinton Turman and what a blessing he was and continues to be to all of us. He was such a sweet baby. The girls were pleased they had a baby brother to play with.

Bonita was twenty-two months old so she did not yet realize how much he would mean to her. She says now that she was put out of her little bed and had to take care of herself and even had to wash her own diapers. She is just kidding of course. She and Ted grew up very close and when we would look across the farm to see where they were, they were always close together, playing and they still are.

Ted really loved his Grandparents and when he was big enough to walk, he would go to see them with an extra diaper under his arm. He really loved his grandma's cooking and would always ask for some to take to his sister, Bonita.

Our private road into the farm was now a state maintained gravel road. It had been straightened out much and improved. Dad had to buy a corner lot from John Bowman and another corner lot from Mr. Dave Scott to get the right of way to straighten out the two short turns in the road before the state would build it. The Parkway objected to the road crossing their land and tried to stop it. Dad had to get Frank Burton, a lawyer to prove to them that he had a right of way long before they did. Without this road we would have never been able to sell milk and get a truck to come in and pick it up.

Chapter Twenty

The Welsh West Virginia Milk Company wanted milk and I was glad to switch to them. Coble had never treated me fairly. This meant getting a better price the year around for our milk and besides I liked the West Virginia Inspector better.

Our budget was very tight but Marie needed a sewing machine. When she sewed she had to take all three kids to Mother's and use her machine and try to keep the kids quiet and clean up every string and put everything back in place when she got through.

With three children to sew for, we bought her a $49 machine made in Japan. This was in the days before being made in Japan meant any kind of competitive quality. When she sewed she spent about as much time working on the machine as she did in sewing. The little children were always pleased with the clothes she made them. They went with me to the store and help pick out the feedbags they wanted their clothes made from. She made their pajamas and Ted's shirts, too.

The children were really growing and Bonita began to talk and walk at an early age. One day she was calling, "Mommie, Mommie, I want to sit down and dance." The radio was on in her room and she was standing up in her bed, about to shake it down. She was sixteen months old. Marie put her down on the floor and she really danced to the music.

Antoinette was growing and we were beginning to teach her to count and do her A.B.C.'s. She still loved to go see her Grandma and play with her.

We all got to watch the T.V. and got to watch it some at night. I would often lie on the couch and go to sleep while watching it after working hard all day. Marie would get me up and walk me to bed without even waking me up. She got tired of this so.....One night the kids were in bed and it was after midnight. There I was sound asleep peaceful on the couch, having had my Saturday night bath. I was wearing my robe and Marie managed to get me up and was walking me to bed, however as she passed the living room door she had one of her funny ideas. She grabbed my robe opened the front door and shoved me out on the front porch in my birthday suit. The cold north wind was howling, the temperature was zero, she turned on the porch light. I was frantically trying to open the door and yelling for her to let me in. She was laughing and pretending she couldn't hear what I was saying. This lasted for just a few minutes and she mercifully opened the door. I was glad to go to bed without her help after this. I did finally get warm.

The year 1953 was a big year at our house. Eisenhower was elected president. There hadn't been a Republican president for years. Our first television being the first in our community was of great interest to us and many of our neighbors.

They came over and watched the inauguration. We had prepared refreshments for all. Mr. Hub Stanley who was up in years thoroughly enjoyed it, especially since this new president was his choice.

This year our crops had done better as well and milk prices had been a little better.

That winter Bonita got a virus in January. We took her to Doctor Cox in Hillsville and he gave her antibiotics in capsule form for pneumonia. She was very sick and as she began to recover a storm of heavy snow moved in with high winds and zero temperature. The roads were blocked and we had no phone. Her temperature dropped to 92 degrees. We had half-gallon cans of hot water packed around her in her little bed. On this cold night our son, Ted also came down with pneumonia. The doctor could not get to us or could we get to him. The wind was blowing so hard we thought our strong house was going to blow away. We sat by Ted and listened to his rasping, struggled breathing. We could hear it all over the house. His temperature was 106 degrees and Bonita's was 92 degrees. We prayed over and over for the Lord to heal them, to help us know what to do to care for them. The Lord told me to give him the same medicine that Bonita was taking. He was so little, only eighteen months old and could not swallow a capsule. We had to break it open and mix it with applesauce and get it down his throat. He was as limp as a towel.

For three days we did this. On her knees by his bed Marie pleaded to God for her babies. She promised the Lord that if he would spare them she would do whatever He wanted her to do. This is when He told me to give Ted the capsules. After several hours of medication we began to see his temperature coming down. We were also bathing him with cold wet cloths.

After three days the roads were finally open and Doctor Cox finally got here and said they seemed to be improving. He did give Ted a shot with a needle that was dull. Marie had Ted lying across her lap with his bare butt exposed to the needle. The doctor had to punch him three times before he got the needle in. He apologized for it being so dull but said he'd had to come by way of Fancy Gap and so many people had been sick with flu and pneumonia and he'd had to give so many shots his needle was dull. (Thank God this was before Aids)

The good doctor said we did the right thing and the medicine we had given Ted had worked and he probably wouldn't have survived without it. We always wondered why they gave babies capsules. They were hard enough for adults to swallow. The doctors did not carry disposable syringes in those days.

Marie said the Lord had told her that she must go up for salvation and accept Jesus as her Savior and she must keep her promise.

We had been going to Meadows of Dan Church some and really did like the preacher. When he heard about Ted being sick he came out and sat with us. This meant so much to us. He had such a dear wife named Lovie and indeed she did love everyone.

When the children were better we began to go back to church, of course against our parents wishes. We wanted our children to go to Sunday school and learn to study the bible. Much of the time we didn't have any way of going. When Sunday morning came Mother and Dad went to church in the car and we stayed home. The '51 Ford car had been a lemon. The motor went bad on it when it only had a few thousand miles. We traded it for a 1954 Chevrolet car, still in partnership with my parents. We could not afford a car of our own.

Our good neighbor Dorsey Harrell and Clara started coming out and getting us on Sunday morning and taking us to Sunday School and church and then bringing us back home. The third Sunday in April we took Mom and Dad to church at Concord which was about half a mile from out church and dropped them off. We went on to our church and this day Marie followed up on her promise to God. This Sunday she went up at church for salvation and let the world know whose side she was on. I wanted to go up also, but I knew her going would mean enough trouble at home, so I didn't go.

I had mixed feelings. I was rejoicing that she had gone for salvation and kept her promise, but I was also dreading the problems I knew we would have at home.

When we went by and picked up Mom and Dad, Ted who was just two years old and big enough to notice things said, "My Mama cried at church today."

Mother guessed and she said, "Marie did you join the church today?" They were really were upset and told me I had better not if I knew what was good for me. They also reminded me we would have no way of going to church. I decided we would and we went and bought us a second hand pickup.

I found one at Hillsville. I had only five hundred dollars and bought it for that. What a mistake, I had to spend more to keep it running, a wheel came off on the way home. We did have transportation though, all five of us in the pickup cab. Ted sat on a little stool on the floorboard, and we did go to church. We went on Sunday morning and Sunday nights as well as Wednesday night prayer meetings.

When Mother told Marie's Mother all Hell broke loose. She came out to the field where I was plowing. She told me to set my foot down and not let her be baptized, that she was too young to know what she was doing. She was twenty-six years old. She also said to tell her never to set her foot in her house again. I just listened and said nothing. I was caught in the middle.

Marie went straight up there to talk with her parents. She sat down and told them her deep feelings and her promise to the Lord. They never once spoke to her and she got up and came home. Marie was going through much persecution from four parents and it was very difficult for us all.

I was really worried about her. She said if she could not serve the Lord she was going to have a good time. If she were going to hell she would have a good time getting there. I saw what a battle the devil was waging through our parents. So I did set my foot down and told her she had made a commitment and I would stand by her and she would be baptized. If I had not taken this stand I do not know what would have happened to her. She continued to go to her Mother's, carry up water, get stove wood and help them in every way she could. They were still not speaking to her. Sometimes she would go late in the evening when it was almost dark and I told her to drive the pickup. I was afraid someone or something might get her. She said she wasn't afraid.

One night I decided to try her out. There was a big old chestnut stump as high as my head by the path and I decided I would hide there about dark and jump out at her and see what she would do. This scared her so badly she started to fall and I caught her, but not before she dropped a cake her mother had given her. They had started speaking to her by this time.

She did learn to drive the pickup after that and drove it back and forth to her Mother's for a long time before she got her permit.

On the first Sunday in May in 1953 she was baptized in Joel Williams pond at Meadows of Dan when she was twenty-six years old. My parents did not go to her baptizing, however her Mother did. It was a pretty baptizing and several others were baptized at the same time.

I praised the Lord for her taking her stand for her Lord and keeping her promise to Him. Our three children held onto me and saw their Mother baptized.

Antoinette was old enough to go to school but she really didn't want to go. She would complain of being sick in the morning until the bus had passed and then she would feel better. Grandpa caught on to her little game and would take her to school later. Soon she made some friends and got to like school better. We took her out to the main road, 641, where the bus came and waited for the bus with her. We did not allow her to walk as we had when we were little.

Ted knew he was a little man and wanted to be like his Daddy. The girls loved playing with him and they would dress him up in their dresses. One day when I came in from work I said, "What a pretty little girl." They had him dressed up and it made him so mad he tore the dress off.

When he was eighteen months old we took him to the barbershop to get his first haircut. His hair was blond and curly and he walked down the street holding his mothers hand. The barber sat him on a high stool in front of a mirror so he could see himself. When the barber had finished he saw he had been transformed into a little boy. When he walked back up the street he not only wouldn't hold his mothers hand he wouldn't even walk beside her.

Marie was back to her usual fun self, always wanting to pull some surprise on me. One evening I was spraying corn silks to kill the worms on the Shelor place and saw her drive up to her Mothers in the pickup. I decided to wait and ride back with her. While I was waiting in the woods beside the road I sat the sprayer down and decided to take off my clothes and shake the corn tassels off of them. They really made me itch. As I was doing that I heard her coming and crouched behind a laurel bush in case someone was with her. She saw the sprayer and stopped and got it, then she saw my clothes lying on the ground. She quickly got them and got in the truck with them. Before I could get back there she had the door locked. She said I could get in the back of the pickup. I did not trust her and would not get in the back. I didn't know where she might decide to take me on the back of the truck. She drove off and left me. She stopped a little ways up the road.

I just listened and did not hear anyone coming and ran up the road. Just as I was almost to the pickup she drove away and went all the way to the house. I heard someone coming and had to hide in the cornfield until they left. It was dark by this time and I slipped in and found my clothes still in the truck.

Bonita was learning to count and read at a very young age. She would read on the cereal boxes and everything she could find. She would say, "So you believe I can count to a thousand?" If we said "No", we had to listen to her count to a thousand. We learned to say "Yes."

She was learning everything that Antoinette was learning at school. Bonita was old enough to carry water to us in the field where we were working. She always would run. Her grandpa said she would amount to something special she was so bright. He sure did love her. In fact all the Grandparents enjoyed all three children.

I was an active charter member of the Meadows of Dan Ruritan Club. The Ruritans did many good things for the community. I was secretary for the Ruritans then president for two years. We put a play on called "Papa Misbehaves." I played the part of a woman in the play. We had much success with the play and presented-in several other places.

The community cannery was constructed and operated while I was a leader in the Ruritan Club.

Each individual put much money and time into the club. It should not have been built on state property, which caused it to be operated by the state. The state meant for it to make money and the intentions of the Ruritans was to serve the community. It did serve the community for several years and was run by very talented people. Marie and I canned hundreds of cans there as did many families. Later many people quit canning and depended on buying at the grocery store or freezing their vegetables.

Most people don't bother with a garden any more. We as a people are not self sufficient but depend on someone else for everything. However it is more difficult to raise a garden anymore for many reasons.

Soil conservation had helped me so much and I was really sold on it. I was asked if I would be interested in being a soil conservation director. I accepted, and my name was on the ballot for the November election. I received more votes than any political candidate in the county election.

BOARD OF SUPERVISORS — Left to Right: Willie L. Vernon, Vice-Chairman; Alva J. Davis; Silas Turman, Chairman; John S. Huddleston, Secretary, and Paul G. Cox, Treasurer.

We met once a month usually at Hillsville. The New River District at first consisted of Carroll, Floyd, Patrick and Grayson counties. Later Floyd joined another district. I served with a lot of good District Supervisors too numerous to mention. I was chairman of the board for twelve years and felt I accomplished much. We met in Galax after the city became a part of the district.

This was a long way for Supervisors to go from Patrick County. So we decided to form a district in Patrick County. We succeed in doing this and after serving for a while longer I decided to resign. I served thirty-one years and gave a lot of free time to the cause and never regretted it.

Darcey Turman and I cut timber one winter while Johnny and Leon Jessup sawed it. I had a two man Henry Disston saw. It was a reliable chain saw and cranked easily and had plenty of power. Later I replaced it with a one-man chain saw.

I decided to build a silo and hired Levie Cruse to lay the blocks. I waited on him pulling the blocks up to him. John Bowman and I plastered the inside of it. I hired Calvin Shelor and others to fill it. It was very expensive. Marie had the task of preparing a big dinner for all the workers. The use of silage did help milk production. Most everyone had tractors by now and I was still struggling with horses. I continued to sow more alfalfa and was getting hard to keep up with the mowing with the horses.

Bonita could read, add, subtract and spell when it was time for her to go to school. We thought it might be boring for her in the first grade so we asked about her starting in the second grade. The school gave her a test and found she was capable of doing fourth grade work, so they put her in the second grade.

Hurricane Hazel had come through the fall before and was the most destructive hurricane I had ever seen up to that time.

The bus came early and let Antoinette off to walk home in the terrible storm, wind and rain. She was almost drowned and frozen to death when she got home. How careless of the driver. Now that we had two children in school the bus would come out our road and pick them up in front of the house.

Now that the girls were in school Ted had his Mother all to himself and spent much time with her and his grandparents. One day he decided he was old enough to visit Marie's Mother, Grandma Ada, and walk up the hill and through the woods. In a few minutes he returned to say he saw half a dog peeping at him through the fence. This must have been a frightening sight.

Our parents told us we must not have any more children and to make sure we didn't. Marie still wanted another baby. She said Ted was so sweet and she knew another would be just as precious. Our parents did not know she was pregnant again until she had a miscarriage. She was over three and one half month when she started hemorrhaging all of a sudden and I picked her up in my arms and carried her to the car and was in the emergency room in twenty minutes. She was passing out by the time I got there with her. She had a close call but with Dr. Lawrence's good care and a blood transfusion she came home the next day. Thank God for someone else's blood. She was home in time for Christmas and was able to sit by the tree as we opened our gifts.

I had bought her a pretty watch in September when I found out she was carrying another of my babies. I lay the gift in her hand and she was so pleased.

Not long after this she was pregnant again and no one but she, I and the doctor knew about it for several months. She was never sick. Finally one day in the fall I had taken Mama and Aunt Bertha to the doctor in Roanoke. As we were coming back Marie saw some pretty apples on the trees beside the road and Marie was trying to get me to stop and pick her one. She said she just had to have one. Mama and Aunt Bertha knew she was pregnant and were really upset. They said there was no way we could support another child.

Everything went fine and Marie was going to Doctor Early at Hillsville. Minnie Jessup, Marie's cousin's wife, was expecting about the same time and was going to the same doctor. She went to the hospital one day before Marie did and had a lovely baby daughter. She was there to welcome Marie to the maternity ward and to stand by her.

On the morning of April 28, 1956 Marie awoke early. She said, "Listen to the mocking bird singing." We lay there and listened awhile and she said, "I think I'll go to the hospital." She got up and was hurrying around when I said, "I've got to have something to eat before I go."

She gave me a disgusted look but she faithfully headed for the kitchen and in a few minutes called me into breakfast. Then she came to see why I hadn't come to eat and found I was dressing in my best suit, white shirt and tie. She laughed and asked, "What's this all about?"

I said, "First impressions are important and I want to make a good impression on this little fellow." (I knew it would be another boy). Marie laughed all the way to the hospital between pains. I intended to stay but the good Doctor encouraged me to go home. He said it would be late in the evening before it would be born. I think he just wanted to get rid of me. I came home and worked real fast a hard until twelve o'clock sowing grass and oats. I hurried back to the hospital and when I entered I heard a baby yelling. I asked the first nurse I met whose baby it was that was crying. She said, "I think it's the Turman baby." Oh what a joy to see our fourth baby. It too was a boy all fine and healthy. Now we had two girls and two boys. The Lord had blessed us wonderfully.

This time Marie came home the fourth day. What a beautiful spring day when she came home with a baby in her arms. The big apple tree on our front lawn was in full bloom and the birds were singing. The girls and Ted were thrilled about this new son Duke Cundiff.

Duke after our dear dentist who had taken care of us so many years and whom we loved so much and Cundiff after me, my middle name. Marie wanted a Junior and I said one Silas was enough.

157

We were attending church regularly and I loved Sunday school. Our preacher Mr. Deatz and his wife were great friends of ours. With all the blessings the Lord had bestowed upon me and my family and with my four children I needed to guide. I knew that I must give my life to the Lord and be a witness to others. I had knowledge of the bible and had read and studied it all my life and understood his message to me. Yet I wanted to know so much, much more.

It was a difficult choice but the bible teaches that we must put the Lord first, even before our parents and families. My parents reminded me that our house was built on their land and they could cut me out of their will if I went to "That Church" and joined it. Even with that hanging over my head I knew I must. It was August of 1956 after a good revival on a Sunday morning when the invitation was given and Antoinette was in the choir. I saw her going to the altar, and found myself stepping out and going to the altar also. I always sat near the back of the church so maybe I could escape quickly and miss the preacher. The Holy Spirit had been working on me for a long time.

I didn't think anyone else knew the struggle I was going through or would go through.

When I came home I went to tell my parents while Marie was fixing lunch. When I walked back up the hill I don't think there was a dry thread on my white shirt. I suffered as Marie had three years before. My precious daughter Antoinette was baptized soon after that on a Sunday night as well as I and many others who had also joined on that Sunday.

Some members of the church there at Meadows of Dan had been feuding and had one another in court over land deals. When I walked the aisle they too came to the altar crying and hugging and asking forgiveness of one another. They said they had been praying for me so long and when I finally did come they thought the end of time must be near and they had better get themselves straightened out. What a rejoicing there was at church. There were fifteen that joined that day. I must have been holding them back.

As time passed my relations with my parents healed and Mother seemed happier than she had been for a long time. Neither she nor Dad was well and neither were Marie's parents. There was never a week to pass that I did not take one of them to a doctor. Marie and I never had much time for each other what with taking care of the kids, parents and the farm work.

We installed a private phone line between Marie's parents and our home so they could talk any time of day or night without someone listening in.

I finished up the downstairs rooms, which we needed, with our four children. We really needed a bathroom badly so I put the fixtures in and installed a hot water heater. I dug a septic tank and the ditches leading to it by hand as well as all the ditches coming from it into the field. I don't know if anyone else did that or not. I had to save money somewhere.

H.L. Webb brought his cement mixer out and helped me frame and pour the concrete septic tank. At last we had a bathroom! How much the children did appreciate it and us too after coming in from the barn.

Chapter Twenty-One

We wanted and needed a new car, however the milk company was requiring a bulk tank to hold and cool milk and would no longer pick up milk in the cans. So we had to buy a tank that was the price that a new car would have cost. Marie said we had a new car it just didn't have wheels on it.

We were producing more milk now but needed to produce more to fill this big tank. I needed farm machinery. I was wearing myself out farming with horses while everyone else had tractors and equipment.

In February of 1958 a tragedy struck. My Mother had a fatal heart attack. I had just finished milking on a Sunday evening and I was washing the milkers when she came by the milking parlor to get a gallon of milk. We were talking and I was telling her about the good church service I had attended that morning and she was telling me how much she had enjoyed the services at her church. All of a sudden she said something bad is wrong and I caught her as she began to fall. I carried her in my arms to the house and called Doctor Cox after laying her on the bed. The good doctor came and she regained consciousness by that time. He said she had a serious heart attack and he doubted if she would make it to the hospital.

He gave her medication and I carried her to the car and drove her to Mount Airy to the hospital. She was saying, "Don't drive so fast."

She lived until Wednesday morning. I had come home to milk when Mr. Sam Terry came by to tell me she had passed on. This was a hard blow to me and my Dad. He moved in our house with us and never did live in his house anymore. The little children were a great comfort to him and they really loved their Grandpa. It was hard to see the old house empty that I had loved so much.

John Bowman's wife Lola died at the same time hurricane Hazel came through. She had suffered for a while with cancer. John decided to sell out soon after that and I bought the forty-five acres with all the savings I had and we still weren't able to buy a car or tractor. The place was growing up with briars and scrub pines. Some of it was so poor it only had moss and broomsage on it. I had a lot of work cleaning it up, liming and fertilizing it and then getting some fences on it so we could graze it. All of this took time to get it where it would produce anything. Dad helped me all he could in cleaning it up.

After Mother's death I had not felt well and had stomach cramps with dysentery much of the time. After going to Dr. Martin several times he decided I might have cancer and sent me to Roanoke Memorial Hospital. I drove over there and parked my old pickup in the parking lot.

Marie went with me and stayed in a boarding house nearby. She did not have a driving permit at that time. I was put in a ward with nine other patients in the old section of Roanoke Memorial Hospital. I underwent a number of tests and was there for a week. They finally decided I had colitis and put me on a strict diet and medication. It was a relief to walk out and get in my old pickup with Marie and knowing I did not have cancer. After a few weeks I felt better and was grateful to God for hearing our prayers.

We could still get to church with the five of us in the pickup cab. Ted was still setting on the stool in the floor and Bonita was in Antoinette's lap and Marie was holding the baby. We could use the car at other times when Dad did not need it and later Dad started driving the pickup wherever he wanted to go. He visited Mother's people and his relatives too.

Duke and Dad had become good friends. How Duke liked to go to bed early with Grandpa at night and he would tell him stories. Also Dad would read Duke's little books to him and at other times they would go walking. Wherever Grandpa was there was Duke. We sold some timber to Sam Terry. I bought a one man chain saw and cut timber. Frank Love helped me some but would not use the saw. Wesley Terry logged it with a tractor and wench. One day in February of 1962 I was cutting trees by myself. I fell and let the chain grab my wrist. My arm was badly cut.

Wesley was going up the steep hillside with a log and I could not make him hear me. When I finally caught up with him at the sawmill and he looked around and saw me, he had to sit down for a minute to recover from the shock of the way I looked. I was covered with blood and the sight of blood made him sick. He got me in his truck and went to the house and let Marie know. She was rocking the baby to sleep after lunch. What a shock for her. Wesley took the baby to her Mother's and Marie helped get me ready to go to the hospital. He drove us to Mount Airy Emergency room. Doctor Lawrence said he would have to take me to the operating room and put me to sleep. I said, "Why not sew me up right here. I've got to get back and milk."

He said, "O.K., if you say so." He went right to work numbing it and working in my arm. All the tendons in my wrist were cut except the ones to my forefinger and thumb. It took him a little over an hour to attach all the nerves and tendons back and then he said he was glad he had not put me to sleep. He wanted to see if they worked and if he had crossed anything up before he closed the gash. They worked, and he put my arm in a cast like it was a broken arm. I got down off the table went home and helped milk that night. After a few weeks the cast was taken off and my fingers worked fine. I never missed a day of milking the cows and doing other work. I finished cutting the timber that spring before putting out the crops.

Our family will be forever grateful to Dr. Lawrence who was always there at our most stressful times. He was a fine Christian man. Like the time he did surgery on Marie after her miscarriage. He told her he had to stop and pray for her before he could stop the bleeding.

I had the measles in March before Duke was born in April and we called Doctor Martin. I had not been exposed to them in school or in the air force and had not taken them. This time I did not know where I got them. At the age of thirty-six the measles really hurt me. I was seriously ill for a period and almost out of it. In fact for about three hours I could barely whisper and Marie said I turned dark purple. We told the doctor later about this and he said that I had broken out inside my lungs. Marie faithfully waited on me and worried with the baby only a month away. Again with God's help we came through this. Another valley and we're forever grateful. All the children had shots and did not have to have the measles.

We attended church twice on Sundays and on Wednesday night and we really enjoyed training union on Sunday nights. We put on a training union program at our church and other churches in the association. Marie had a big part in the program. A young minister was attending our church and he wanted me to introduce him to my sister. He was shocked when he learned it was my wife.

Sometimes strangers thought she was my daughter and could not believe she had four children. Once we were having the Blue Ridge Association Meeting at our church and I was helping park the cars. Marie and our four children went on in and sat down with our four children. A man that she did not know came in with his four children about the same ages as ours and sat in the same pew with Marie. She overheard one lady in the pew behind her say. "Did you ever see such a sight?" She thought they were one family.

That day we carried our car trunk loaded with food and every one at our church did the same. After lunch that day 0 was really disgusted when I helped clean up the garbage. There was so much food wasted and not eaten, just thrown into the garbage. Many people had overloaded their plates and not eaten it. We taught our children to take out only what they thought they would and not to waste food.

Lee Telephone Company began a new line into our area and finally we had a dial telephone and could call anywhere in the country and had very good service. However we were on a ten party line and that was not good. You could not get the phone and someone was always listening in or answering your ring before you could get to it. Even so it was an improvement and it continued to improve as time went by.

By now we had three in school and all were enjoying it and doing well.

Dad seemed to enjoy living here in our home and enjoyed visiting his and mother's relatives. His problem with emphysema seemed to get a little worse each year and he had to visit the Doctor often and take a lot of medicine.

We raised collie puppies and the children really loved all the farm animals. They loved playing with the puppies until we sold them. Duke especially loved his collie and with the other children gone to school he spent many hours with his dog Jack. One day Marie was looking for him and stood on the lawn calling for him. She could see the tall grass moving in the hayfield and as she watched she knew it was Duke and his two dogs. She knew they would take good care of him. When his mother had to spank him he went outside and lay down, Jack would come and lie beside him and put his paws over him. Dog is indeed man's best friend.

Ted had missed his Grandma so much; he was five years old when she died. He had gone to see her often and she had played games with him. He would eat an early breakfast with us and hurry down there. His Grandmother would ask, "Have you had breakfast, Teddy?"

He would say "Not much" and eat again. Grandma's cooking was always better.

The children would ask why she didn't cook like Grandma. She would tell them that someday when she became a grandma she would. And sure enough she did.

By now Duke had taken Ted's place with Grandpa and he felt jealous, and he picked on Duke. He really enjoyed jumping out from behind a door and scaring him, especially in the dark.

Mr. Asa was not well and much of Marie's time was spent going up there to help her Mother. She went once or twice a day to carry wood and water and do many other things. I rented Mr. Asa's land and limed it and gave Mr. Asa half of what was produced. I plowed the garden for Marie's Mother for she really enjoyed her garden. She also continued to milk a cow and kept chickens.

Finally! I bought a second hand tractor, a plow, a disc and a mowing machine to use with it. I didn't have a baler or rake and continued to put the hay up loose. I bought an old two-row corn planter but still cultivated with a horse for another year or two until I could catch up on my bills. We bought some cheap furniture for the house and a large freezer.

Now with the tractor I could do more work but it cost more money and I came out about the same, however it was easier than following the horses. The girls and Ted were now old enough to hoe in the garden and pick beans. They also helped dad hoe corn a few years before I began to spray it.

They also each had a calf they were responsible for and had to feed it. This calf would be sold in the fall and they would use the money for school supplies or clothes.

I built a second silo and Gene Barnard helped me fill my silos in the fall. I bought a fifty-foot elevator to fill the upright silos. I helped Gene fill his trench silos in return for his work. We also filled Ed Love's silos.

I bought a power take off manure spreader and it doubled as a silage wagon. I put a high bed on it and it could unload the ensilage into the elevator cute or in the trench.

Marie was canning for the family while I was canning for the cows. She put up hundreds of cans of beans, pickles, peaches, applesauce, tomatoes and berries as well as freezing lots of sweet corn. All this she did between milking the cows morning and night. In addition to this she made clothes for herself and the children, including shirts and pants for the boys.

The children enjoyed going to the store with me. I would get them a treat of a drink and candy. This was a rare treat for them, because we all drank the good cold milk we produced at home for meals.

Finally I bought a new pickup that dad enjoyed driving. We used the car to go to church now and used the pickup to haul feed and other things in.

We always observed our wedding anniversary on the twelfth of July. We made this a special day for our children. We would get up quiet early and get the milking done and pack a picnic breakfast and sometimes a lunch and take them someplace special. Sometimes it would be one of the parks like Pilot Mountain, Luray Caverns, Hanging Rock Park, Hungry Mother Park, White Top Park or maybe to the movies or Blowing Rock or Tweetsie. We wanted them to know they were special and that they were a real blessing in out marriage. They really did enjoy this.

We do regret not taking our children on a real vacation and I hope they will learn to take more time to play with their own families. The main reason we did not go more was because of the health of our parents. We could have gotten someone to milk for a few days but not to take care of our four parents. Today when our children go on their vacations we are thrilled for them.

In the spring the children always started asking, "When is our anniversary?" It was precious to them, too. Many times we had a baby in the bassinet that we sat on the table while we ate. One time we went to visit Old Salem, In Winston-Salem, and took the children to eat lunch in a cafeteria. Marie had nursed Duke just before going in so he wouldn't have to eat while we were in there, however he saw us eating and he thought it was his turn again. We were seated near the long line of people entering the cafeteria.

Marie had a blanket over his head while he was nursing. He did not like this and would pull the blanket away to see what was going on. The other children were embarrassed by little brothers actions. People coming through the line would stare and look shocked. Well that baby was hungry and that was his bottle.

Marie was beautiful and always attracted attention under ordinary circumstances. She was also full of energy and fun and could always keep me in line. One evening as we went to milk I had been complaining and was in a bad mood. She warned me to straighten up and get in a better mood. As I entered the barn I kicked the cat that happened to cross my path all the way across the barn. And I loved cats, too. Well that was a mistake. A moment later I was in the feed room opening bags of feed. Suddenly Marie was behind me, slamming me over on to the big sack of feed bags, jerked my suspenders loose and wore my bottom out. Ouch!

This was between looking after the milers on the cows, about two minutes time I figured. By the time I finally got dresses and all back together she was out there attentively watching the milkers as if nothing unusual happened. I didn't kick any cats that she knew about for a long time. She caused me to be careful in what I said or did knowing what she could do, any time or anywhere.

I continued to be active in the Ruritan Club and we were active members of the P.T.A. at school. I was chairman of the P.T.A. I was beginning to realize I could get active in too many organizations so I dropped out of the Ruritans and became less active in the P.T.A. I loved the church and all that was going on there and wanted to be a full part of that.

Our beloved preacher Rev. Deitz and his family were leaving and we sure hated to see them go. They had been a great influence in our life and we loved them very much. I had been asked to serve on the pulpit committee to look for a new minister. I knew this would be a great responsibility.

The winter of 1960 would be one we would never forget. January had been a very rainy month. We said if this had been snow we would have had a lot. The mud and fog were really something as we tried to take care of the milking. Then February came. On the twelfth we had twenty-four inches of snow and then a week later we had twenty-four more inches. We had to shovel a path for the cows to enter the barn to be milked and then shovel a path for them to leave. The wind blew and blew straight out of the north and the snow drifted. It kept on, every day until the end of March. The roads were blocked and there was no school for a month. All the fences were buried under the snow. The clothesline was buried three feet under a drift.

There was one place in nearby Vesta where the power lone was buried. As soon as the state opened the roads the wind blew and the snow came and they were buried again. Finally nothing could get through but a bulldozer and even they would get hung up. I worked with the front-end blade with the tractor and the state finally got our road open so the milk truck could get in. However the roads were completely blocked for days at a time. We had to milk the cows and feed them, shoveling the snow out of the barn doors and out of the lane each morning. Now the milk tank was level full with milk and no way for the truck to get in. We opened the valve and let it—hundred gallons of it go down the drain. Ouch! We did skim some of the thick cream off and Marie churned it and made lots of butter to go in the freezer. But before the truck could come back we would have to dump another tank.

We were thankful we stayed well through this bad weather and no one needed a doctor. There were helicopters that flew over and dropped food to places where they saw no paths. We called our neighbors to come and get some milk. One day little children carried milk all day in deep snow, some of our neighbors had run low on firewood and when they tried to cut a tree it fell and buried in the snow and they couldn't find it to cut it up.

When the roads opened a little Opal and Bill came and brought us a big bag of groceries, fruit celery, lettuce, tomatoes and many things they knew we loved and hadn't been able to get out and get. What a welcome sight to see visitors in this frozen land.

Chapter Twenty-Two

Working on the farm was a family affair, all working together. Before Antoinette went to college she helped with the milking as did Marie, Bonita and Ted, so when I had to work late they did the milking. We raised many calves on the bucket or bottle and we sold the calves for veal. The children worked faithfully doing the farm chores and they saved their money for school clothes and other things they needed. It was hard to have money enough to cover everything. Sometimes Marie searched under couch cushions for lunch money and somehow just before the bus came she would find some.

Now it was Bonita's turn to talk about going to college and trying to decide where. There never was a question of if but where and faith that we would help her although Antoinette was still in college. Ted knew he was going to college and had his eye on Virginia Tech. We knew we would have to sacrifice and were glad to do so since we did not have the privilege of going. We thanked the Lord for good health and knew that with His help we would make it.

It was on rainy days that we went to town to buy supplies for the farm and to buy groceries for ourselves and our parents. When we had a dry spell and were so busy on the farm we really got behind in our shopping.

Mr. Asa, Marie's stepfather became very sick and was sick at home a few days and then we took him to the doctor. He had a bad case of shingles and we had to take him to the doctor many times. This time something else was wrong and Marie insisted he go to the hospital. I took him in the car with his son's Levi and Dorsey's help. Marie brought her Mother home with her. Mr. Asa has a cerebral hemorrhage and lived only a short while. Marie's Mother would live with us the rest of her life. The children loved Grandma Ada and she spent many happy hours talking with them.

Grandma Ada loved to work in a garden so I plowed up her one behind our house and she enjoyed growing things in her garden. She loved to share her good things with others. I can still see the beautiful banana cantaloupes that we all enjoyed eating all summer.

Now the old blue Chevrolet had seen many miles and it was time to shop again. I bought a midnight blue Plymouth Fury. It was the best car I ever owned. We had it setting in the driveway when Ted came home from school. He was sixteen and had just gotten his drivers license. He was thrilled to see the new car, however he was surprised to see the old one still here and asked why we didn't trade it in on the new one. I didn't say a word and he looked at me for a moment and finally said, "My car?"

He threw his books down and ran out to look at his "New car." He stood and rubbed it all over and kept saying "My car!" It had over a hundred thousand miles on it.

I knew Ted was capable of having his own car and since he was involved with lots of sports and school activities he needed transportation. When he came back in the house I handed him the keys. He will never be as proud of a Cadillac, if he ever has one.

Bonita graduated from High School with high honors and decided to enter college at Richmond where Antoinette was. Bonita loved the farm and farm animals so much and we were really going to miss her.

In the fall of 1967 we were off with our second daughter to college in Richmond. We really had the car packed with both the girls and all their precious possessions.

When we left Bonita there to return home she looked so sad I wanted to tell her to get back in the car and we would take her back with us. Bill who was seven years old had gone with us also. He lay down in the back seat with his pillow over his head and cried all the way home. He told us later that he felt like we had taken his mama off and left her far away. She had really been a Mama to him and he her baby doll. Marie was in the front seat with me and she cried the first hundred miles. I told her the next time she could drive and I would cry.

Bonita made good grades in high school and was surprised to find college was different. She soon settled down and did well. We did have to give Antoinette credit for helping her settle in. They had a portable sewing machine that was quiet heavy but they shared it and carried eight blocks when the other one needed it.

Now our responsibilities seemed to increase. With two in college and my Dad and Marie's mother to look after. We were having a hard time keeping up with the bills. We received a letter from Antoinette asking permission for her to sell her blood to help pay her bills. We borrowed some money from grandpa and sent it to her. Marie started putting in applications for work, anywhere. A job at Mount Airy came up at Quality mills and she went to work. Now we were working harder than ever but we paid our bills and paid Dad back.

Marie would leave before daylight and I would be milking by myself and hurry back to the house to get the boys on the bus and check on Dad and Mother. Then I would hurry out to the fields and hurry back and fix lunch and rush back to the fields. The boys were big enough and they certainly did their part down at the barn. They couldn't do much in the morning because the bus came along so early. Marie cooked for supper enough for next day's lunch and did the laundry. In the summer I made the garden and harvested it. Dad and Ada would break beans and etc. Marie would can or freeze them before she went to bed.

Sometimes it would be after midnight. We got a few hours sleep and we were blessed our health was good so we survived.

We still found time to attend most all meetings at the church. One week Marie was working ten hours a day and we were in a revival at church. She would come in, wash her face, and I would have the milking done and we would go out the door to church. Many nights our supper was at eleven o'clock, but being in our church was worth it.

Marie's mother had a heart attack and was in the hospital at Mount Airy in intensive care. It was difficult for Mother Ada to be in a strange place so Marie and Opal stayed with her in the hospital day and night. Mostly Marie for Opal still had small children she couldn't leave. She was there on Christmas Eve and a big snowstorm came on that night. Opal went and stayed with her on Christmas Day.

When she finally got back here she said the years spent in our home were the happiest she ever had in her life. She had a warm house and all the comforts she needed. No power bills to pay or groceries to buy and surrounded by loving grandchildren. We also took her wherever and whenever she wanted to go someplace. She loved to do handwork and make pretty pillows and Afghans that she gave to her grandchildren. Her favorite pass time was reading her Bible or the children's bible storybooks. She had a big family bible from which she often read.

She loved flowers and had them planted all around the house. One day I came home for lunch and was mowing the yard and was clipping the weeds that had grown up around the edges and accidently got two of her flowers. I was sorry about that.

Antoinette graduated from college in the spring of 1968 and took a job in Richmond. Soon she met a young man she would later marry. She soon brought him home and we were nervous wondering what this city boy would be like and I guess he wondered what these strange mountain folks would be like. He, too, had graduated from V.C.U.

When they drove up the boys were looking out the window and like in "The Waltons" they yelled, "Here they are!"

There was a mad scramble in the house, I had rushed into our bedroom to change my smelly barn clothes, and just as I did Mother Ada shoved past me to look out the window, not even noticing that I was there. She wanted to see this fellow her precious grand daughter was bringing home. I quickly dressed and she had not noticed that I was wearing my birthday suit and without a tie.

Antoinette's friend, Harry Mustard was well liked by the family and I am sure he found the sense of humor of the Turmans trying at times.

The evening meal was going as well as could be expected with all the family trying to put forth their very best manners for company, until Duke, at the age of thirteen decided that Harry was getting a little too much attention. He had a way of pointing at anything at this age and it would move. This time it happened to be his glass of ice tea that suddenly jumped off the table and into his Dad's lap. Well this broke the ice, so as to speak, after I recovered from the cold tea. We all loosened up and had a few good laughs at my expense.

They continued to see each other and set the wedding date for November 15, 1969. Harry, being the well brought up Southern gentleman that he was, asked for my daughter's hand in marriage. I told him they were both old enough to know what they were doing and gave them both my blessings.

The day before the wedding I had to go to the bus station in Danville and pick up Bonita while Marie and the boys did the milking of the dairy herd. The weather had turned very cold and I knew Marie needed a new coat, so I stopped in J.C Penney's to see if I could find something in five minutes. I prayed as I entered the store, Lord help me. I looked in the display window as I passed and saw a very beautiful blue coat with a fur collar, which was in style at this time. In my hurry I asked, "Lord please let that be her size".

I asked the clerk and she said it was the size I needed. I said, "I'll take it and do you happen to have a warm suit to go with it?"

She found a pretty light blue three piece knit suit and I was out of there in less than ten minutes, hoping Marie would be pleased. She loved it and it was a perfect fit.

Lowell Willis performed the ceremony at Meadows of Dan Church. The reception was at the community building. Seeing our daughter get married and giving her away was both a sad and happy occasion. I was also remembering our own happy wedding twenty- three years before.

Harry was employed in Atlanta, Georgia, and they would be going there to live. It was hard to give up Antoinette and wave good-bye as they drove away in his little light blue Triumph sports car. I knew I would not be seeing her as often since they would be living in Atlanta.

At this time Mike Wood, Rick Hall, Garry Smith and Duke were getting together and forming a Rock music band. We did not care for rock music. They would practice upstairs in the boys' room and we could appreciate it if we were down the hill behind the barn.

Lowell Willis our beloved pastor and his wife Phyllis were planning to leave the church. He was planning to return to seminary in Texas and we would be without a pastor for a while.

I hated to see them leave for they had done so much for the church. Again I was on the pulpit committee. I met Dr. Court Flint who was living at Ground

Hog Mountain with his wife Ilene. We became good friends. He preached at our church, filling in while we were without a pastor. The church liked him so well he continued to be asked to be out temporary pastor. The church finally voted him as pastor without the pulpit committee taking any action. He did a great work especially with the young people and built up the church membership. He had a great outreach ministry to other churches. Great crowds were coming every Sunday from long distances and the church was packed. Every Sunday people were being saved and most Sundays there were baptizings. People came regularly from Blacksburg, Chatham, Martinsville, Eden, Winston-Salem, Reidsville and many other places. Our youth went and held revivals in other Churches. The church was growing by leaps and bounds and Burl Eastridge was putting a large addition on the front and doing a great job.

Dr. Flint was a gifted speaker and teacher as well as being good with young people. He was good at visiting and teaching members how to visit. He was also a gifted writer and had written several books. I wondered how he found time to do so much. He often visited Dad and Mother Ada. They appreciated it very much. He gave them much time and attention and seemed to have time to listen to them.

Marie had worked at Quality Mills for two and one half years and now she felt it was time to quit and take care of Dad and her Mother. She did visit for the church with other ladies and sometimes with Dr. Flint in the hospitals. Marie was always doing good for those in need. She could go when I was around and could be in and out of the house to check on our parents.

We cut wood for those not able to get their own wood and were always giving away garden vegetables and canned or frozen food to those in need. We received a great blessing from this and I really felt a greater blessing in this than I did on the money I gave on the building fund and the many projects beautifying the church.

I always tried to decide what would Jesus do about this and found the answer from reading my Bible. Jesus spoke much about taking care of the widow and the needy and spent much time teaching about the kingdom of God. He never did encourage building beautiful buildings or churches. People built high towers and put their name on them to be seen of men and get the praise of men. It is not always to the praise of the Lord.

Ted, Duke and I put up a lot of hay in those years during the summer months. Our own hay and that of several of the surrounding neighbors. It was hard hot work but we enjoyed it most of the time, and we had a lot of fun while we were working.

Sometimes we would work until late at night putting the baled hay into barns. Duke said he was glad his Daddy did not work on Sunday and was a

Christian. We quit on Saturday night about eleven o'clock.

At this time the gospel group "The Joyful Noise" came into being. Duke was a part of this group. They traveled far and near playing and singing praises to the Lord. They were such a blessing to us and received many blessings in this work.

Ted was in the last graduating class at Meadows of Dan in 1970. I had graduated in the first graduating class in 1940. After this the school became an elementary school and the high school moved to Stuart.

I had worked hard and faithfully to prevent the county from consolidating the schools in Patrick. I said at that time at one of the many meetings, "Bussing will be expensive, gas will soon cost a dollar a gallon." Everyone really laughed at my remark since at that time it cost thirty-two cents a gallon. In a few short years it did cost over a dollar a gallon. I still do not think it has been an improvement. We have the big building and the children spend much time being bussed to and from school. County citizens are being taxed to death and the quality of education is going down every day. Where is the improvement?

Chapter Twenty-Three

Things on our road had changed. We were now the only houses on our road #779. Mother Ada lived with us after Mr. Asa's death and his children had inherited his property. The Quesinberrys, Gerda and Macie had moved to Blacksburg after Garcie's death. John Bowman moved away after his wife's death and I bought his property. The Dave Scott family had all moved out after the parents died and I rented their land. We were the only ones on our road and that was all right. We liked it that way.

I loved my family and my church and I loved people and being with people, but I also liked being alone at times.

Bill liked school and did well. He had some trouble with his homework. He liked to do his own thing rather than do what was assigned to him. Before he was of school age he disappeared one evening just before dark and we could not find him. We were looking everywhere for him and calling his name, no answer. Just at dark we found him. He was in the building with his pet calf and had lay down beside it and gone to sleep wearing his grandpa's big gloves.

Another time he hid in the big cornfield and his Mother could hear him. She ran and ran through the corn, listening awhile and running awhile until she caught up with him. By this time she was itching something awful with the corn pollen.

This was almost as bad as the time Antoinette got lost in the big field of kudzu grass. It was very tall and looked like corn. We raised it so when the weather was dry we could turn the cows in it to eat. One evening she and Bonita went to get the cows out and Bonita had them up in the barn and Antoinette had gotten lost and couldn't find her way out. It was so tall she couldn't see the house.

On the day Marie's Mother died, Bill fell at school and hit his head. The Doctor told us to wake him up every hour that night. Well, that night Marie told the girls to go to sleep and she would look after him, they said they would. The next morning they found that at different times all during the night they had all gotten up and walked him through the house never realizing the others were doing the same thing. Bill thought they were doing what they were supposed to do.

Ted made plans to go to V.P.I, and he had been working for the Blue Ridge Parkway at Rocky Knob service station. The girls had worked at Mabry Mill. Ted would be entering college and Duke would be entering high school. We made arrangements for Duke to go to Carroll County High School. It was seven miles nearer than the new consolidated school at Stuart and he did not have to go up and down the mountain. He did not like it at first but soon got to liking fine.

In fact the principal sent us word that if we had six more like Duke to send them on. Bill continued to go to Meadows of Dan through the seventh grade.

In September we took Ted to V.P.I, and were glad it was not so far away. Ronnie Wood would be his roommate. They were certainly well acquainted since they had started in the first grade together. After a few weeks he wrote us he had developed Dunlap's disease. On the college food his belly had dun lapped over his belt. Like the girls, when he had gotten settled in, he took part in the Campus Crusade For Christ. He had the joy of seeing many souls won to the Lord.

One day, February 15, 1971 Mother Ada was standing on the porch playing with the collie dogs and she started to fall. I carried her to the living room couch and then to her room and lay her on her bed. Suddenly she was gone. Marie rushed to the phone to call Dr. Flint, our pastor. When she went back to tell her she said, "Ah yes he's the doctor that I need now." Then she closed her eyes so peacefully never to open them again in this life. On the day before, Sunday she had called Ted into her room and talked with him and told him how to live. She ended up by telling him she loved him. Later he said he knew she was telling him Good-by, she had loved him very much. Her bible was open to John chapter 14, "In my Father's house are many mansions." What a comfort this was to us later.

She was buried at Bell Spur between her sisters Ruth and Rosalie as she had instructed us to do. We had always honored her request and this was the last one. She'd had a hard life having lost her husband when her daughters were just babies and having to raise them by herself. She had waited on her parents in her younger years and had not married until she was forty years old. Then she had cared for her second husband in his last days. Her life had been one of waiting on others.

I was glad she could spend her last six years with Marie and I in our comfortable home. I was glad I could do something for her, after all, she had cared for and raised the daughter that was to be my lovely wife. We erected the simple monument she had always requested.

Now it was Marie and I and Dad and the two boys who were left at home. We were still active in church and Marie spent much of her time visiting for the church. She worked in the nursery and enjoyed working with the little ones.

Dad continued to visit his relatives and Mother's relatives and always enjoyed his fellowship with them. I took him to his church when he did not feel like driving or when he attended a distant church. That meant that Marie and I were going separate ways sometimes. We never could be together enough, and our love grew deeper as the years passed. We had very few arguments.

We now had three in college at one time after Ted went to V.P.I. Bonita was making top grades in school and was working at Arby's to help pay her expenses. Ted could have his car at school the second year and that helped so we didn't have to go get him when he could come home on the weekends. He was driving a second hand Chevrolet that we bought for him but it was a lemon.

In the spring of 1971 Bonita graduated from V.C.U. Marie and I and Opal went to her graduation. Bonita made many friends while in school, some she would keep in touch with over the years.

That summer I traded Ted's old Chevrolet in for a Plymouth Fury and gave Ted the 1967 Fury. This car was the best car and Ted would drive it for years. I bought Bonita a 1971 Valiant on the same day. She would make the payments and I had done the transaction for her.

She came home from Richmond and saw these new cars in the driveway and thought we had company. She was surprised to learn one of the cars was hers.

She had accepted a teaching position at Martinsville and would have to learn to drive her new car in ten days before school started. Marie rode with her in the daytime and I rode with her at night. She took her driving test and passed. Now at twenty-one she was joining the working force. So off to Martinsville she went to drive in the early morning work traffic.

After teaching one year she decided she did not want to teach school for the rest of her life.

Ted was taking political science at V.P.I, and getting into his second year he decided he could not go into law. He was working closely with the Campus Crusade and had received his call to the ministry. He came home one weekend and we rejoiced with him.

It was at this time that Duke and his rock group decided to join Bill Banks and become a gospel group. Our prayers were answered when we saw the Lord changing Rock to Gospel. Bill Banks had the greatest voice and with him as a leader Duke, Mike and Garry began playing in churches and would travel to many revivals with Dr. Flint preaching. Many souls were saved. They traveled through this area and North Carolina and made many friends. The Joyful Noise made a tour of Florida the year Duke was seventeen and they played and sang in many churches and sold lots of their albums.

Duke had a special friend in Carroll County, Kylene Barker that traveled with the group some when they were in revivals. She too, was saved one night in a revival in Martinsville. They were good friends through high school and later she went on to achieve fame as Miss America of 1979. The "Joyful Noise" group still exist but Duke lives too far away to play with them.

It seems my mouth opened at church and always said "I'll be glad to," and first thing I knew I was chairman of the board of deacons and Sunday School Superintendent at the same time. I was still farming too!

One night I rushed in from the barn trying to dress and attend another meeting, Marie was laying out my clothes and helping me --- I thought. I complained of being so tired (Man should never complain). Well my wife with so much compassion in her heart said. "Just go to bed and rest."

"No, I have a job to do and I'll do it."

As she went past our dresser she saw the key to our room and that sudden impulse hit her. She picked up the key and locked me in. No, I did not scream or say a word, but I wasn't to be outdone by a locked door, either. Since my Mother had taught me to be prepared for emergencies I looked in the dresser drawer and pulled out a screwdriver and went to work on the door hinges. It took no time at all to have that door off the hinges and set in the living room. As I came out I asked the kids, "Where is that Mama?"

"Daddy, she's in the den helping Bill with his homework." It had been a hot day and she was comfortably wearing her shorts and halter, with her feet bare.

I picked her up and carried her on my shoulder to the car, and said, "You're going with me to church and sit on the front seat and tell them why I am late."

"Oh Honey, don't make me do that." All the way to the highway she was pleading, "Please let me out." I did at the end of the road and she had to walk all the way back to the house bare footed. (She did not try this any more.)

Duke played football in Carroll County High School and broke his foot and had to wear a cast for weeks. It was in the cold wintertime, so Marie made him a large sock from a red towel to wear over the cast. We attended a few games, but were not football fans. We did not get to go to the basketball games much either or take part in the school activities as we had at Meadows of Dan.

When the High School left Meadows of Dan it took the very heart from the community. Later in life when the schools were consolidated I could see that too much money and time is spent on sports and outside activities. Our first three children that graduated from Meadows of Dan had a much easier time in college than the two that graduated from Carroll County.

Through the years I had kept in touch with only a few of my old air Force buddies. Gene Lalamand and his family came to see us and spent a week one summer. His doctors had told him that he did not have long to live and he wanted to see me again.

We enjoyed his family and him very much. They came after Marie had become a Christian and before I was baptized. He urged me to accept Jesus as my savior as he had long ago. It was his influence and encouragement that helped me to make my profession of faith soon afterwards. We had hoped to visit them in Nashville. The doctors were right, soon after he left here he went to meet his maker when he had a fatal heart attack.

Marie and I took Bill with us to see Harry and Antoinette in Atlanta. It was early in the spring and everything was beautiful down that way when it was still wintertime up here in the mountains. We put Bill in the car asleep and he did not wake up until we were in South Carolina.

This was our first trip to Atlanta since we were married. Antoinette and Harry lived in mid-Atlanta and after we had driven so far through the city, Marie told me I was lost. She was reading the map. I had studied the map thoroughly before we left home and I knew where I was. She still insisted we were really lost. I told her I felt I was right since I saw Harry standing in the back yard with his yellow Gremlin automobile. She said it was nice to be married to someone who is always right.

We enjoyed our visit for a few days and we saw many places of interest in Atlanta. This is the first time we had seen real hippies. As we drove through Hippie Town we were shocked at what we saw. This was the beginning of the hippie movement.

We did not know at that time just how many would come marching through our doors later. We also visited Warm Springs and Calloway Gardens and enjoyed the many beautiful flowers.

On a second trip I found Ike Croft's telephone number in the book and decided to phone him. I knew he was living in Atlanta since we had corresponded with each other some since we were in the Air Force. His wife answered the phone and I was shocked to find he had passed away with a heart attack a few weeks before.

Harry and Antoinette, as social workers, were required to attend a black church along with another couple. Marie and I went with them to the Wheat Street Church in the middle of Atlanta. It was a huge church with over two hundred in the choir. We sat down near the back so we could make a quick exit, just in case we had to do so. The ushers were very gracious and moved us up front, right under the preacher. We were the only white people there and at first felt very small, but we were treated like royalty. The preacher and service were great and we felt a complete spirit of unity. One Spirit, One God, and his great love over us all. It was a great experience.

Antoinette was one of seven students at Atlanta University and took classes in addition to work and received her master's degree. I asked her if she didn't feel small being white in a predominant black college. She replied, "Dad, I don't see color."

This daughter of ours had great compassion for all people and did much for others.

On one of our trips to Atlanta we went back to Moultrie, Georgia, where I had been in the Air Force and saw our former landlady. We also visited David Monk and went out to Spence Field. It was almost unrecognizable. It was not an Air Force base anymore, and was really run down. But we did enjoy the trip and the fond memories.

Once I attended a Dairyman's Convention when Jimmy Carter was governor of Georgia and he spoke at the convention. We stayed at the Regency Hyatt Hotel one night and dined in the revolving restaurant on top of it. There they really had a good view of Atlanta.

Marie attended one Dairyman's Convention in Louisville Kentucky. She flew from Bristol to Louisville. It was her first flight and she loved it. Another year we both flew to Louisville and Ted, who was in school in V.P.I, and in the middle of exams, managed to come home between classes and did the milking so we could go. We really did appreciate this very much as we seldom ever got to go anywhere together with the responsibility for our parents and the milking. One of us almost always had to stay home.

The very first time Marie and I saw hippies was in Richmond when we took the girls to college.

We saw what we thought was a lady pushing a baby carriage down the sidewalk and we were admiring her beautiful long hair, which she had tied with a pretty ribbon. Then as we passed we noticed that the lady had a full beard and a mustache. Later we saw them in Atlanta and then of all places, Meadows of Dan! Some of the hippie crowd attended church and finally were in our home as guest, then overnight, then for a week, and then all summer!

We had one Catholic Brother who stayed all summer and always attended the church and was faithful in going to revivals with the "Joyful Noise" when they went to other churches. I was able to get some work out of them on the farm. Marie did the laundry and cooked them good meals and spent many hours listening to their problems. A Christian friend of Marie's asked her one day, "How can you have this mess in your home and not get hurt?" This shocked Marie but she recovered to answer, "Love, just love covers it all."

What a revival took place in our church and many of them were saved and are living in different areas of the country and are living for the Lord. There were many homes besides ours that were open to this group of fine young people who were seeking something. We knew God was sending them here to be fed His word. We felt responsible.

Some of the girls wore mini skirts, skirts so short that on a cold day they could freeze everything.

I wondered what my Mother would have said to see women wearing skirts up to their hips. She thought up to the knees were scandalous. Sometimes you could not tell if they were wearing a dress or just a blouse. Yet worse some of them really needed a bath, you could tell before they got very close. One day Marie said, "I sure am thankful our sons cut their hair properly and don't look like such slobs." She learned her lessons, not to thank God for what you don't have because in no time we had three bushy headed sons. They did take baths though.

Ted said in V.P.I, they would stand in front of barber shoos and make fun of the barbers. His hair was so curly and some of the guys were asking how he got it so curly. They were rolling theirs wet, on socks at night to make it curl like his. He told them God curled his before he was born.

One store manager in Mount Airy told of the young lady who was grocery shopping with a small son. The little boy got lost from his mother and came up to the store manager the third time looking for his mother. He told him, "Son, why don't you hold on to your Mother's skirt." He said he couldn't reach it.

Marie gave much time to the church in visiting and witnessing and I did all I could, giving of time and money.

When Duke turned sixteen we went to Galax and bought him a Grasshopper Green Gremlin, brand new. He said it was the same color as his girlfriend's eyes.

Well, he was proud as well as mature enough and responsible enough. He was traveling with the "Joyful Noise" and they were a blessing to the Lord.

Marie continued to look so young and so pretty. When we went to buy Bonita some luggage for college the clerk asked me which of my daughters was going to college, meaning Marie or Bonita. One night Marie carried a beautiful bouquet of Dahlias to church. Of course we were late, having to milk the cows and the church was full when she arrived. She went right up to the front and set them on the table and as she did the zipper broke in her pretty black dress and her back was bare. She gracefully made a hasty retreat and sat quietly in the back pew.

Doctor Flint did a great job for the church and the community. He overextended himself and some did not like him. The good he did far outweighed the mistakes he made. None of us are perfect but I often see those who think they are.

Many things are said about becoming grandparents but no one really expresses how it really is. It gives you a feeling of security knowing there is someone to carry on the family name and traditions. It gives you someone to love at an age when you appreciate more love.

On March 11, 1975 our first grand daughter was born to Antoinette, Amelia

Kathryn Mustard. Harry and Antoinette had moved from Atlanta to Greenville, South Carolina.

They as well as her Grandparents had looked forward with great anticipation to the new baby. She was a perfect and healthy baby. Marie and I did not get to be there for the blessed event. Harry said that was a great experience. Antoinette told him he could have the next experience.

At the age of three weeks Amelia Kathryn was brought to see the family. She was such a pretty, healthy baby and we were so proud of her.

Duke was nearing graduation from Carroll County High School. The girl he dated for three years would one day become Miss America. On the evening of June 7, 1974 Duke graduated from high school and we were late getting home. The next morning Ted was to graduate from Virginia Tech at eight in the morning. This meant getting up at 3 A.M. to milk the cows and to be there at seven so we could get a seat. I said for the others to go and I would stay here and milk. My dear wife said, "No way," and she meant it. She was out of bed with her flashlight and was off to the cow pasture to round up the sleeping herd. Nothing unusual happened and we all were leaving promptly at six o'clock. We made it. We were standing outside the stadium and watching the graduates march out, trying to pick out Ted. We knew there would be no problem and were watching for his curly hair sticking out from under his cap. "There he is," I said pointing, but discovered there were several hundred that had curly hair.

I really figured they rolled it well the night before. This was an all day affair, there were so many to graduate. Duke was not with us as he had gone to the beach with his friends.

I planned to treat the family to a nice lunch and we looked for a nice restaurant, everything was closed but a very crowded hot dog stand. We were all tired and disgusted. We did not get one picture of his graduation. We had used all the film the night before at Dukes graduation. Nothing was open so I could buy some.

The two girls were out of college but would both go back as would Ted and Duke. After Bonita's teaching experience she came home and worked at Mount Airy for a while until she decided what she wanted to do. She decided to get a degree in medical records and went to Lynchburg to college and got her degree there. She graduated second in her class with very high grades. Duke was studying hard at V.P.I, and working in a juvenile detention home to have money for his books. Ted was preparing to go to Louisville to the Baptist Seminary. He was delayed and did not go until January. He stayed home to help me after I had broken my shoulder. I had fallen off the truck helping to load my tractor. I was in the hospital ten days after Dr. Lawrence did surgery on my shoulder. It recovered after physical therapy.

On the last of January Ted went to Louisville to enroll in college and Marie went with him to see where he was and how everything looked. His car was fully packed. Marie returned on the bus.

Now it was just Little Bill, Grandpa, Marie and I left at home. There was no one else living on the road.

Bill did not take part in sports as the other boys had because he said his daddy needed him to help on the farm. When we had hay to get up he would say we can get it up without help and we usually did. We still milked the cows and it was a large task for Marie, Bill and me. When really bad cold rainy weather would come Bill would say to his Mother, "Now you don't have to go out, I'll go in your place."

How his mother appreciated this and would cook him a good dinner.

We were still active in church although we missed our children who were in other places. Marie loved to visit the sick and those who had moved into the area and make them welcome and invite them to church. We gave our time and money and tried to help those in need.

After graduating from Lynchburg College Bonita went to work at the training center at Woodlawn, Virginia keeping records for Southwestern Training Center, she helped some on the farm.

Ted did well in school at the Seminary and he worked part time. He would come home on breaks, which was not very often. We had a time keeping tires on all the cars on the roads. Once when Ted was home we noticed his were down to the fabric so we put tires on his car while he was home.

Bill did well in Carroll County high School and Duke was doing great at Tech. Marie and I were blessed with good health so we could run the farm and keep the bills paid. Dad was sick and required a lot of time and attention. He was in the hospital and doctors office quite often.

Ted decided suddenly to get married to a girl he met at the seminary. It was love at first sight. A June wedding was planned and we were planning to attend.

Harry and Antoinette had moved to Roanoke and we were glad we could visit them on weekends or they could come see us. Amy was such a pretty little girl now and was learning to read and swim.

In a cool June morning Bonita, Marie and I left to drive to Greenville, Mississippi for Ted's wedding. We left Bill with all the responsibility of milking the dairy heard and taking care of Grandpa. I handed him a hundred dollar bill and told him if he needed it to use it. (He returned it to me when I got back). I did give him a love offering for his effort.

At sixteen he was trustworthy and had his own car. We left much in his capable hands.

Harry, Antoinette and Amy left on a different route at the same time. Duke and his girlfriend were riding with them. Amy was a cute girl with a head full of golden curls.

We went through Tennessee by way of Knoxville, Nashville and Memphis. We stayed in northern Mississippi that night and on to Greenville the next day. After leaving home on this cool June morning we arrived to a very hot temperature of 104 degrees. We just got back in the car and turned up the air conditioning. I had forgotten how hot it could be there in the summer time. We had some car trouble and when we got it fixed on Monday we started for home remembering the beautiful wedding. Duke and Lynn were riding back with us in the back seat. He was singing "Carry me back to old Virginia."

We were seeing the Mississippi delta where the cotton and rice fields were abundant with newly planted seeds. The fields were so level and you could see far away, so different from our mountains.

Bill had done his job well, taking care of Grandpa and the cows. How we always hated to leave a family member behind. Ted and his new bride moved to Galax to live a year, but she missed her flat lands and her family so they moved to Mississippi.

Dad's health continued to get worse and then he fell and broke his hip. Just before this Duke came to tell Grandpa he was getting married. He wanted to tell him himself. He and Grandpa were close. This pleased Grandpa and he said, "I'll be at the wedding."

The date was set for May 7, 1978, one year after Ted's and Tricy's wedding. One day Dad started to sit down on the bed and slipped off and broke his hip. We took him to Mount Airy to the hospital where he had surgery. He recovered very slowly and for the first time was mixed up in his mind. They sent him home unable to walk and with pneumonia. We sat by his bed around the clock for several days here at home and then took him to the V.A. Hospital in Salem for Veterans. They did all they could and said they would have to put him on a respirator if he lived and then he would never get off it, and would not even recognize us. I had to make the decision with much prayer and help from the V.A. chaplain and Dr. Flint. I had to make the final decision. I felt neither Dad or the Lord would want him here like that, and I decided not to keep him on the respirator. It was a very heart rending decision for me. He and I had been very close and all the family had been close to him.

Duke was especially hurt and wanted to put off the wedding. I had a very badly abscessed tooth during the funeral and the day before the wedding had it pulled.

It had to be ground out a piece at the time. It took the dentist over an hour. I suffered very much with it.

Duke and Lynn Phillips had both graduated from V.P.I, and were making their home in Christiansburg, Virginia. She was a beautiful bride and we loved her very much.

Marie, Bill and I were still milking the cows. Marie and I dreamed of one day we would be able to retire and travel some from the cows but we were working harder than ever. We had lots of fun days on the farm and had been blessed with good health. My Dad always said, "Life is full of many ups and downs." I find that to be true. More in some lives than in others it seems.

In the fall of 1980, Marie was diagnosed with cancer. I loved her so much it would not have been as shocking if it had been me. It was rough for each of us. When we went for a second opinion it was the same. Her left breast must come off, and then the treatment was uncertain. We had always believed in answered prayers and we prayed much. Marie asked the new pastor and deacons for a prayer for her healing. We were shocked when they refused, especially when the church had prayed for others. We prayed for her as a family. The children all came and stood with her in the hospital at Roanoke. I stayed with Antoinette who was still living at Roanoke. Ted came from Mississippi although his wife was expecting their first baby any day.

We will always be grateful for Ted's wife Tracy sending Ted to be with his Mother at this time.

The surgery seemed to be successful with the left breast and all the lymph glands stripped away. She came home in eleven days and now must take a year of chemotherapy, which she would do in Galax. The chemotherapy treatments were not easy to face. Our prayers were answered and Marie was not sick. After each one I bought her a meal of steak and baked potato.

It's amazing the remarks some people can make when one is having problems. One lady said, "I thought you were a good woman." Marie's answer was, "No just a sinner saved by grace."

We felt our work was finished at Meadows of Dan Baptist Church. The next Sunday we attended Reed Island Springs Baptist Church and we found a home there and work to do. Praise God we found love and acceptance and a place to serve. David Horton was the young pastor and really did preach some blessed sermons. It was difficult to leave our church after twenty-eight years but we knew God was leading us to do so. But that church will always be dear to us because we had such a spiritual investment there.

On January of 1981 we had our first grandson born in Jackson, Mississippi. They named him Clint Turman. What a joy when Ted called and told us the good news. Clint was the first baby of the year in Jackson and received many great gifts from the stores and a free hospital bill.

Ted had prayed he would be born the last of 1980 so he could count him as a tax exemption but this was even better. He said the bible says, "Ye know what ye ask."

When Clint was three months old in March Bonita, Marie and I went to see him in our car. We were blessed again to have Bill and our neighbor to take care of the cows.

What a joy once again to hold another grandchild in our arms and to see such a perfect baby. It was sweet to see Tricy hold him and rock him in her favorite rocking chair and how proud she was of her little son.

Bonita had decided prior to this to further her education and had attended Seattle University in Seattle, Washington for six months. After having her here with us for a while and to see her go again pierced our hearts. We never did get use to our kids leaving home. She had excelled there in school and was offered a teaching position in Stanford University in California. However she returned home and took a four-hour exam at Wake Forest University in Medical Records. She tied for first place nation wide. She then accepted a position in Western Carolina University. We took her there in the spring and saw the beautiful campus all covered with blooming shrubs and flowers.

Bill had graduated from Carroll County High School and was going to Wytheville Community College. His head was set on being in police work and was taking courses in Police Science.

Marie and I were all alone now for the first time ever. Bonita and Bill were in college, how very empty our ten rooms seemed.

We continued to milk the cows and talked of quitting milking and getting some beef cows. We knew we had to make a decision and we could not continue, without help. Bill was here in the summer but he would soon be getting a job and moving somewhere else. While Bill was in college he was blessed to be living in a very comfortable home in Wytheville. It was a house owned by a judge who was living out of town and wanted someone to house sit. Bill was very comfortable in this completely furnished house and felt a big responsibility to care for it. He and several boys lived there and took good care of it. Bill knew he wanted a job in the police department and was trying for an outstanding record. He made it on the dean's list all through college.

When an opportunity came up for him in the Chilhowie Police Department at last he saw his dream come true. The police chief, his boss introduced him to his young sister-in-law. This was the cream to Bill's dream, this was it!

Bonita was doing well in her teaching position but was overworked and missed her family very much. She resigned her job and returned home, much to our shock. She had taught there four years and we had been to see her several times. So for two years she worked here on the farm trying to decide what next.

The government came up with a plan to get the small farmer out of the dairy business and I began to give it much thought. I signed up for it. The government would pay you a small amount of money for five years if you would sell your herd and never milk again. I signed the contract and wished I had not when I found you must brand the cattle on the face so no other dairyman would buy them. They had to be slaughtered. We had to brand all the cows and heifers with an x on their face. We had to buy a branding iron. The government took a fee of 50 cents out of every 100 pounds of milk sold to get the money to pay the farmers who sold out. This was over a five year period and they collected millions more than they paid out. Meanwhile the public was made to believe their tax money was paying for this program. Actually no tax money was used but the 50 cents levy on the milk.

I was really sick at heart when I sold the cows. We had been told we could sell the cattle on any market. What we didn't know was that only designated slaughterhouses could buy and slaughter them. They were bought for less than half price, 25 cents per pound, beautiful cows and heifers for less than $250 a head. We came out with less money than we would have, had we not signed up and sold them without the brand.

The government made millions on them also. They sold the processed meat to foreign countries for big profits. I learned from this that you cannot trust your own government.

Many of our servicemen also learned this. We had looked forward to getting out and now we were out!

We had loved the cattle and hated to see the last truck pull out with the last load. Words cannot be spoken to reveal how we really felt.

On a beautiful August 21, 1983 in Chilhowie, Virginia, William Turman and Darlene Poston were married at 2 P.M. What a joy to meet such a wonderful family who were so filled with so much love for one another and they all seemed to love Bill, too. They were married in the church and had a police escort out of town. The Police Chief was his brother-in-law. Amy was here and she went with us there on the night before the wedding to the rehearsal. Bonita early that morning had sprained her ankle and had to go to the doctor and she was wearing a cast up to her knee and was walking with a cane. We knew she wanted to steal the show.

That night all of us gathered in one motel room just having a fun time, about fourteen of us. A friend dropped by and asked, "Are all of you staying in here tonight?"

Harry with his Southern sense of humor said, "Yes, we are a close family."

Bill and Darlene lived and worked in Smythe County. On March 17, 1987 our lovely Sarah Elizabeth Turman was born. Marie and I were there for her birth.

What a joy to see a brand new grand baby come into the world, and what a beautiful name. I am forever grateful that we could be there and see the joy on the face of these two parents.

In August of 1990 Marie went with Ted to get Clint and Callie in Mississippi and they came back by Tweetsie Railroad and they really did enjoy this. These children of Ted's are really growing and it is such a joy for them to come to the mountains to see their Dad and all the family. I wish they could come more often. They really are well-behaved and loving children. The first thing they do when they come into the house is to. go to the dining room and measure and see how much they have grown. Marie painted the dining room but she could not paint the edge of the door, there history is recorded.

When Callie was three and rode the bus up here with her Dad Marie showed her all over the house, and she said, "Now I want to see the kitchen." When Marie had shown her the kitchen she said, "I'll help you wash the dishes," and she did.

Bill and Darlene were so happy and were really enjoying Sarah Elizabeth so they were praying for God to bless them with another child. Then along came Amanda another lovely daughter with a personality all her own. I really think she must be like Grandma Marie with all her energy. When she enters a room we all see her and hear her. These little girls really are drawn to Auntie Bo (Bonita) and follow her like little puppies.

They love to go with her to see the farm animals and help feed them. They like to take long walks with Bo and she dearly loves them too.

Bonita and Marie were there for Amanda's birth and Sarah sat right in the waiting room with all the rest of the family members. What a joy to hear her first cry.

I could not be there as I had come down with a rare illness called Myasthenia Gravis, which took a year and many doctors to diagnose. They had suspected a brain tumor.

This was the end of my very active and enjoyable life and I will not attempt to write about it and the time I spent in the hospital. I've also had a heart attack and am now a diabetic and have to give myself insulin and take thirty to fifty pills a day. I have been on a walker for four years, but I cannot dwell on that.

So I am forever grateful for all the good doctors and nurses, shots and all the pills and for the walker with which I am able to move about. Also I am grateful for the love of my church, pastor and friends. Indeed I am forever grateful for my family who has been so good to me and give me so much love and support. I am forever Grateful for each card I receive and my wife has one wall completely covered with them. I look at them and thank God for so many friends who pray daily for me.

For my wife more than anyone, she's still a beautiful and active woman who has stood by me, loving me, nursing me, cooking and housekeeping for me and neglecting the things she would love to do, so for her I am forever grateful.

There are some things I cannot write about, they are too painful to me and to those who might read about it. Ted and Duke's divorce, Antoinette's tragic auto accident and suffering in the hospital before her death September 6, 1989. There is also the great destruction of the storm Hugo two weeks after our daughters death, the buildings and forest that were destroyed.

I go back down memory lane and think of the good things like in September when Ted had returned to college and Marie had to come back to the barn. It was a very foggy morning and one of our big Holstein cows, which were expecting her calf, was missing from the barn. Marie, who I knew was having a pity party because she had to come back to the barn and milk again, said I would go and see if I can find her. I finished milking and she had not returned so I went looking for her and the cow. I found the cow and calf all doing well but I could not find Marie. I called out, "I've found her."

On a distant hill I heard her and found her in the dense fog. She was lying on the ground crying and disgusted that she had not succeeded and sorry for herself.

I picked her up and put a hundred dollar bill in her hand and said, "Here, wipe your tears with this."

She looked and could not believe it. I told her it was hers to keep. So she came to the barn with the bill in her faded jeans pocket. I could not always do this. All of our $100 bills went to buy books for college kids and we were thankful to do this.

On another occasion I remember when Marie was searching the hills for another lost mama and baby and came upon a tall field of stickweeds in full bloom in September. She stood and saw such a beautiful sight, the migrating Monarch butterflies, thousands of yellow butterflies arose up off the weeds.

There are still many happy moments in my life and many things for which to be grateful.

On December 16, 1989 we had the privilege of attending the wedding of Duke and Margaret Turley in the new house they had been building for a year. The day was so very cold and the snow was so deep I was debating whether to go or not because of my health conditions. Ted brought his car right up to the door and helped me down the ice-covered steps and we were there after three hours of traveling over icy roads to their home. As I sat there in the living room and saw this beautiful ceremony, with them standing in front of their fireplace I will be forever grateful.

There were no curtains at the windows and every way I looked, there in the woods that surrounded their house, was a beautiful scene. Snow was hanging on every twig. Margaret was a lovely bride and while I listened to the ceremony, I thanked God for another precious daughter-in-law.

In a few short years Duke called to tell us Margaret was in the hospital with a new baby daughter. She was one month early and all was well. I'll be forever grateful that God let me live to see yet another beautiful granddaughter, Catelin Mae, with such sparkling blue eyes. Now I get to see her and Amanda play together, so it is with a grateful heart I thank God for these five precious grand-daughters and my one grandson.

Yes, and in April of 1990 Harry and Amy Mustard had a large deck put on the back of our house. I enjoy many happy hours sitting on the deck furniture and at the table having lunch in the summer time. I'll be forever grateful for this kind gesture from them. I can walk out on the deck and the ramp leading to it and get into the old pick up and drive over the farm.

It is from this deck I can enjoy the scenery, looking south and over the rolling green hills. On a clear day I can see over into North Carolina, the beautiful blue color of Pilot Mountain. Hanging Rock Park and Sauratown Mountain.

I can also watch the sunrises and sunsets and sometimes we watch the thunderstorms in the far distance. We can see the streams of lightning going down, all God's handiwork.

Nearby I see the green fields I have worked over many times. Now I see the beef cattle grazing and late in the evening we see the deer come out and play.

I look down on the lawn and see Marie working in her beautiful flowers that she loves so much. But most of all I Love to watch my lovely wife as she cares for the lawn and flowers and making things beautiful around her.

Then to sit on the deck on a warm spring night and hear the little creatures of God begin their singing, the crickets chirping and the katydids all praising God in their musical way. In the distance I hear the whip-poor-will calling his mate. The lights appear in the distant cities and beyond the lights we see the planes landing in the regional airport at Winston-Salem. Sometimes a jet going over to land at the airport breaks the peacefulness.

As I sit there I picture in my mind the places I can't go anymore. The orchards now gone almost, the smell of the blossoms in full bloom in the spring. How wonderfully sweet they smelled! A beautiful memory I have of one spring day as I passed through my neighbor's orchard and saw Marie sitting beneath the apple tree, which was in full bloom.

I guess she was sitting there daydreaming and I did not disturb her thoughts. I stood in the distance and saw what a beautiful woman she had become and hoped that one day she would be mine.

I travel back in memory down Squall Creek, back to where I crossed it so many times on my way to the store or to Bell Spur school and hear the rippling waters as I watched it flow over the mossy green rocks, remembering the many trout in it. I remember crawling through the thick laurels as I went downstream, then coming to an open area where the big pines grew near by. I look at the old south slopes where Marie and I enjoyed picking blackberries, wild and sweet and juicy in the hot summer sunshine. Then we would wade in the cool stream at the foot of the hill before we came home with our buckets full.

On down the stream I ventured as a teenager and later in life, where the water became more swift and where more streams entered Squall Creek. Then on down to the falls you can hear, long before you can see it pouring over the mountain to Kibler Valley.

Life is like the water in Squall Creek, it begins as a small stream and it goes on its course, sometimes flowing slowly and sometimes faster, sometimes quietly and sometimes completely out of control following a storm, sometimes clear and then again muddy from outside sources, growing and gathering knowledge as it goes along, picking up speed as it goes along. Squall Creek will plunge over the falls, there is no turning back. It could be dammed up for awhile but it would soon overflow and go on its way.

So is life. We have a path to follow and there it is, no turning back and then we will go to the Great Maker from which we came. Just as Squall Creek goes on to Dan River and eventually to the ocean from which it was evaporated and fell as rain here in the mountains. Now the creek is polluted by its surroundings and whatever is poured into it, or with whatever it comes in contact, so are we, waiting to be cleaned by our Lord.

Silas Turman, 1920 - 2002

8439036R0

Made in the USA
Charleston, SC
09 June 2011